Virtues and Economics

Volume 8

The series is dedicated to virtue ethics and economics. Its purpose is to relocate economic theory to a domain where the connection between the virtues and economic decisions, as that connection is actually experienced in everyday life, is an organic component of theory rather than some sort of an optionally added ingredient. The goal is to help develop a virtue-based economic theory which connects virtues with the contents of economic activities of individuals, unincorporated and incorporated economic agents. The primary context is Catholic Social Teaching but other faith traditions (especially Judaism, Islam, Hinduism, Buddhism, and Confucianism) will also be explored for their construction of virtues in economic action. Special attention will be made to regulatory and policy issues in promoting economic justice.

The series connects virtue ethics with the core of economic theory and practice. It examines the basic and irreducible intentionality of human activities concerned with the production, distribution and consumption of goods and services. It considers the incommensurability of values as the central problem of economic decision making and examines whether that problem can be overcome by any means other than practical reason.

This series covers high quality edited volumes and monographs. The majority of the volumes are based on papers developed for the Economics as a Moral Science Program of Blackfriars Hall, University of Oxford.

Péter Róna • László Zsolnai
Agnieszka Wincewicz-Price
Editors

Homo Curator: Towards the Ethics of Consumption

Springer

Editors
Péter Róna
Director of Las Casas Institute's Economics Programme
University of Oxford
Oxford, UK

László Zsolnai
Business Ethics Center
Corvinus Institute for Advanced Studies
Corvinus University of Budapest
Budapest, Hungary

Agnieszka Wincewicz-Price
Polish Economic Institute
Warsaw, Poland

ISSN 2520-1794 ISSN 2520-1808 (electronic)
Virtues and Economics
ISBN 978-3-031-51702-0 ISBN 978-3-031-51700-6 (eBook)
https://doi.org/10.1007/978-3-031-51700-6

This work was supported by Porticus Foundation

This Springer imprint is published by the registered company Springer Nature Switzerland AG
The registered company address is: Gewerbestrasse 11, 6330 Cham, Switzerland

Paper in this product is recyclable.

Foreword

On August 15th 1221, a band of thirteen Dominican friars walked into Oxford to open a house in the nascent university city. It was to be a centre of learning and teaching in philosophy and theology, the fruits of which study were not reserved to an academic enclave, but were to make a difference in the lives of countless men and women up and down the land. A leading professor (a Regent Master), Robert Bacon was soon attracted to join the community, and by the early 1230s King Henry III was supplying oaks to roof the friars' lecture hall. Such was the importance accorded to the project that not long afterwards work began on a much larger priory just beyond the city walls by the river. Meanwhile, Dominicans from Oxford had begun to found numerous other houses in England, Ireland, Scotland and Wales, each of which were centres for preaching and teaching.

These preachers were valued not least for their concern with economic justice, with the right use of money and material goods, with what was owed to a worker and his family, with what was owed to the poor by way of neighbourly charity, and for their warnings against usury, greed (*avaritia*) and self-indulgence (*luxuria*). The Hereford Dominican, John Bromyard, who probably studied at Blackfriars, Oxford, wrote extensively in his fourteenth-century *Summa Praedicantium*, against these two vices as amongst the most serious and widely prevalent in every sector of society. Avarice is seen as a key motivator to all kinds of malpractice, and case-stories about it make up little under half of his *exempla* on the deadly sins. Nor was greed simply about temporal goods; it included the refusal to share lecture notes and knowledge!

The Oxford Blackfriars was suppressed at the Henrician Reformation. So, too, were all the other Dominican priories in England and Wales. For several hundred years, scarcely a handful of Dominican friars ministered discreetly to recusant Catholics in missions attached to foreign embassies or country estates. Yet, from the mid-nineteenth century, it became possible to open new religious houses with urban parishes which served members of the impoverished working classes, many of them Irish immigrants, employed in mills, factories and shipyards. In the early twentieth century, their cause was championed by a fiery Northern Irish Dominican, Fr Vincent McNabb, whose speeches and newspaper articles explained to a lay Catholic audience the radical social teaching of Pope Leo XIII in his encyclical *Rerum novarum*. McNabb presented his teaching not as a defence of private property owned by rich industrialists, but an urgent call for the redistribution to the poor of property unjustly held by the tycoons. At much the same time, the Dominicans refounded Blackfriars, Oxford, as a centre for learning and teaching, laying the foundation stone in 1921. Once again, it was to be a centre from which knowledge could be disseminated through the work of countless preachers across the generations to make a difference in ordinary lives.

From this perspective, the research on Economics as a Moral Science led by Professor Péter Róna at the Las Casas institute for Social Justice at Blackfriars Hall, Oxford, stands in deep continuity with the Dominicans' mission in Great Britain and beyond. It seems particularly appropriate that the octocentenary of the friars' foundation of Blackfriars, Oxford, should be the occasion of an international colloquium on the ethics of consumption. At a time when climate change, and the patterns of consumption which drive it in large measure, have become matters of grave importance for this and future generations, it is immensely valuable to draw on the resources offered by the philosophical and theological tradition that runs from Aristotle through St Augustine and St Thomas Aquinas. The dedication of this volume of edited chapters to mark the octocentenary of the Dominicans in Oxford is a welcome reminder of that tradition and of the vital mission in which it features.

Director, The Las Casas Institute for Social Justice
Blackfriars Hall
University of Oxford
Oxford, UK

Richard Finn OP

Introduction

The ubiquitous, ever-accelerating and increasingly demanding calls for prompt and concerted action to tackle the global problem identified as "climate change" are deficient – at least on the level of proposed institutional and political remedies – in one important, if not crucial aspect. What is missing is the apparent underappreciation, or misconception of constitutive parts of human nature and its tendency – on the one hand – to produce excess in a myopic pursuit of self-gratification, and – on the other hand – the capacity and inherent need for self-correction and self-betterment for the sake of oneself and others. In other words, the lacking element is the apparent ignorance (disbelief?) of the moral nature of the human being who is capable of both good and evil. Those involved in the seemingly noble (if debatable in its execution) project of global "green transformation" fail to get to the heart of the problem of misuse, abuse and overuse of earthly resources which is to be found in human vice, hubris and naiveté. Likewise, in the catalogue of proposed remedies, they do not seem to find space or rationale for genuine conversion of hearts and minds that would go beyond replacing consumption of plastic or coal with equally excessive consumption of so-called renewables, into a more profound realm of revisiting the goals and limits of consumption as such. It is the understanding of the editors and the authors of the chapters included in this volume that no grand scheme of universal change of technology and even of material habits will succeed at saving the planet and – more importantly – humankind within it, if it does not account for the ultimate source of waste and damage, and the necessary condition of change, both of which are spiritual and ethical.

Taking aside the contested point of the actual role of human action in the anomalies of nature that we have observed around the globe in the last decades, we argue that the problem at stake is much larger. For when we pay closer attention to the harm that is caused by deficiency of reason and virtue, we see it does not only manifest itself in pollution and depletion of resources but also in the enormous disparities of wealth and well-being as well as moral and social damage of the gluttonous societies aptly summarised by Easterlin as "paradox of happiness". Looking back on the history of major revolutionary endeavours of the past – political, social and economic alike – we see that there is a real danger that this green revolution of our age (for a revolution it is) will fail at producing any meaningful change and improvement on any front, if it is based merely on material stipulations. What we need is an adequate conception of the good for the sake of which we are asked to partake in this great revision of the old ways of production and consumption.

It is symptomatic, however, that this very conception, the cornerstone of ethics, has been entirely missing from the very branch of knowledge, and indeed of social thought, that was designated with explaining how the processes of production and consumption work, and devising how to organise them to overcome the longstanding problem of scarcity. That discipline is naturally economics. In its modern articulation modelled on "value-free science", it stays clear of any normative issues which could blemish its scientific purity. Previous volumes in this book series have indicated at length that it has not always been so, for economic questions used to be part of and in fact originated in a broader field known as the moral sciences. In our effort to track and explain the indisputable crisis of modern economics, we take a step further and pose a challenging and bold question of whether this purported science with all its ontological and methodological deficiencies has not been given too large of a role in informing, and indeed redefining what is good. This would truly be a paradox, given the economists' ethical and moral agnosticism, but as the reader will see in the chapters that follow, this agnosticism is often fictitious as is economics' normative neutrality. The imperatives of economic growth, calculated rationality and efficiency affirmed in economic policy of liberal democracies, serve as case in point.

Yet, examination of the ethical foundations of any economic policy or model has not been a meaningful part of economic theory until recently. Even less attention has been given to the harm that overreliance on philosophically and ethically deficient economic dogmas has brought about. This overreliance is not present on the theoretical level only. It is arguably carried forward into the realm of policy advice, and through mainstream-dominated public discourse it also affects daily practice of consumers and producers who learnt to believe that the more they buy and the more they make will not only benefit themselves but also their societies. Environmental damage and growing inequalities show that this belief needs qualification. In other words, greed is not good and economics is not the place to look for ethical guidance. To fill this gap in knowledge and understanding of how misconceived economic notions misinform and bias human action away from its proper goal requires an extraordinarily cross-disciplinary effort. Such is the approach of the book before you in its objective to revisit the ethical resources of modern economic life. It represents voices of philosophers, ethicists, economists, theologians, social theorists and natural scientists.

The wide range of disciplines and topics involved in this discussion show that mainstream economics stands in need of a dialogue with many more areas of scholarship than it has been recognized to date. Together they can help economics identify the limits of its often meaningless abstraction and break free of its narrow confines. This seems the only way to better understand the real nature of economic processes and their potential outcomes. Such multidisciplinary and revisiting effort seems particularly needed in the economy of today, facing a series of unresolved crises that can no longer be solved by conventional tools.

The book consists of three parts. The first part goes back to the Christian tradition of stewardship and sketches out multiple ways in which rich societies of today fail to measure up to that standard. Special attention – both philosophical and theological – is given by both Joshtrom Kureethadam and Stefano Zamagni to the analysis of the root cause of unbridled consumerism which is to be found in the vice of gluttony, also known as avarice or greed. Some important insights are also given into the role of economics in turning this basic human vice into virtue, including criticism of Adam Smith's hailed principle of the invisible hand where good economic outcomes are not intended but result from pursuits of self-interest. It is not, however, self-interested consumption per se that is castigated here as much as it is wasteful consumption that does not take responsibility for the good of others, both our contemporaries and future generations. It is also suggested here that the unbridled consumption is encouraged on a broader social and policy level where the dogma of limitless growth, enabled in big part by mass consumption, is hailed. Frugality, self-restraint and discerning separation of want from need are suggested as an ethical minimum to counterbalance thoughtless overconsumption. That such attitude is not easy and self-evident is well illustrated in the very much needed analysis of what is enough and how we can establish this unmeasurable measure for individuals and social entities. What should be particularly insightful for economists in Sister Margaret Atkins' contribution is how it addresses the problematic and unrealistic – if taken seriously – economic concept of utility maximisation. The last two chapters in this section provide two very different in origin, yet somewhat consistent in their core messages, accounts of consumption rightly understood. Sister Laura Baritz's is based on the works and thought of Thomas Aquinas, László Zsolna's is rooted in an altogether different tradition of Buddhism.

The second part tackles in more detail the big question of mainstream economics' contribution to the ecological harm of today. In a thought-provoking debate (and quite heated in some places), two strong attempts to defend the mainstream economic paradigm are confronted with challenging and exacting criticism of the basic economic tenets which goes as far as pointing to "the corrupting effects of economic sciences". The first defence, prepared by David Rose, argues that Homo Economicus and excessive consumption are not the root of the global ecological problem, for the non-normative model of a rational agent is inclusive enough to incorporate attitudes that would in fact protect the environment from further degradation, and the concept of individual utility maximisation does not equal selfishness but rational maximisation of one's welfare (which could include other people's welfare too). The other defence, voiced by Hayden Wilkinson and Geoffrey Brennan, is equally understanding towards the concept of Homo Economicus and its use in economic theory; it is also complementary of some economic theory tools that can be useful in solving a number of ecological issues (e.g. Pigovian tax, provision point mechanism). Its authors argue that problems of climate change do not arise from agents being indifferent to environmental harms, but instead because each harmful action is so strongly in the agent's interest; as such these are collective action problems. The same authors are not however entirely uncritical of modern economics for they admit that economists are prone to use an implausibly narrow account of human motivations and adopt a similarly narrow conception of what matters morally. While they find it problematic, the authors are sceptical as to the possibility and usefulness of accounting for a broader scope of human motivations in the existing models for this could lessen their predictive powers. Still, they do agree that material motivation should not always be the guiding feature of human behaviour in economic models.

Both defences indirectly admit that economic theory built around the concept of instrumentally rational, utility maximizing agent is void of any recognition of the agent being a moral being, capable of both good and evil. The problem with this approach, explored in detail in the response by the Editor of this series, is twofold. On the methodological level, it prioritizes the rigour of the logic with which economic theory's or model's conclusions are reached over empirical confirmation of the theory or the model – in other words, facts are made to conform with the model rather than the reverse. On the practical level, the claim that economics' scientific status is based on its value-free methods stands in direct contrast to the empirical fact that these non-normative theories nonetheless encourage economic growth and consumption within it, and as such obviously make value judgments. Those value judgments are by no means neutral to real economic phenomena such as distribution of wealth and income, neither are they neutral to the environment. The adverse effects of economic theory on the environment are, in Péter Róna's view, to be traced back to the modern economics' focus on exchange value (and neglect for use value) and pricing mechanisms that account only for "economic" goods, that is those goods that can be made the subject of exchange. At the same time, in a value-free economic discipline, there are no restraints on what may be turned into an exchangeable good. The result is a radical misrepresentation of the actual costs involved in production, distribution, and consumption of the factors of economic life.

The reason for including Edward Skidelsky's chapter at the end of this part might not be immediately obvious to the reader, but upon closer familiarity with the content of the two above-mentioned defences of mainstream economics, his original treatment of the concept of prudence becomes a most helpful illustration of why the precious rational economic agent might not deserve as much praise as was given to it first by Rose and then by Wilkinson and Brennan. Skidelsky does not stop short of criticising the homo economicus for being unlike *Homo sapiens*. He goes deeper in his analysis and engages more profoundly with the very nature of this rational agent's quality of prudence (applauded by most economists). He argues that contrary to the official line, economics does have a normative doctrine of practical rationality, and that it is a flawed one because it is rooted in satisfaction of current preferences. Yet, utility maximisation ceases to be an obvious strategy when one takes into account concern for the past and for the future along with all possible ethical dilemmas involved in those considerations.

The chapters included in the third and last part of the book offer some hope and wide-ranging, constructive insights into how to go forward and what needs and can realistically be changed in how economics is done and understood. Dominic Burbidge includes his discussion of economic methodology in a broader criticism of modern social sciences and notices how the increasing distance from empirical realities decreases analytical rigour in this field. One particularly significant instance of this in economics is its reliance on the concept of self-interest which is assumed to be a common drive of human action across cultures and generations, when in fact what, according to Burbidge, is a uniting feature of human motivation is trust, defined here as intentional unity. He further argues that this obvious aspect of human conduct should form the basis to social inquiry whose focus would then become the study of horizontal coordination of interests between persons in common pursuit of social ends, and of vertical coordination of people's interests with how they view themselves. Turning the reader's attention to the contingency of human scenarios, the complexity of human interactions, and the inability to distinguish between the cognitive capacities of researchers and the researched, his chapter makes a refreshing, if humbling observation that economics – like other social sciences – is unable to approach sufficient causal knowledge, but is nonetheless able to point out necessary conditions that brought about past events.

Continuing the theme of social goals and interactions, Joseph Rice locates the question of human consumption in the perspective of human vocation to participate in community. He proposes to base economic modelling (broadly understood) on anthropological and therefore ethical assumptions concerning the question of what it means to be human. Wojtyła's concept of participation allows him to find the answer to this question in the capacity of a human person to act together with others in a way that respects them as persons, and to recognize the same property in the humanity of others. He stresses that thus understood participation is not as an abstraction, but a concrete value, grounded, and recognized in conscience. The formation of the latter, in turn, and the very first experience of participation in the *communio*, takes place in the family. Recognition of this fundamental aspect of one's development as a person leads Rice to second Frank Knight in his argument that it is the family, not the individual that should be considered the primary unit for social policy. He warns, however, against the danger present in that perspective of viewing a person merely as subject of an economically quantifiable unit and not of non-quantifiable morality, and against temptation to define our worth by material standards. With John Paul II he locates the dangers for ecology and economy as secondary effects of succumbing to this temptation and suggests that the ecological crisis cannot be therefore sufficiently addressed by better management of resources but by turning away from consumerist attitudes and refocusing on how humans can continue to live in harmony and mutual respect of human dignity. Education in responsibility is one way to achieve that goal.

A more practical way to address the ecological crisis, one that nonetheless requires an ethical consensus of foregoing excessive material gain, is offered in the last chapter in this volume. Its author, Eors Szathmary, an evolutionary biologist, identifies grave negative social and economic consequences, exacerbated by the climate change, in what many readers might find surprising, namely the way central banks regulate interest. Using mechanisms known in biology, he develops an alternative way to calculate compound interest, one that implies sub-exponential, rather than exponential growth. Putting this new formula in practice would make asset growth self-inhibitory which, as the author argues, would temper greed by slowing down the growth of wealth of the rich.

While we do not suppose this volume will give sufficient answers to the critical dilemmas and questions we are currently facing regarding not only the ecological but also energy, economic and humanitarian crises, we nonetheless believe that it is a much needed voice in a wider debate concerning the goals of policy and society in the era marked by uncertainty and collapse of scientific and political dogmas. Given that many unprecedented economic policy moves that we have witnessed at least since the outbreak of the Covid-19 pandemic are defying many of the core tenets of mainstream economics (e.g. exorbitant increase of public deficit spending, more numerous protectionist measures resulting from increased mistrust of global trade, promotion of new, ideologically rather than profit-driven corporate governance oriented towards green investment, attempts to involve central banks in facilitating the latter) provokes the question of why those core economic principles cannot stand the test of time, and what are the more profound truths that allow us to question those principles. Now might be a better moment than ever to revisit what is truly scientific in economics and what might be considered mere ideology that not only makes it a bad science, but also causes misconduct and harm for those who blindly follow it as well as those who are subject to them.

Oxford, UK Péter Róna

Warsaw, Poland Agnieszka Wincewicz-Price

Contents

Part III Way Forward

Part I
From Gluttony and Avarice to Moderation and Virtue

Chapter 1
"Blessed Are the Gentle …": Moving from Gluttony to Sobriety

Joshtrom Kureethadam

Abstract Earth, our common home is in a precarious state as we have transgressed important geo-bio-physical limits of the planetary boundaries. Among the root causes of the destruction of our planetary home is the endless orgy of profligate consumption and waste. We have appeared to lose any sense of limit whatsoever. We live in a society that exalts luxury and reckless consumption of resources, resulting not only in the degradation of life-sustaining ecosystems but also in widening levels of socio-economic inequalities.

We need to embrace the virtues of simplicity and moderation, if we are to conserve Earth as a home where all forms of life, including the humans can flourish. Fortunately, we do have important resources within our own religious and ethical traditions in this regard. Faith traditions insist on the importance of frugality and measure in the use of material resources and call upon their adherents to cultivate the virtues of voluntary restraint and self-discipline. As one of the Gospel beatitudes reminds us: "Blessed are the gentle, for they shall inherit the earth" (*Mt* 5:5).

In this paper, we shall proceed according to the "See-Judge-Act" methodology. We will begin with the precarious state of Earth, identify its root causes in unbridled consumerism sustained by the vice of gluttony, and propose a radical ecological conversion towards sobriety by walking gently on the very land that sustains us.

1.1 The Precarious State of Our Common Home

As Pope Francis reminds us in *Laudato Si'* "we need only take a frank look at the facts to see that our common home is falling into serious disrepair" (Pope Francis 2015, 61). We have inflicted great harm on our common home "by our irresponsible use and abuse of the goods with which God has endowed her", and "she 'groans in

J. Kureethadam (✉)
Dicastery for Promoting Integral Human Development, Vatican, Vatican City
e-mail: j.kureethadam@humandevelopment.va

P. Róna et al. (eds.), *Homo Curator: Towards the Ethics of Consumption*, Virtues and Economics 8, https://doi.org/10.1007/978-3-031-51700-6_1

travail' (*Rom* 8:22)" (Pope Francis 2015, 2). According to the Pope we are already seeing alarming "cracks in the planet that we inhabit" (Pope Francis 2015, 163).

It is our common home that is crumbling around us of which the manifestations are multiple and interlinked. The signs of the collapse of our common home are evident in the disruption of the geophysical cycles as well as in the progressive degradation of the ecosystems that sustain life on Earth. We can see signs of it on land and sea. Seventy-five per cent of the land surface is significantly altered with a third of it severely degraded, 66% of the ocean area is experiencing increasing cumulative impacts, and over 85% of wetlands (area) has been lost (IPBES 2019, 11). The scale of human impacts on Earth, our home planet, is immense.

Globally, human activities move more soil, rock and sediment each year than is transported by all other natural processes combined. We have cut down nearly 3 trillion trees, about half of those on the planet. Factories and farming remove as much nitrogen from the atmosphere as all Earth's natural processes. These changes rival those in Earth's geological history [4]. … If you weighed all the land mammals on Earth, 30% of that weight is us humans, 67% would be the farm animals that feed us, and just 3% are mammals living in the wild. A sixth mass extinction in Earth's history looms (Maslin 2019).[1]

The fingerprints that human activities have left on our common home of life are conspicuously evident in a diverse range of records in land, ocean and atmosphere for which empirical evidence is on the increase. According to Michael S. Northcott:

(T)here is not a stretch of ocean and very few areas of forest which do not show signs of the industrial and commercial transformation of the earth into a materials bank for human exploitation. The extent of human interference and disruption of natural systems can be measured three miles above the North Pole in the loss of protective ozone, and one mile deep in the rift valleys of the ocean floor in the polluted sediments which trickle down from the waste products of modern consumerism (Northcott 1996, 32–33).

A very good and comprehensive indicator about the perilous situation of our planetary home on account of human activities is provided by the landmark study entitled "Planetary Boundaries". This important report shows how our common home is pulled down by several and interlinked physical crises.

The study of the Planetary Boundaries was carried out by a group of 28 scholars associated with the Stockholm Resilience Centre, among them prominent Earth scientists like the Nobel for chemistry Paul Crutzen and James Hansen of NASA. Their findings were published in a paper entitled "A Safe Operating Space for Humanity" in the September 2009 issue of the prestigious scientific journal *Nature* (Rockström et al. 2009a).[2] The aim of the authors was to determine and quantify the safe operating space for humanity with respect to the Earth system and its associated

[1] See also: Crowther et al. (2015) and Lewis and Maslin (2018).

[2] A more detailed version of the same study came to be published later in *Ecology and Society*. See Rockström et al. (2009b).

biophysical sub-systems. The "planetary boundaries" are the limits or thresholds that must not be transgressed in order to avoid irreversible ecological damage. The authors identified planetary boundaries in nine key areas: climate change, rate of biodiversity loss, interference with the nitrogen and phosphorus cycles, stratospheric ozone depletion, ocean acidification, global freshwater use, change in land use, chemical pollution, and atmospheric aerosol loading.

According to the study, humanity may soon be approaching the boundaries for global freshwater use, change in land use, ocean acidification and interference with the global phosphorous cycle. The most alarming conclusion of the report was that with regard to the areas of climate change, rate of biodiversity loss and interference with the nitrogen cycle, humanity has already transgressed the limits. With regard to climate change, some of Earth's subsystems appear to be moving outside their stable Holocene state, like the rapid retreat of the summer sea ice in the Arctic ocean, the retreat of mountain glaciers around the world, and the accelerating sea-level rise during the past couple of decades. As for the rate of biodiversity loss, where the transgression appears to be most flagrant, species are becoming extinct at a rate that has not been seen since the last global mass-extinction event. As for the nitrogen cycle, it appears that industrialized agriculture has already poured more chemicals into the land and oceans than the planet can process (Rockström et al. 2009a). A 2015 update of the study published in the *Science* (Steffen et al. 2015) showed that we have now transgressed a fourth area, namely, land system change.

The study on the planetary boundaries conveys a very important message, namely, that it is the entire common home of humanity that is threatened. The Earth system is a single, integrated complex system, with many inter-related and inter-dependent sub-systems. The contemporary ecological crisis in this regard is unparalleled in the geological history of the planet. It is the first time that humanity's own dwelling is threatened in such a comprehensive way.

A constant preoccupation of the scientific community in recent years has been about the risk of crossing the thresholds in tampering with the Earth's climate and its natural processes. It is important to remember that the tipping points are themselves "interconnected across different biophysical systems, potentially committing the world to long-term irreversible changes" (Lenton et al. 2019, 592). Tipping points are indeed points of no return. Many scientists agree that if those boundaries are crossed, it would be difficult, perhaps impossible, to reverse the process, at least for thousands of years. As the scientific community warns us: "if damaging tipping cascades can occur and a global tipping point cannot be ruled out, then this is an existential threat to civilization" (Lenton et al. 2019, 595). Humanity is indeed treading today on a slippery slope.

What humanity is sleepwalking into is a possible collapse of our very home, with dire implications for the members of our common household (Kureethadam 2014, 57–58). As Lynn White noted already in 1967 in his epoch-making article: "surely no creature other than man has ever managed to foul its nest in such short order" (White 1967,1204).

1.2 Consumerism and the Collapse of Our Common Home

The fundamental issue at the heart of humanity's increasing environmental footprint in the planet is consumption (Maslin 2019). Today, we have become addicted to profligate consumption, so widespread in economically advanced societies and spreading like wildfire to the rest of the world with the globalization of the current neo-liberal economic model. What is polluting our common home and bringing the planet to the brink to the climate breakdown and the biodiversity crisis, are our life-styles of inordinate and wasteful consumption of natural resources.[3] In the case of climate change, for example, it is estimated that consumption behaviour and house-holds are responsible for 72% of greenhouse gas emissions (Dubois et al. 2019). The most affluent countries are mainly responsible for the historical GHG emis-sions and generally have the greatest per capita emissions (Ripple et al. 2020, 8).

A yardstick that is being increasingly used to measure human impact on the planet is that of the Ecological Footprint Analysis.[4] "Ecological Footprint account-ing measures both the biocapacity available as well as the demand people put on it through all of our activities: from food and fibre production to the absorption of excess carbon emissions" (Almond et al. 2020, 56). It is widely considered as the most comprehensive aggregate pointer of human pressure on ecosystems to date.

Ecological footprints measure a population's demands on nature in a single met-ric: area of global biocapacity. By comparing humanity's ecological footprint with the Earth's available biological capacity, ecological footprint analysis (EFA) sug-gests whether or not our use of crop lands, forest lands, pasture lands, fisheries, built space, and energy lands can be sustained (Venetoulis and Talberth 2005, 2).

The Ecological Footprint Analysis can be used to determine the exact date that the global community begins to live beyond the means of what the planet produces each year. Overall, humanity's Ecological Footprint has doubled since 1966. While economies, populations and resource demands grow, the size of the planet remains the same. There is a limit to the resources that Earth can produce and the waste it can absorb each year. The problem is precisely that human demands on planet's services are exceeding what it can provide. Till very recently, humanity's use of nature's services was within the means of what nature could regenerate. But, some-time in the mid-1970s, humanity appears to have crossed the critical threshold. Since then, humans have been in ecological overshoot, using resources faster than they can be regenerated and putting carbon into the air more rapidly than it can be reabsorbed. The Ecological Debt Day or the Earth Overshoot Day marks the precise day when humanity's demand for ecological resources and services in a given year exceeds what the Earth can regenerate in that year (WWF 2010, 8).

[3] "Profoundly troubling signs from human activities include sustained increases in both human and ruminant livestock populations, per capita meat production, world gross domestic product, global tree cover loss, fossil fuel consumption, the number of air passengers carried, carbon dioxide (CO_2) emissions, and per capita CO_2 emissions since 2000" (Ripple et al. 2020, 8).

[4] The Ecological Footprint Analysis was pioneered by William Rees and Mathis Wackernagel (1996).

The ecological footprint analysis clearly shows a consistent trend of over consumption. Humanity's consumption of Earth's regenerative capacity has grown from 73% in 1960 to 170% in 2016 (Lin et al. 2008, 58) with substantially greater per-person consumption in countries with highest income. In 2020, this overshoot dropped to 56% above Earth's regenerative capacity as the Ecological Overshoot day fell on 22 August. It meant that between January and August 2020, humanity consumed as much as Earth can renew in the entire year, and with staggering inequality among people and countries (Bradshaw et al. 2021, 4).

Currently, humanity as a whole consumes or rather over-consumes 1.56 Earths a year. This means the human enterprise currently demands 1.56 times more than the amount that Earth can regenerate.[5] The situation is projected to get even worse in the future looking at current levels of consumption and waste. It is calculated that we are on track to require the resources of two planets well before mid-century. But of course, we only have one Earth.

Our current unsustainable levels of consumption take a toll on the natural world and on the bodies of the poor. We see it in the the increasing degradation of the land and in the fast depletion of the natural resources beyond their capacity for regeneration. The over-exploitation of the land is clearly evident in the form of modern 'intensive agriculture' which has led to land degradation and even to desertification, in some parts of the world. We over-exploit our fellow human beings too, as evident in the increasing prevalence of cheap labor, factory chains and call centers where people work round the clock to increase the profits of a minority. As we live in an interconnected world there is also the increasing phenomenon of "telecoupling" – with resource extraction and production often occurring in one part of the world to satisfy the needs of distant consumers in other regions.

In *Laudato Si'*, Pope Francis is particularly critical of current levels of consumption by the rich which have led to the exploitation of our home planet beyond acceptable limits. He writes: "We all know that it is not possible to sustain the present level of consumption in developed countries and wealthier sectors of society, where the habit of wasting and discarding has reached unprecedented levels" (Pope Francis 2015, 27).

Ecological overshoot is possible only for a limited time before ecosystems begin to degrade and possibly collapse. This can already be seen in global climate change, water shortages, reduced cropland productivity, erosion, overgrazing, deforestation, desertification, collapse of fisheries, rapid extinction of species, to name a few. The multiple manifestations of the ecological crisis point to the truth that we are already using up more than what the common habitat that sustains us can provide. Such wasteful profligacy of living beyond our means is also returning to haunt us in the form of the contemporary ecological crisis. Our levels of rapacious consumption are indeed pillaging our common planetary home. The consumption of many important natural resources is clearly beyond their renewal capacity rates. In the case of

[5] Global Footprint Network, Calculating Earth overshoot day 2020: Estimates point to August 22nd. Lin et al. 2020; Almond et al. 2020, 56.

important natural sources like fisheries, forests, biodiversity, and especially fresh water, we are fast approaching crucial thresholds.

Today, our unbridled consumption patterns have reached frenzied levels as against all levels of sustainability. At the same time, we are subtly coaxed to consume ever more by media advertising - the poster boy of modern consumerism. Like a tsunami, consumerism is engulfing human cultures and Earth's ecosystems. The modern consumerist lifestyle of the developed world, increasingly aspired to by the burgeoning upper and middle class populations in developing countries, is a profligately wasteful one. The sheer quantity of waste produced by modern economy and our consumerist life styles is striking. As Pope Francis points out in *Laudato Si'*, if we do not intervene, "the paradigm of consumerism will continue to advance, with the help of the media and the highly effective workings of the market". (215)

The rapid depletion of our home planet's natural resources in blissful ignorance of the larger ecological context is a sure recipe for global disaster. Carrying on with the current paradigm of infinite economic growth on a finite planet is the perfect recipe for dystopia. As Seán McDonagh notes: "the Earth's ledger, which in the final analysis is the only real one, tells us that the Earth is finite and vulnerable, and that natural systems will be seriously depleted and possibly collapse unless human beings begin to shape their lives in the light of this reality of ecological accounting" (McDonagh 1986, 45). No previous generation has survived the ongoing destruction of its natural supports. Nor will ours. Instead, we go on liquidating our home planet's finite natural assets to fuel our reckless consumption.

1.3 From Hubris to Gluttony

The roots of greedy consumption and profligate waste do have deep "human" roots. These roots ultimately spring from our refusal to accept our self-identity as creatures along with its associated limits. It is the sin of human *hubris*. In fact, the refusal to accept any limit that arises from our creaturely status was the 'original' sin of humanity, as we read in the third chapter of the Book of Genesis. As Michael S. Northcott rightly notes, the contemporary ecological crisis results ultimately from our refusal to see ourselves as creatures.

At the heart of the pathology of ecological crisis is the refusal of modern humans to see themselves as creatures, contingently embedded in networks of relationships with other creatures, and with the Creator. This refusal is the quintessential root of what theologians call sin. And like the sin of Adam, it has moral and spiritual as well as ecological consequences (Northcott 2007, 14).[6]

In ancient Greek thought, immeasurable growth and excessive development, beyond natural limits, were considered as expressions of *hubris* – coinciding with elements of haughtiness and disrespect (Ecumenical Patriarch Bartholomew I

[6] See also pp. 5 and 16.

2009a, 195). The *hubris* of denial of natural limits, and of our creaturely dependence, is clearly evident in the oft quoted words of Lawrence Summers, former U.S. Secretary of the Treasury: "There are no limits to the carrying capacity of the earth that are likely to bind at any time in the foreseeable future. The idea that we should put limits on growth because of some natural limit is a profound error."[7]

Our refusal to accept creaturely limits is evident in the hubris of modern anthropocentrism and widespread individualism. In a totally self-centred vision of reality, any consideration of the planet's sustainable limits or of the common good is seen as irrelevant. We may cite here the attentive diagnosis offered by Pope Francis in *Laudato Si'* of the roots of our reckless consumption patterns:

When people become self-centred and self-enclosed, their greed increases. The emptier a person's heart is, the more he or she needs things to buy, own and consume. It becomes almost impossible to accept the limits imposed by reality. In this horizon, a genuine sense of the common good also disappears. As these attitudes become more widespread, social norms are respected only to the extent that they do not clash with personal needs (Pope Francis 2015, 204).

Our current ecological predicament results from our stubborn refusal to accept any limit whatsoever – be it regarding the carrying capacity of the Earth in the case of the 'ecological footprint' of individuals, communities, and nations, or in the case of the 'carbon footprint' directly linked to climate change. Our "refusal to accept limits placed upon humanity on account of its creaturely status" (McGrath 2002, 79) is manifest in the sin of gluttony.

Today, the consumerist society that we live in exalts the vices of excess and gluttony. The currently reigning paradigm of consumerism does not contemplate or even tolerate limits to our insatiable desires to possess and to use material resources. We live in a society that thrives on unbridled consumption, wasteful prodigality and opulence, built on the myth (and the bubble) of infinite economic growth – considered as paramount - which in a finite system like the planet is an impossibility, as rendered evident by the contemporary ecological crisis.

As early as 1975, John Taylor wrote *Enough is Enough*, a book "in which he explored the sins of excess, especially in cultures where consumption of food and accumulation of goods become the highest values, and in which waste and pollution, our plundering of the planet's natural resources of fuels and minerals (Taylor 1972)."[8] Most people define their identity today, first and foremost, in terms of what they have, as they continue buying and throwing away material goods, swayed by the enthralling promises of the multi-billion advertisement industry which has made consumerism the cult and religion of our age. Today we have lost the values of moderation and simplicity, we have lost our sense of proportion. Our homes are much bigger than what we need voraciously consuming energy and resources, our cities are far too big with problems ranging from pollution to congestion and not the

[7] Attributed to Lawrence Summers, U.S. Secretary of the Treasury under President Clinton. Cited by Toolan (2001, 45).

[8] Cited by Atkinson (2008, 80).

least increasing stress disorders among inhabitants, our consumption patterns are wasteful with citizens in developed countries throwing away nearly a third or quarter of food already purchased. The disproportion is best epitomised in the standard of living of the first-world cities versus third-world slums, the swollen stomachs of starving people versus increasing levels of obesity around the world, and the sprawling homes of the billionaires versus the wretched abodes of the poor - in the city of Mumbai, the financial capital of India, the 27-story house of billionaire of Asia's richest person Mukesh Ambani sits uncomfortably with Asia's largest slum, Dharavi, with open sewers and crammed huts, home to more than a million people! Pope John Paul II offers a telling critique of the culture of consumerism and the inequalities associated with it in his social encyclical entitled *Sollicitudo Rei Socialis*:

> … side-by-side with the miseries of underdevelopment, themselves unacceptable, we find ourselves up against a form of superdevelopment, equally inadmissible, because like the former it is contrary to what is good and to true happiness. This superdevelopment, which consists in an excessive availability of every kind of material goods for the benefit of certain social groups, easily makes people slaves of "possession" and of immediate gratification, with no other horizon than the multiplication or continual replacement of the things already owned with others still better. This is the so-called civilisation "consumption" or "consumerism" which involves so much "throwing away" and "waste" (Pope John Paul II 1987, 28).

Our wasteful life styles are indeed a far cry from basic Christian values that called upon people to live in moderation, to avoid excess, to share our resources with those less fortunate rather than to hoard them for a flagrant display of wealth. "We trample the earth and the poor with a kind of disregard that in earlier days would cause one to blush and feel a healthy kind of shame" (Aeschliman 2008, 95). As the ecumenical Patriarch Bartholomew I reminds us it is precisely "this excessive acquisitiveness in today's world is greatly responsible for a large part of the ecological destruction of our planet human greed and acquisitiveness cause ecological destruction on the one hand and the irresponsible and unequal division of goods on the other" (Ecumenical Patriarch Bartholomew I 2009a, 198).

The contemporary ecological crisis is a result of our modern lifestyles built on the shaky pillars of greedy accumulation, profligate consumption, and waste. Our present lifestyles, especially those of the developed world, are totally unsustainable, as they are beyond the carrying capacity of the Earth and have detrimental effects both on our home planet's life systems and on the poor. Our lifestyles are placing unbearable pressure on our common home, which appears to be on the verge of a collapse.

1.4 Recovering the Virtue of Sobriety

The antidote to gluttony is sobriety. We need to embrace the virtues of simplicity and moderation, if we are to conserve Earth as a home where all forms of life, including the humans can flourish. We stand no choice of saving our common home, unless we are able to regain a more simple life style, based on the essentials and really necessary. As Mahatma Gandhi said decades ago, with a ring of prophecy "Earth has sufficient for everyone's need, not for everyone's greed"! While humans have 'natural' rights to avail of the biophysical goods to satisfy human needs and fulfil their cultural potential, they also have moral responsibilities to use these resources frugally, fairly, and prudently, living within the boundaries of planetary capacities, respectful of both present and future generations of life (Nash 1991, 137).

Faith traditions, on the whole, insist on a certain amount of austerity and asceticism in the use of material resources and call upon their adherents to cultivate the virtues of voluntary restraint and self-discipline. In fact, to be truly 'religious' is to dispossess oneself of the superfluous and to be content with essential things in life. Frugality of life style is a core teaching in almost every religious tradition of humanity. Frugality connotes moderation, temperance, and simplicity. Down the centuries, the Hindu and Buddhist *sanyasians*, the Christian hermits, indigenous and aboriginal communities, and countless wise persons have shown in practice how simplicity of life-style is indeed a sure road to inner freedom, a concrete expression of solidarity with the poor and needy, and an effective way to harmony with the rest of creation.

The Biblical writings exalt the virtues of simplicity and moderation and Christian tradition is replete with shining personal examples of persons who have tread the path of asceticism of austerity and frugality, in order to attain holiness. The Old Testament tradition of the Sabbath was indeed an institution founded on the virtues of sufficiency and contentment. In the law of gleaning, for example, the farmer was not to reap to the very edges of the filed, but to leave something "for the alien, the orphan and the widow" (*Dt* 24:19) (Atkinson 2008, 80). In the great Sabbath of every 7 years the land itself was to be left fallow for an entire year allowing it to recuperate (*Ex* 23:10). Prophets like Amos condemned the social evils of excessive accumulation of wealth in the hands of a few and their extravagant life styles at the expense of the poor. In the New Testament, we find Jesus, the Son of God, an epitome of simplicity: the man who was born poor, lived poor and died poor. As the ecumenical Patriarch Bartholomew I reminds us, Jesus "commanded us to use the world's resources in *a spirit of ascetic restraint and eucharistic sacrifice*, to transform our way of thinking from egocentrism to altruism in light of the ultimate end of the world" (Ecumenical Patriarch Bartholomew I 2009b, 284). The early Fathers of the Church emphasized the importance of remaining within the limits imposed by our basic needs. As Nilus of Ancrya wrote in the *Ascetic Discourses*, *Philokalia*: "Once we are carried beyond these limits in our desire for the pleasures of life, there is no criterion to check our onwards movement, since no bounds can be set to that which exceeds the necessary" (Nilus of Ancrya 2008, 100).

If the contemporary ecological crisis is the result of greed and unbridled consumption of resources, it can be overcome by rediscovering the virtues of simplicity, temperance and the measured use of resources. We need to rediscover the virtue of frugality. As the National Council of Churches document affirms: "Frugality is the corrective to a cardinal vice of the age: prodigality – excessively taking from and wasting God's creation. On a finite planet, frugality is an expression of love and an instrument for justice and sustainability: it enables all life to thrive together by sparing and sharing global goods" (National Council of Churches 2005). We need to rediscover the spirit of asceticism and of self-sacrifice. Asceticism, what Eastern theologians have called *enkrateia* (self-restraint) is an essential element of our responsible stewardship of God's creation. "Each of us is called to make the crucial distinction between what we *want* and what we *need*. Only through such self-denial, through our willingness sometimes to forgo and to say "no" or "enough", will we rediscover our true human place in the universe" (Ecumenical Patriarch Bartholomew I 2009c, 274–275). We need to fast from actions that pollute and degrade our common home. But asceticism goes deeper. From a theological point of view, asceticism reveals the cross dimension of human life, namely, that of self-sacrifice and sharing in love, which alone can lead to abundance of life. The contemporary ecological crisis invites humanity to rediscover the tree of life. If the selfish and unbridled desire to consume the fruits of the tree of life in the garden of Eden caused the original sin, whose ripples continue to be felt in our voracious consumption of planet's natural resources, the embrace of the Tree of Life – the Cross – in a spirit of sacrifice and sharing, following the example of the kenotic Christ, can lead to the restoration of life. Ultimately, only the spirit of asceticism can save us and our home planet. The ecumenical Patriarch Bartholomew I writes:

The cross is the singular, ultimate, and absolute solution to the ecological crisis. The cross reminds us of the reality of human failure and of the need for a cosmic repentance. In order to alter our attitudes and lifestyles, what is required is nothing less than a radical reversal of our perspectives and practices. There is a price to pay for our wasting. It is the cost of self-discipline.

This is the sacrifice of bearing the cross. The environmental crisis will not be solved simply by sentimental expressions of regret or aesthetic formulations of a creative imagination. It will not be altered by fashionable programs or ecumenical catch-words. It is the "tree of the cross" that reveals to us the way out of our ecological impasse by proposing the solution of self-denial, the denial of selfishness or self-centredness (Ecumenical Patriarch Bartholomew I 2009d, 296).

As our planetary home is wrecked by our totally unsustainable life styles, dictated solely by the values of modern consumerism which take a heavy toll on the bodies of the poor and of the planet's ecosystems, a genuine ecological conversion will need to lead to a profound change in our life styles. We need nothing short of radically new lifestyles if we are to save our common planetary home for ourselves and for future generations. We may cite Pope John Paul II once again in this regard:

Modern society will find no solution to the ecological problem unless it *takes a serious look at its life style*. In many parts of the world society is given to instant gratification and consumerism while remaining indifferent to the damage which these cause. … Simplicity, moderation and discipline, as well as a spirit of sacrifice, must become a part of everyday life, lest all suffer the negative consequences of the careless habits of a few (Pope John Paul II 1990, 13).

Against unhealthy consumption patterns that tear down the physical and social pillars of our common home, Pope Francis in *Laudato Si'* calls for a radical "change in lifestyle" which "could bring healthy pressure to bear on those who wield political, economic and social power" (Pope Francis 2015, 206). He encourages us to choose lifestyles which are "countercultural" (Pope Francis 2015, 108). He recalls in this regard examples of consumers movements who boycotted certain products which forced businesses "to consider their environmental footprint and their patterns of production" (Pope Francis 2015, 206). According to the Pope there is "great need for a sense of social responsibility on the part of consumers" (Pope Francis 2015, 206). and calls on people to change their consuming and purchasing behaviour.[9] Pope Francis recalls an important affirmation of Pope Benedict: "Purchasing is always a moral – and not simply economic – act" (Pope Benedict XVI 2009, 66; Pope Francis 2015, 206). In fact, given the gravity of the crisis, simple solutions like a bit of recycling or occasional bicycling will not do. As Mark Dowd writes: "We should not fool ourselves into thinking that 'deckchair-rearranging' activities such as giving up plastic bags and changing light bulbs will be enough to put the tanker that is environmental degradation off course" (Dowd 2015, 4). We need to embrace simple, just and sustainable life styles.

1.5 Conclusion: Walking Gently on Earth

"Blessed are the gentle, for they shall inherit the Earth" (*Mt* 5:5) is one of Jesus' Beatitudes for happiness. In order to truly live in harmony with the rest of creation, and to "inherit" Earth for us and for children and grandchildren, we need to tread gently on Earth.

We need to do it with utmost reverence as the land on which we stand is "holy ground" (Ex 3:5) which has been sanctified by the incarnation of "God who loved the world so much" (Jn 3:16) so as to "pitch His tent" (Jn 1:14) on our little planet – "this tiny blue dot", to say it with Carl Sagan - in the supreme event of Incarnation.

We also need to do it with profound humanity, rediscovering our our self-identity as *imago mundi*, created from the dust of the Earth, from *humus* (like the Hebrew *adamah*). Only the honest recognition of our origin from the *humus* (soil) of the Earth, will enable us to stand with 'humility', before the Creator and in fellowship with the rest of creation. Such creaturely humility will indeed be a sure antidote for the *hubris* with which we are consuming and depleting Earth's finite resources.

References

Aeschliman, Gordon. 2008. Loving the Earth is loving the poor. In *The Green Bible*. London: Harper Collins.

Almond, R.E.A., M. Grooten, and T. Petersen, eds. 2020. *Living Planet Report 2020: Bending the Curve of Biodiversity Loss*, 56. WWF: Gland.

Atkinson, D. 2008. *Renewing the Face of the Earth: A Theological and Pastoral Response to Climate Change*. Norwich: Canterbury Press.

[9] See in this regard Hoffman (2015, 12–13).

Bradshaw, Corey J.A., et al. 2021. Understanding the challenges of avoiding a ghastly future. In *Frontiers in Conservation Science*, vol. 1.

Crowther, T.W., H.B. Glick, K.R. Covey, C. Bettigole, D.S. Maynard, S.M. Thomas, et al. 2015. Mapping tree density at a global scale. *Nature* 525: 201–205.

Dowd, M. 2015. For Every Living Creature on Earth, *The Tablet* (13 June), 4.

Dubois, G., et al. 2019. It starts at home? Climate policies targeting household consumption and behavioral decisions are key to low-carbon futures. *Energy Research & Social Science* 52: 144–158.

Ecumenical Patriarch Bartholomew I. 2009a. Greeting at the commencement of the fifth summer seminar on Halki, June 14, 1998. In *Cosmic Grace Humble Prayer: The Ecological Vision of the Green Patriarch Bartholomew*, ed. John Chryssavgis. Grand Rapids/Cambridge: William B. Eerdmans.

———. 2009b. Address during the official Sophie Prize presentation ceremony, June 12, 2002. In *Cosmic Grace Humble Prayer: The Ecological Vision of the Green Patriarch Bartholomew*, ed. John Chryssavgis. Grand Rapids/Cambridge: William B. Eerdmans.

———. 2009c. Closing address during the concluding ceremony for the fourth international and interreligious symposium on the Adriatic Sea, June 10, 2002. In *Cosmic Grace Humble Prayer*, ed. John Chryssavgis.

———. 2009d. North Sea symposium, Keynote address at Utstein Monastery (June 23, 2003). In *Cosmic Grace Humble Prayer*, ed. John Chryssavgis.

Hoffman, A.J. 2015. The Pope's encyclical letter and its implications for business. *Environment: Science and Policy for Sustainable Development* 57 (6): 12–13.

Intergovernmental Science-Policy Platform on Biodiversity and Ecosystem Services (IPBES). 2019. The global assessment report on biodiversity and ecosystem services. In *Summary for Policymakers*. Bonn: IPBES secretariat.

John Paul II. 1990. *Peace with God the Creator, Peace with All of Creation*. Message for the World Day of Peace (1 January).

Kureethadam, Joshtrom I. 2014. *Creation in Crisis: Science, Ethics, Theology*. Maryknoll: Orbis Books.

Lenton, Timothy M., et al. 2019. Climate tipping points – Too risky to bet against. *Nature* 575 (28 November): 592.

Lewis, S.L., and M.A. Maslin. 2018. *The Human Planet: How We Caused the Anthropocene*. London: Penguin.

Lin, D., L. Hanscom, A. Murthy, A. Galli, M. Evans, E. Neill, M.S. Mancini, J. Martindill, F.-Z. Medouar, S. Huang, and M. Wackernagel. 2008. Ecological footprint accounting for countries: Updates and results of the national footprint accounts, 2012–2018. *Resources* 7 (3).

Lin, D., L. Wambersie, M. Wackernagel, and P. Hanscom, eds. 2020. *Calculating Earth Overshoot Day 2020*. Oakland: Global Footprint Network.

Maslin, M.A. 2019. Climate change: Essential knowledge for developing holistic solutions to our climate crisis. In *Emerging Topics in Life Sciences*, vol. 3/2.

McDonagh, S. 1986. *To Care for the Earth: A Call to a New Theology*. London: Geoffrey Chapman.

McGrath, Alistair. 2002. *The Reenchantment of Nature: The Denial of Religion and the Ecological Crisis*. New York/London: Doubleday.

Nash, James A. 1991. *Loving Nature: Ecological Integrity and Christian Responsibility*. Nashville: Abingdon Press.

National Council of Churches. 2005. *God's Earth is Sacred: An Open Letter to Church and Society in the United States* (14 February).

Nilus of Ancrya. 2008. Ascetic Discourses, vol. 1, *Philokalia*. Cited by Matthew Sleeth, "Teachings on Creation though the Ages" in *The Green Bible*, London: Harper Collins.

Northcott, M.S. 1996. *The Environment and Christian Ethics*. Cambridge: Cambridge University Press.

———. 2007. *A Moral Climate: The Ethics of Global Warming*. London: D.L.T. – Christian Aid.

Pope Benedict XVI. 2009. Encyclical Letter *Caritas in Veritate* (29 June).

Pope Francis. 2015. *Laudato Si': Encyclical Letter on Care for Our Common Home*. Vatican City: LEV.
Pope John Paul II. 1987. Encyclical Letter *Sollicitudo Rei Socialis*.
Rees, W., and M. Wackernagel. 1996. *Our Ecological Footprint: Reducing Human Impact on the Earth*. Philadelphia: New Society Publishers.
Ripple, William J., et al. 2020. World scientists' warning of a climate emergency. *BioScience* 70/1: 8.
Rockström, J., et al. 2009a. A safe operating space for humanity. *Nature* 461 (24 September): 472–475.
———. 2009b. Planetary boundaries: Exploring the safe operating space for humanity. *Ecology and Society* 14/2: 32ff.
Steffen, Will, et al. 2015. Planetary boundaries: Guiding human development on a changing planet. *Science* 347 (8 January): 1259855. https://doi.org/10.1126/science.1259855.
Taylor, John. 1972. *Enough Is Enough*. London: SCM.
Toolan, David. 2001. *At Home in the Cosmos*. Maryknol: Orbis Books.
Venetoulis, J., and J. Talberth. 2005. *Ecological Footprint of Nations: 2005 Update*. Oakland: Redefining Progress.
White, L. 1967. The historic roots of our ecologic crisis. *Science* 155: 1203.
WWF International – Institute of Zoology – Global Footprint Network. 2010. *Living Planet Report 2010: Biodiversity, Biocapacity and Development*. Gland: WWF.

Chapter 2
Avarice in Post-modern Society: The Meaning of the "Homo curans" Anthropological Assumption

Stefano Zamagni

Abstract The paper deals with the most "economic" of all capital vices and argues that it represents a typical case of "failure of reason". Indeed, the greedy hoards wealth by removing it from circulation and in so doing does not enhance prosperity, rather it thwarts it. The absence in economics of a proper theory of rational motivations is what explains the difficulty of the discipline to understand the greed phenomenon and its multiple negative consequences. Economics possesses a theory of the *reasons* for doing what the *homo economicus* believes it must do, but not a theory of the *motives*. The paper speaks in favour of the introduction in economics of the anthropological assumption of *homo curans*, and indicates which implications would follow, the most relevant of which would be the consideration, in the analytical discourse, of the principle of reciprocity.

2.1 Introduction

This paper deals with avarice, a capital vice that is rarely revealed as such, wearing from time to time the clothes of usury, concupiscence, greed, hunger for gold. From the annoyance that the greed of others arouses, the greedy can assume what others feel towards him/her. In pursuing his/her own self-interest, the greedy is led to behave as if he/she were not such. The mimetic capacity of greed is such that in certain circumstances it can even take the form of virtue as Juvenal had already foresaw. When the Spanish Prudentius in his famous "Psychomachia" (405) – an allegorical work in verse that tells of seven fierce battles for the conquest of souls, in each of which is involved one of the deadly vices and the related virtue – deals

S. Zamagni (✉)
University of Bologna, Bologna, Italy

SAIS Europe of the Johns Hopkins University, Bologna, Italy

Pontifical Academy of Social Sciences, Vatican City, Italy
e-mail: stefano.zamagni@unibo.it

P. Róna et al. (eds.), *Homo Curator: Towards the Ethics of Consumption*, Virtues and Economics 8, https://doi.org/10.1007/978-3-031-51700-6_2

with avarice, he writes that the souls of the faithful (priests included) that greed fails in conquering by force, it will take by deception. Pretending to have a certain nobility of mind, greed manages to conceal its true traits, so much so that greed and stinginess will be attributed to the noble purpose of providing for the needs of the sons. By laying down its arms, greed will then take on the role of parsimony, becoming – writes Prudentius – "that virtue that is called economics". (In the end, however, *operatio* will win definitively *avaritia*!)

Avarice is defined in many ways: if one wants to understand its specific nature it is necessary to look transparently at its many variations and consider its meanings, as they have been articulated over time. In what follows, I will try to stir up those sedimentations of thought related to greed; these are especially present among economists who tend to credit the idea of a minor vice that can be easily corrected using appropriate incentive schemes. It is not by chance that in economic textbooks, from the most refined to those of the widest dissemination, greedy behavior is never discussed; nor does it make sense, according to mainstream economics, to wonder whether the preferences of *homo economicus* are avaricious or not. The latter must only think of behaving rationally, maximizing, under appropriate conditions, its own interest, whatever it may be. On the contrary, I will show that this is not the case: greed – the most "economic" of the capital vices – represents one of the most frequent cases of "failure of reason". Since it lacks a well-conformed reasoning process, the greedy does not know how to direct the "passion of having" that dwells in each human being; in particular, he/she does not know how to direct such passion – physiological in itself – to the goods that it is reasonable to desire. The greedy hoards wealth by removing it from circulation; it does not facilitate production, rather it thwarts it because of its dissipative behavior.

In what follows, I will argue that the absence in economics of a theory of rational motivations – i.e., what *motives* do we have to do what we acknowledge must be done – is what explains the inadequacy of this discipline to understand the greed phenomenon in its multiple expressions. (So much so that it does not deal with it at all). Why does the greedy continue to accumulate insatiably, knowing that the power that wealth bestows on him/her can never be realized? Economics possesses a theory of the *reasons* for doing what the *homo economicus* thinks he/she must do, but not a theory of the *motives* for doing what he/she recognizes he/she must do – which explains, by the way, why mainstream economics lacks a proper theory of rational decision, while it has a well-developed theory of rational choice.

2.2 Who Is the Greedy Today?

In the postmodern society, how does greed manifest itself? To answer this question, it is appropriate to investigate the relationship between greed and scarcity and to ask what is scarce today particularly, in western societies. It is clear, in fact, that in the land of plenty where, by definition, there is no scarcity, the greedy would not be able to find a living space. The scarcity is considered bad since it deprives mankind not only of what is necessary, but also of all that serves to its development.

There are two types of scarcity. As Albino Barrera (2005) points out, the primary one is scarcity due to human finiteness. It is because the human being is finite that he/she must make allocative choices: if he/she chooses one option, he/she must give up the others. This is the meaning of the notion of opportunity-cost: giving up an alternative that has value, always entails a cost. This has been well explained by the Buridan's ass paradox in which the donkey starved because it could not decide from which of the two piles of hay that the owner had placed next to it in the stable it should feed. This paradox teaches that it is sometimes the abundance of resources available and not their insufficiency – as was the case of the Garden of Eden – to lead to dramatic results. The primary scarcity is therefore also present in the realm of plenty, since Adam and Eve, being finite and therefore limited beings, cannot escape the logic of choice. What is the meaning of this scarcity? As the scholastic thought had already illustrated, the primary scarcity is necessary if the gift of freedom must have some meaning: in the absence of the opportunity-cost, in fact, the exercise of freedom would become empty.

Then there is the secondary scarcity, which is typical of the post-Eden situation. It is moral evil the source of this type of scarcity, which can manifest itself in different forms and degrees, up to the extreme Malthusian form that is what generates misery and deprivation. Both Augustine and Aquinas had argued that the Original Sin does not cause ontological changes in the creation. The sin's impact on the secondary scarcity does not occur through nature, but through free human action. As if to say that it is not the Original Sin in itself that generates greed, but rather an unreasonable and disordered reason. That is why Jean Thomas (1995) says that the Original Sin constitutes a failure of economic reason; i.e. the consequence of an incorrect calculation in order to obtain an equally erroneous advantage. "The Original Sin – writes Thomas – is not the origin of economics [since the economic problem also exists in the Garden of Eden], but rather of the difficulties of economics".

According to the Judeo-Christian tradition, greed, which is typical of the post-Eden social configuration, is the capital vice most responsible for secondary scarcity and the consequent distributive conflicts. There is a clear link between greed and scarcity: on the one hand, the latter acts as a stimulus for the adoption of increasingly self-interested behavior, given that the possession of scarce goods increases prestige and social consideration; on the other hand, greed tends to aggravate the various forms of secondary scarcity due to the negative impact on the availability of goods and the difficulty in distinguishing between needs and desires. It may be interesting to recall, in this regard, that the Hebrew word for money – the principal object which the greedy longs for – is "*damim*", which in the Talmud and Kabbalistic tradition means "blood" in the plural form. Blood leads to life only if it circulates; if it stagnates it leads to certain death.

What lies at the bottom of stingy behavior? More specifically, what are the reasons for giving in to the call of greed and what are the reasons for an individual to act as a greedy individual? According to David Hume's theory of motivation, one is motivated to do something only if one has the desire to do it – since cognitive states alone are not enough to push us to act. It is therefore a matter of understanding the nature of the desire to possess, to accumulate obsessively goods or money. Not all obsessive people are greedy, but it is certain that all greedy people are obsessive. The position of the ancient "Franciscan voluntarism" and, nowadays, of authors such as Bernard Williams and Thomas Nagel seems convincing to me: the reasons to act depend on the desires of the person who acts. At the origin of every intentional action there is therefore a desire that provides – so to speak – the drive to action, while the direction of the action clearly depends on the means available to the agent.

What is the nature of the greedy desires? For the sake of clarity, desire is not a mere feeling that is expressed in some physiological state or an emotion that vanishes rapidly. Rather, to desire is to miss. To satisfy a desire – in the present case the desire to have – means (as the etymology of the word desire suggests) "to do enough" to appease it. The greedy, however, is not content to satisfy his/her desire for possession, wants to realize it, that is, he/she wants to make it a thing, thus eliminating the tension towards its fulfillment. Why? If we consider the nature of the economic problem, we shall have a convincing answer. Convenience is the basic principle of the economy. Economic convenience comes from an agreement reached by free choice ("convening" means, literally, "being with others on the same point" and metaphorically "agreeing"). It is convenience that makes man a social animal that needs the systematic collaboration of so many other people. The principle of convenience is the indispensable precondition for the division of labor. In this collaboration, everyone is led to make his/her own contribution by considering a purpose that everyone wants to achieve.

The purpose can be one own's profit, or the common good or something else; the important thing is that the purpose is endowed with objective utility. Now, this collaboration between free subjects in which a plurality of individual choices, dictated by subjective interest, converge towards a unitary purpose endowed with objective utility, is carried out through that universal instrument, money, considered the ultimate set of means. So much so that in common language it is said "that one is a person with many means" meaning "a person who has a large amount of money". Money is therefore the measure of convenience and for this very reason it effectively becomes a value: *the* economic value as such, i.e., what is needed to buy the valued goods. As a generalized exchange value, money is something able to buy everything. It has therefore an infinite power and as such it is preferred compared to the use values in which it can be incorporated. It is true that money is only a symbol, and yet this symbol is not only sought after, but, as a symbol of freedom of choice, it is preferred to the *real good* with which it is exchanged. That is why the greedy would like his/her money never to solidify and at the same time, that it could grow in liquid form, which is obviously impossible, because money can only multiply if it disappears into the use value, turning itself into real goods.

As it is well known, spending can be painful, paradoxical as it might be, because if one spends, that implies he/she judges that the value of the benefit obtained is at least equal to the value of the money paid. Well, the greedy person is one who puts, in its scale of preference, the opening to the potential over the closing of the reality.

In the greedy mind, therefore, what is part of human action tends to pose itself as the whole or its own whole. Not only that, but the part that should be a function of the anthropological whole reduces the latter to be a function of the part. In essence, the greedy is an individual who is unable to "educate" that *passion of having* which in itself is a positive source of spontaneity and energy. In other words, the greedy is an individual who does not know how to show to his/her passion the goods to desire according to their specific qualities. In this sense it can be said that the greedy exhibits a serious deficit of practical reason in the Aristotelian sense. Like all men, the greedy possesses the passion to acquire but the absence of a well-conformed reason prevents him/her from transmitting to it the sense of what is really good.

2.3 Can the Greedy Be Happy?

If in the wake of Jeremy Bentham (and today of Daniel Kahneman), we identify happiness with mere pleasure, the answer to the question posed in the title can be affirmative. Indeed, to the extent that the greedy takes pleasure in the repetitive and obsessive accumulation of goods or money, to the same extent he/she can be happy. This describes the situation of psychological selfishness, typical of a person who, having self-destructive desires, has as its ultimate goal (that is, as a non-instrumental purpose) only its own self-interest. Therefore, if in line with hedonistic thought, happiness is defined as the psychological state founded on pleasure, the greedy can be called happy.

Not so, however, if we accept the Aristotelian definition that conceives happiness as human "flourishing": the well-known *eudaimonia* cited by Amartya Sen, Martha Nussbaum, and a wide array of scholars. *Eudaimonia* includes pleasant emotions, those that give pleasure, but not only. In fact, it is necessary to add both the activities endowed with intrinsic value, and the activities that give rise to relational goods. Happiness – Aristotle taught – cannot be reduced to an instant, it cannot depend on an event, but must last in time. Therefore, happiness presumes virtue as something that makes good life possible and enjoyable; but it is not enough to possess virtue, it is also necessary to exercise it constantly. Unlike the moralistic tradition, of stoic derivation, which has done everything to make the virtuous life unattractive charging it with weights and prohibitions sometimes unbearable, the advantage offered by the Aristotelian ethics of virtues is to show that the virtuous life is the better life not only for others, but also for oneself.

It should be recalled that virtue is fully such when it is civil virtue, that is, when its field of action is the *polis*, or even better the *civitas*. There is no good life and therefore happy life in isolation, without a relationship, albeit conflictual, with the other. Happy therefore, is the subject who excels in the art of building bridges and so constructing human relationships, since it is only in community life that the human being – social animal – can blossom in fullness. It is a fact that up to Bentham it is indeed the Aristotelian idea of happiness that dominates the scene. Think also of Spinoza, the philosopher who more than others fought against the sadness generated by sad passions such as greed. Although the causal link between virtue and happiness is reversed – it is happiness that allows the control of the passions, that is, the virtuous life, not vice versa – Spinoza strongly reiterates that the strengthening of happiness happens in the collective sphere: the happier I am, the happier I will make others, and vice versa. It is because of reductionism – the identification of happiness with pleasure – operated by utilitarianism that it was taken for granted, from the nineteenth century, that the greedy can be happy. The greedy yearns for what he/she cannot achieve. Hence his/her melancholy, that condition produced in the greedy by the growing gap between experience and expectation, between what he/she already has and what he/she expects to have.

Two extraordinary diagnostics of modernity, Stendhal and Tocqueville, had well understood the close correlation between what we now call the "paradox of happiness" discovered by Richard Easterlin (1974): beyond a certain threshold, further increases in *per capita* income not only do not increase, but even decrease the aggregate happiness index and the mass-culture spread of utilitarian calculus. The central idea that the myth of individualism of singularity (not to be confused with individualism of belonging) – on which that calculus is based – conveys is that the realization of the life potential of the subject depends solely on his efforts. But in this way, the individualist *a priori* renounces enjoying "relational goods": goods generated by encounters in which the identity and motivations of the other with whom he/she interacts are essential elements.

It is indeed admitted that, in order to achieve its aims, the individual must enter a relationship with others, but this is justified only by considerations of convenience, to obtain more consent or more power. Yet if my relationship with the other remains purely instrumental, I will never get out of that "insufferable sociability" of which Kant spoke. With the consequence that I will never succeed in taking a path at the end of which there is my full realization and therefore my happiness. Since there is no happiness without others, I need the other to find that it is worth that I preserve myself. And the other also needs to be recognized by me as someone who must *blossom*. Since we need the same recognition, I will act towards the other as I would before a mirror. Self-realization is the result of such interaction. The original resource that I can make available to those in front of me is the ability to recognize the value of the existence of the other, a resource that cannot be used if it is not shared.

The recognition of the other implies not only his/her *right* to exist but also the *need* for him/her to exist so that I can exist, in relation to him/her. Recognizing the other as a purpose and recognizing him as a means with respect to the purpose of our common realization, unifies. This solves the reductionist dualism between a Kantian morality, which demands that the other is to be seen only as a purpose and a theory of instrumental rationality that instead sees the other as the mean to its own purpose. The benefit of self-realization is achieved when mutual recognition between persons is assured. For the sake of clarity, the fact that the recognition of the other brings with it the mutual recognition which I too need, does not make such a provision merely instrumental. In fact, the Self is also constituted by the recognition given by the other. In view of this, it is understandable why greed is the antipode of happiness.

The reason, in essence, is that well-being, depends on two components complementary to each other and not substitutable: acquisitive, the first one, and expressive, the second one. The first one binds the individual to the possession of goods capable of increasing utility. It is therefore rational the individual who, being able to judge what he/she likes, sets out to seek ways of maximizing his/her utility function, under specified constraints. The second component, however, indicates that people have expressive needs to satisfy, and not only material ones. Needs that express the constitutively relational nature of man, his/her profound identity. The betrayal of possessive individualism is all here: in making one believe that to be happy, one must just increase the utility. While we know that you can be a perfect maximizer of utility even in solitude, to be happy, however, it takes at least two, as Aristotle was the first to acknowledge. The reduction of happiness to utility is at the origin of the belief that the greedy would, after all, be a rational subject. Yet many social interactions acquire meaning only thanks to the absence of instrumentality. The sense of a courteous or generous action towards a friend, a son, a colleague lies in its being free. If we were to learn that this action stems from a utilitarian and manipulative logic, it would acquire a totally different meaning, with the result that the response would be changed by the recipients of the action. The "Chicago man" – as Daniel McFadden (2006), recently called the most up-to-date version of *homo economicus* – is an isolated, solitary and therefore unhappy person, even more so when he looks concerned about the others, since this solicitude is nothing more than an idiosyncrasy of his preferences. *Homo economicus* is the perfect identikit of the social idiot: a subject whose sphere of economic rationality is reduced to the sphere of rational choice as if the only valid theory of human action were the theory of intentional action. Now, as economists have known since at least Adam Smith's time, much of human action stems not only from intentions but also from moral dispositions and sentiments.

Therefore, the serious limit of applying rationality only to the category of intentional actions is to end with judging irrational all those actions that stem from dispositions such as the disposition to reciprocity. The result of such a methodological move is truly paradoxical: in many situations, an "irrational" response based on the principle of reciprocity leads to better results than those that can be achieved by following behavior inspired by the exchange of equivalents principle; yet the latter is the behavior judged rational by mainstream economics. This paradox is exactly the opposite of that exemplified by the Smithian invisible hand, where self-interested agents promote, although not having the intention, the general or collective good. In the present case, individuals who practice reciprocity also gain personal interest beyond their intention.

It is now clear why the greedy cannot be happy: since he/she is greedy first of all *with himself/herself*; because he/she denies himself/herself that value that the principle of reciprocity could assure him/her. It is only within reciprocity that recognition and self-respect between humans takes place, i.e. the *self-esteem* of which

Adam Smith speaks at length in his *Theory of Moral Sentiments* (1982, [1759]). Secondly, the greedy cannot be happy because he/she reduces the plurality of needs to a single fundamental need, that of possessing. Yet, it has long been known that man's needs are structured, that is, that they are hierarchized, arranged in scale. In resolving the heterogeneity of needs – if the needs are on a scale that means that they are heterogeneous – in the homogeneity of a single general and abstract need, the greedy precludes the possibility of enjoying the good and the beauty of diversity.

To express the same concept in a different and more robust way, we may consider that thymotic passions are totally absent in the greedy person. The notion of *thymos* is due to Plato, who in the IV book of *The Republic* conceptualizes it as the identitarian need for social recognition that human beings feel in order to place themselves within society. *Homo tymoticus* aims at being acknowledged by the others by acting positively towards the social group he/she belongs to. The act of recognition lays at the core of any process of socialization, as well as of subjectivation. It is never an entirely intentional action, as the actor receives social recognition only by strategically aiming at other goals. The greedy person does not want to be recognized; whence his/her unhappiness (Bellanca and Pichillo 2014, 13–38).

2.4 The Pinnacle of Greed: From "Free Market" to "Greed Market"

Having crossed the threshold of what is needed to ensure a decent life, the spring of greed resumes its vigor until it turns the market from a place of exercise of positive freedom – freedom *to*, that is the *libertas electionis* – to a place where greed finds an open field. The financial crisis, which began in the summer of 2007 in the United States and then spread to the rest of the world, is the clearest and most recent confirmation of this. Let us get this straight. It is a fact that ever since the momentous phenomenon of globalization began to take shape, finance has not only gradually increased its economic influence, but it has progressively helped to change people's values' system and with it their cognitive maps. Basically, this is the meaning, of the financialization of the economy, a real ideology – disguised with a supposed scientific mask – according to which, starting from the anthropological assumption of *homo economicus*, one would come to the conclusion that, under certain conditions, markets (including the financial ones) are institutional set-ups capable of self-regulation, i.e., institutions capable of both giving themselves rules and enforcing them.

The bridge that connects that assumption to such a conclusion is the *ethos* of efficiency, a veritable regulatory principle of postmodern society. It is from the pervasiveness in our culture of the principle of efficiency that the "performative myth" for which *to say* means *to do*, derives. And therefore that something becomes true just by the fact that we do it. It is this general state of mind that fuels the speculative machine which has been able to use financial instruments and products with a "firepower" never seen before; it is furthermore clear that a speculative bubble with the proportions of what we know today could never have happened without the "mental bubble" which led a large number of people to believe that it would be possible to reduce the risk to zero, only if it could be shared among many operators. However, financial risk – contrary to *natural risk,* which is exogenous, i.e. independent from the human will – is endogenous, i.e. it grows as the volume of financial transactions increases. This sense of omnipotence, nourished for several years by the financial euphoria, has taken possession of the mental habitus not only of traders and financial institutions but also of the political authorities, of the social media, and of research centers. The self-referentiality of finance – finance that becomes a purpose in and of itself – has thus made us forget Plato's maxim that "the only good currency with which we need to change all the others is *phronesis*", i.e. wisdom. A maxim that the illustrious American economist John Galbraith made much more prosaically: "It is good that money is sometimes separated from imbeciles", given the fact that many innocent people are paying for the *hybris* of imbeciles.

As history teaches us, almost always the *phronos zeon*, the wrath of the gods that accompanies the *hybris*, always falls on the lasts and the most vulnerable; which is simply scandalous when this happens in societies that maintain to be *open* in the sense of Karl Popper and *decent* in the sense of Avishay Margalit. The spreading *ethos* of efficiency as the ultimate criterion of judgment and justification of economic reality, on the one hand, ended up legitimizing greed: the greed market that replaces the free market. "*Greed is good, greed is right*" stated Gordon Gekko, the protagonist of Oliver Stone's famous film *Wall Street* (1987). On the other hand, the same *ethos* of efficiency is at the origin of the systematic alternation of greed and panic. One cannot oppose to this assertion the argument that panic is the result of irrational behavior on the part of operators; for panic is nothing more than a euphoria with a *minus* sign in front; so, if the euphoria is rational, so too is panic.

Clearly, the process of which we are today astonished spectators could not have reached the level of pervasiveness and current incidence without the scientific support of a certain way of setting the economic discourse. Unlike what happens in the natural sciences, economic science is strongly influenced by the thesis of the double hermeneutic, according to which economic theories on human behavior affect, more or less, sooner or later, the very behavior of man. As to say that theorization in the area of economics never leaves unchanged its field of study, since it not only shapes the cognitive maps of the economic operators, but also indicates them the way that must be followed if the goal is to be achieved in a rational way. Now, if the latter is the ever-increasing accumulation of goods or money and if, as it is obvious, the purpose of an action prescribes the means required to achieve it, the hermeneutic circle is soon closed. It is for this fundamental reason that whoever studies economics cannot hide behind a supposed axiological neutrality when building models and theories, especially when one is aware that the products of the scientific work potentially spread a certain way of thinking and are taken as a reference by political decision-makers. This is precisely what happened in the two great crises of modern capitalism, in 1929 and in 2007: individual greed and success have been erected to the impossible ideal that everyone can be better off than the others. Which is clearly impossible.

It is not difficult to identify the basis of so much intellectual arrogance still so frequent in many financial circles. This is the inability to understand, perhaps for a lack of philosophical background, the distinction between rationality and reasonableness. An economic argument may well be rational, mathematically impeccable, but if its premises, that is, its assumptions, are not reasonable, it will be of little help; on the contrary, it can lead to disasters. The philosopher of science Georg von Wright (1971, 87) wrote: "Judgments of reasonableness are oriented toward value; they are about what is considered good or bad for man. What is reasonable is undoubtedly also rational, but what is purely rational is not always reasonable". Reasonableness, in fact, is the rationality that makes the reason, reason *of* the man and *for* the man. As such, it is an expression of wisdom and not only of intellectual ability. Charles Sanders Peirce – the founder of American pragmatism – wrote in 1893 that economic science had succeeded in overthrowing to its own advantage – thereby demonstrating all its extraordinary camouflage capacity – the evangelical maxim of fraternal love, transforming it into what the famous philosopher called the *Gospel of greed* (1999).[1]

Faced with today's *res novae*, it is not difficult to see where the social danger of greed lies. The problem that the greedy creates is not so much the fact that the things he/she longs for are an expression of selfish preferences, nor that they are his own desires, but rather the fact that all his/her desires have as their object goods *for him/her*, only. That is why the greedy is a parasite. He/she can be what he/she is if *others* are different from him/her. The greedy fulfills his desires and realizes his/her plans only within some social context. But society, to exist, postulates that there are (at least some) subjects who consider the interests of others as a claim to themselves! Paradoxically, this means that greed would not exist if all individuals accepted and put into practice the maxim of Horace: "O citizens, citizens the first thing to look for is money. Virtue comes after money." We read in the famous "Economic Possibilities for our grandchildren" by J.M. Keynes (1963, [1930]): "When the accumulation of wealth is no longer of high social importance, there will be great changes in the code of morals. [...] We must have the courage to give the motivation "money" its true value. The love of money as a possession — as distinguished from the love of money as a mean to the enjoyments and realities of life — will be recognized for what it is, a somewhat disgusting morbidity, one of those semi-criminal, semi-pathological propensities which one hands over with a shudder to the specialists in mental disease".[2]

---

[1]A few years later, in 1898, the American steel king, Andrew Carnegie, will publish his *Gospel of Wealth!*

[2]Epistle I, p. 1.

2.5 The Gift as Gratuitousness

There is in the human being a feeling that drives the passionate search of what suits his/her needs, which has the name of desire. Human desire, when it is not deviated, turns to things as to what satisfies it. But it can be set on the wrong target. This is to say that some of the targeted goods are apparent goods, that is, evils: goods that seem to satisfy, but that bend towards disorder and push towards unhappiness. Desire is the energy of life, but you can desire things that make us bloom and things that make us wither. Well, greed is a wish that withers. It is the derailment of desire that grows on itself, just like the desire of power after power that Hobbes was talking about. We know why. Goods become actual goods, that is, good things, when they are put forward for the common good.

Goods not shared are always ways to unhappiness even in an opulent world. Money held tight, as jealous possession, impoverishes its possessor, because it strips him/her of the ability to give. The greedy, by definition, cannot give and therefore cannot be happy. He/she can make donations, that is, can engage in philanthropic practices if this serves him/her, instrumentally, to increase his/her possession. The greedy, in other words, may come to cover himself/herself hypocritically with the veil of the charitable alibi, but this has nothing to do with the authentic gift. In fact, it is well known that the strength of the gratuitous gift is not in the given thing *per se* or in the given quantum – as it is the case in philanthropy – but in the fact that the gift constitutes an encounter, a relationship between people. That is why, while philanthropy almost always generates dependence in the recipient of philanthropic action, the authentic gift stimulates reciprocity and therefore frees the recipient of the donative action of "shame".

The action of those who, by virtue of their intentions, do not allow the beneficiary to counter-act is not exactly free. If the recipient is not placed in a position to reciprocate, he/she will end up feeling humiliated and in the long run, will hate his/her benefactor, as Seneca in his letter to Lucilio reminds us. Thomas Aquinas argued that to be able to correspond to a (real) gift, the one receiving the gift must present another (real) gift, not a mere equivalent of what has received. The gratuitous gift, by its nature, always causes the activation of the inter-subjective relationship par excellence, that of reciprocity. It is only with reciprocity that mutual recognition is implemented, which is precisely what nurtures self-respect.

In this consists the generating principle of human sociability, to distinguish it from non-human sociality. The donative action is that which practices the difficult art of treating with respect the perceived need of the other. The logic of the gratuitous gift, in fact, is based on the circumstance that the bond accompanies the gift and that the first component is more important than the second. This is not the case in philanthropy, where what counts is the entity (or value) of the donation. That is why the intent to benefit others, *per se*, is not enough to characterize the authenticity of the donative action. The greedy gives to receive – this is the meaning of the so-called exchange of gifts.

In the reciprocity that comes from the gratuitous gift, however, the opening towards the other determines a modification of the *ego* that, in its return to its own interiority, is found richer for the encounter that took place. The departure of the *me* towards a needed *you* is what defines the gratuitousness of the authentic gift. Indeed, if, contrary to the individualistic conception, I construct my identity in relation to the other, then my ego is produced only through a process of relationship with the other. I cannot define myself if I do not feel responsible for whomever is different from me. In this sense, I always need the other.

Giving gratuitously to another is always giving oneself to another, whatever the object you give. Not so in the exchange of equivalents of value, which arises from the contract, whose founding principle is rather the perfect symmetry between what you give and what you can claim to get in return. It is because of such property that the law can always intervene to give execution to bonds born by contract. Why is this clarification important? Because as the French school of the MAUSS (*Mouvement anti-utilitariste dans les Sciences Sociales*) has made clear, there is a conception of the gift typical of premodernity, which, however, still exists today, according to which the gift should always be linked to an underlying exchange structure. This is the conception of the gift as *munus*, as a tool to engage the other, to the point of enslavement. Because of such a conception, gift becomes, paradoxically, an obligation to preserve the social bond: life in society deems as a necessity the practice of the gift, which thus becomes a social norm of behavior, as binding as all such norms.

Think of social practices such as *potlach* and *kula* so well described by Marcel Mauss and Claude Lévi-Strauss: those who return the gift try to overcome in magnificence the gift received, forcing, in fact, the first donor to do even better and more. It does not take much to understand how such a conception of donation can be reconciled with the behavior of the greedy to the point of making the latter pass as a philanthropist. In this regard, Tolstoy's specific statement in the essay *The Destruction of Hell and its Restoration* is evocative; "the evil of philanthropy instills in men the idea that if they rob and give crumbs to the robbed, they do beneficial work and they no longer have to long to be better". Donation is not at all incompatible with the interests of the giver, if this is understood as an interest in being in the relationship with the other. The gratuitous gift is not a finite act in itself, but represents the beginning of a relationship, a chain of reciprocal acts. As if to say that the gratuitous gift is done with good reason, in view of the establishment of a bond. It is the interest *for* the other (and not *at* the other) that comes from the desire for the bond. An idea that was masterfully understood and illustrated by Giovan Battista Vico (*La Scienza Nuova*, Augusta, 1725) when he foresaw that the decline of a society begins when men no longer find within themselves the motivation to tie their own destiny to that of others.

The "greedy-philanthropist", however, does not have this interest, so much so that he/she is not even interested in knowing the identity of those to whom his/her charity is addressed. The person involved simply "is not seen". In another way, the fact that on the surface the opposing terms "interest" and "gratuitousness" inevitably appear intertwined with each other does not in any way erase the specificity of the free gift as such. In fact, there is a more radical dimension of the gratuitous gift that presents itself as that dimension of depth in which a person is "constituted" or is brought into the world only if and when another person recognizes it or satisfies its needs. Here gratuitousness exceeds the calculation of interest for the simple fact that there is no symmetry between the subjects involved. The fact is that the culture of modernity is so steeped in utilitarian mentality that whenever we hear about a bi-univocal relationship between two subjects we are instinctively led to read an underlying, albeit indirect, relationship of exchange of equivalents of value. This is one of the heavy intellectual legacies of modernity. "For there to be a gift – writes Jacques Derrida – it is necessary that the gift does not appear, that it is not perceived as a gift". But such a gift cannot exist, it is impossible, because man, to Derrida, is an ontologically self-interested being, that is, greedy. If the gift has an intention, if it means something to the donor, it is no longer a gift. For Derrida, the only possible gift should not be motivated, it should be completely disinterested. Which is not true at all, as argued above.

It may be of interest to recall what B. de Mandeville – the Author that coined the word "Capitalism" – wrote in his famous work *The Fable of the Bees: or, Private Vices, Publick Benefits* (1988, [1713]): "I flatter myself to have demonstrated, that neither the Friendly Qualities and kind Affections that are natural to Man, nor the real Virtues he is capable of acquiring by Reason and Self-denial, are the Foundation of Society; but that what we call Evil in this World, Moral as well as Natural, is the grand Principle that makes us sociable Creatures; the solid Basis, the Life and Support of all Trades and Employments *without Exception"*.

Having to weigh up the intrinsic and extrinsic value of those dispositions that guide human action, the moral appraisal of agents' conduct is a particularly burdensome exercise, Mandeville believed, also because no metric exists for such purpose. Thus it is understandable (but not justifiable) why Mandeville's conceptual framework was welcomed by all those who wished to show that the forms of behaviour condemned by tradition were in fact the very ones needed in order to achieve "public benefits". One can certainly morally disapprove of greed – the strong expression of the vice of avarice – but if it is shown that under certain conditions, favouring such behaviour can reduce poverty more effectively than the promotion of self-sacrifice can, then it is clear that said behaviour will ultimately be considered beneficial. The profound nature of capitalism – its ontology as a philosopher would say – will never be fully understood without realising that this socio-economic system, in order to function, employs to a previously unseen degree hidden mechanisms resulting in undesired, unforeseen consequences. This had significant political and cultural consequences: from that moment on, the moral protests raised by those who were not aware of, or did not understand, such mechanisms were either set aside or, indeed, ridiculed. It is of great interest – I believe – to recall what Don Patinkin in his influential 1956 book *Money, Interest and Prices* wrote: "We can consider the individual – with his given indifference map and initial endowment – to be a 'utility computer' into whom we 'feed' a sequence of market prices and from whom we obtain a corresponding sequence of 'solutions' in the form of specified optimum positions".[3]

2.6 Epilogue

The dominant culture, places the gift as a sort of an absolute which, precisely because it is such, is then forced to declare itself impossible to achieve. It is the question – central in the contemporary philosophical debate – of the gift's "suspicion" as a gesture that would claim to be gratuitous and that nevertheless appears constantly crossed by elements of interest that pollute its purity. The only possible act would then be that of philanthropy, which is perfectly compatible with the individualistic anthropological assumption. Not very different, as to the outcome to which it leads, is the position of postmodern philosophers like Emmanuel Levinas, centered on the idea of exile, of nomadism. For the French philosopher, the orientation towards the other, in which the self is the hostage of the other, means that we forever live beyond ourselves. One is saved only in this movement towards the other. But this position is unacceptable, and even dangerous. Because the basis of human sociality cannot be the "exile" (the *kenosis*), since if it is true that the hosting host must accept the hosted host, it is equally true that the host must receive the hospitality offered. Not only that, but to arrive at demanding, as Levinas does, "the ingratitude of the other", since gratitude would be "the return of the movement to its origin", means to deny that human sociability is not only desire *for the other*, but also desire of the *other for me*.

As Davis and MacMaster (2020) indicate, care challenges the conventional rubric of economic organizations predicated on greed. Economists of all sorts – with the exception of feminist economists – have either overlooked or failed to appreciate the centrality of care to human existence. Care is marginalized in economic thinking since the location of the domain of care is viewed as non-economic (the home) and hence not priced in the marketplace. But care is not a commodity; it is a relational good. The sooner mainstream economics overcomes its unreasonable reductionism, making room in its theories and models to the figure of "homo curans" better for all (see also Zamagni 2021).

I would like to conclude with a general consideration. The fact that a society in which the assumption of "homo curans" is lost, and where everything comes down to optimising transactions based on the exchange of equivalents principle, on the one hand, and to increasing the transfers made by public welfare organisations on the other, is not a sustainable society, has been forgotten, would explain why it is that despite the quality of the intellectual forces at play, no credible solution to present day challenges has yet been forthcoming. A society in which the principle of

[3] Quoted in Pabst (2021, 57).

reciprocity is neglected, is a society with no future; that is, a society cannot progress if it is only capable of "giving to receive", or of "giving as a duty". This is why neither the liberal-individualist vision of the world, in which everything (or nearly everything) is exchange, nor the State-centric vision of society, where everything (or nearly everything) is based on a sense of duty, can safely lead us out of the shallows, where globalization and the digital revolution are severely testing our existing model of civilisation.

References

Barrera, Albino. 2005. *God and the Evil of Scarcity: Moral Foundations of Economic Agency.* Notre Dame: Notre Dame University Press.

Bellanca, N., and G. Pichillo. 2014. Identitarian passions: The overwhelming power of the human recognition need. *International Review of Economics* 61: 13.

Davis, J., and R. MacMaster. 2020. A road not taken? A brief history of care in economic thought. *European Journal of the History of Economic Thought* 2: 209.

de Mandeville, B. 1988, [1713]. *The Fable of the Bees: or, Private Vices, Publick Benefits.* Indianapolis: Liberty Fund.

Easterlin, Richard. 1974. Does Economic Growth Improve Human Lot? Some empirical evidence. In *Nations and Households in Economic Growth*, ed. P.A. Davis and M.W. Reder. New York: Academic.

Keynes, John Maynard. 1963, [1930]. Economic possibilities for our grandchildren. In *Essays in Persuasion,* 358–373. New York: W.W.Norton & Co.

McFadden, Daniel. 2006. Revealed stochastic preferences: a synthesis. In *Rationality and Equilibrium*, ed. C.D. Aliprantis et al. Berlin: Springer.

Pabst, A. 2021. *Postliberal Politics*. Cambridge: Polity Press.

Peirce, Sanders. 1999. *The Essential Peirce*. In *Selected Philosophical Writings (1983–1913).* Indianapolis: Indiana University Press.

Smith, Adam. 1982, [1759]. *Theory of Moral Sentiments,* Indianapolis: Liberty Fund.

Thomas, Jean. 1995. The love of our neighbour and the economics of giving. In *Love of our Neighbour*, ed. A. Pilé. London: Blackfriars Pub.

von Wright, Georg. 1971. *Explanation and Understanding*. Ithaca: Cornell University Press.

Zamagni, Stefano. 2021. The quest for an axiological reorientation of economic science. *Structural Change and Economic Dynamics* 58: 391.

Chapter 3
What Is 'Enough'?

Margaret Atkins

Abstract Economics was invented to deal with material scarcity, and is therefore biased towards increasing materially production. Many of the world's current problems, however, are caused by excessive use of the resources of the natural world, often driven by an excessive desire to accumulate the money that stands proxy for them. In order to respond to these, then, we need to return the concept of 'enough' to the centre of moral and social, and therefore political and economic, thinking. 'Enough' for an individual turns out to be concretely contextual and intrinsically relational. At the same time, it has objective boundaries, set not least by ecological limits combined with justice, both local and global. Therefore we need both good judgement and healthy societies to be truly satisfied, as individuals, with enough. One of the factors that exacerbates our weakness for excess is the monetarisation of goods. Economists, I suggest, might need to be attentive to the importance, the specific complexities, and the risks of quantifying 'enough'.

This paper is dedicated to the memory of Professor Rosemary Mitchell, a dear friend and former colleague who was taken ill unexpectedly and died while it was in preparation. A comment of hers on a recent related paper of mine provides a profound and apt reflective context for my argument: 'The problem also seems that where we should understand finitude (e.g. natural resources), we act as if are limitless – while we marginalise goods which ARE actually limitless (e.g. poetry). For me, part of the problem is our failure to recognise in ourselves that which is mortal and finite, and that which is not, the God-given. Insufficient humility and insufficient adoration ....'
Robert Skidelsky and Edward Skidelsky's superb, *How Much is Enough? Money and the Good Life* (2013) has been both an invaluable aid and a dialogue partner in preparing this paper. Rob Dietz and Dan O'Neill, *Enough is Enough: Building a Sustainable Economy in a World of Finite Resources* (2013) is basic reading for anyone wanting to return sanity to mainstream economic thinking.
I am grateful to Edward Hadas and Malcolm Schofield for very helpful comments on this paper.

M. Atkins (✉)
Canoness of St Augustine in the community at Boarbank Hall in Cumbria, Grange-over-Sands, UK

Research Fellow, Blackfriars, Oxford, UK
e-mail: margaret@boarbankhall.org.uk

P. Róna et al. (eds.), *Homo Curator: Towards the Ethics of Consumption*, Virtues and Economics 8, https://doi.org/10.1007/978-3-031-51700-6_3

3.1 The Madness of Maximising

When I was a child, we used to play a game called 'Simon Says'. The leader told you to perform a simple action, preceded by the words, 'Simon says ...' The challenge was, that if he or she omitted the key words, you were *not* to perform the action. It was surprisingly difficult not to be caught out. For the uninitiated, reading academic literature on economics feels like playing 'Simon Says'. Nearly every time you encounter the word 'rational', you have to remember that it describes someone whose goal is to 'maximise'. In ordinary life, people who try to maximise possessions are called 'addicted', 'obsessive' or 'avaricious': sad, mad or bad. On the other hand, in ordinary conversation the word 'rational' is a compliment: 'endowed with reason', 'having sound judgement, sensible, sane', to quote the *New Shorter Oxford English Dictionary* (2482).

The discrepancy matters not only because it makes economic literature difficult for non-specialists to read. It matters because if you turn an ordinary word into a piece of jargon, or maybe simply confuse it with another word, it is almost impossible for both writer and reader not to import into their thinking the connotations of the richer original meaning. In other words, it is hard not to imply or assume that there is something normal and reasonable, even virtuous or desirable, about the obsessively calculating desire to increase one's material goods. (Indeed, the adjective 'calculating', though not quite conveying the oddity of so-called 'rational maximising', would have tracked its meaning more closely, and been less misleading in its associations.) The pervasiveness of such misleading language is inevitably pernicious in its influence.

There are, of course, now a welcome minority of economists who argue for a broader concept of rationality or question the goal of 'maximising'. Defenders of the 'Rational Economic Man' model have responded by redefining 'utility' as preferences, and arguing that such preferences need not be selfish. This does not help with the problem of maximising. Firstly, although the original model may have been crass, at least it was clear how it was meant to work. If, however, you redefine 'utility' to mean anything that someone might happen to want at any moment (including things that are not in any way in their material interest), you will have no way of grasping what such utility comprises, except the crude measure of financial expenditure. Indeed, it is not clear how you could even identify, let alone count, add up or predict, the actions people are engaging in, let alone their motives for such engagement. Secondly, while statistical generalities about preferences could be useful, they have little to do with 'maximising'. Preferences are just not the sort of thing you can, logically, maximise, for various philosophical reasons, including, as Edward Skidelsky elegantly explains, the way in which our perspectives change over a lifetime.[1]

These confusions, I suggest, spring from the fact that economists use money as a proxy for goods. As St Thomas Aquinas pointed out, following Aristotle, the

[1] Skidelsky [in this volume]. See also Wincewicz-Price (2021).

avaricious person has infinite desires because he forgets that money is a means and treats it as an end.[2] But because money, unlike material goods, has no natural limit, such a person can never be satisfied: ‘Restlessness issues from avarice in that this engenders anxiety and undue worry in a person: *a covetous man shall not be satisfied with money*.’[3]

In the relatively innocent societies in which Aquinas lived, most other desires had natural limits: even the greediest person has to stop eating pork at some point.[4] I have suggested that we too, in ordinary life, recognise that there is something close to madness (or at least pathological addiction) about simply desiring more and more of specific things, which is why we used to make jokes about Imelda Marcos’ shoes. However, in our own society, the machinery for promoting desires that St Thomas would have considered both unnecessary and non-natural is vast, sophisticated and untrammelled to a degree that he could never have dreamed. It works not by directly encouraging us to ‘maximise’ types of things, but by constantly reinventing and persuasively advertising new possibilities for acquisitiveness.[5] Because these possibilities are presented as open-ended, we have a new reason for amassing money. Aquinas’ miser had forgotten the point of the thing he was collecting; present day consumers rarely examine the deeper purpose of their new purchases, and have no idea what the point of their future purchases might be. The indirect but socially approved pressure to keep on accumulating is as powerful, and far more pervasive, than the eccentric desire of the occasional miser.

Good sense, I submit, even sanity, requires that we do not seek to maximise, but aim for the right amount, for ‘enough’. To do that, however, we need to know what enough is. That, however, is often far from obvious. ‘I wish the government would give us a quota for flights, so we know what is fair,’ remarked a friend following a family holiday. Similarly, Edward Hadas (2021, 102), after raising various questions about the precise meaning of the moderation in consumption recommended by Catholic Social Teaching, comments, ‘I would love some more papal guidance.’ How much, then, is ‘enough’? How do we decide? And how, once we have decided, do we move from excess nearer to sufficiency? I propose to explore these questions

---

[2]The wise and profound discussion of wealth in Aristotle’s *Politics* 1.8-10 provides the bedrock and background of this critique, and is highly relevant to the whole topic of sufficiency in economic thinking.

[3]*Summa Theologiae* 1.2.30.4; Ecclesiastes 5.9, quoted in *Summa Theologiae* 2.2.118.8.

[4]Cf *Summa Theologiae* 1.2.30.4 (although Aquinas’ use of Aristotle’s example of medicine and health as a possible example of infinite desire is - to me at least - obscure).

[5]I owe this distinction between the way avarice and consumerism works to Edward Hadas. Cf. J. K. Galbraith (1958, 127): ‘Were it so that a man on arising each morning was assailed by demons which instilled in him a passion sometimes for silk shirts, sometimes for kitchenware, sometimes for chamber pots, and sometimes for orange squash, there would be every reason to applaud the effort to find the goods, however odd, that quenched this flame. But should it be that his passion was the result of his first having cultivated the demons, and should it be that his effort to allay it stirred the demons to ever greater and greater effort, there would be question as to how rational was his solution. Unless restrained by conventional attitudes, he might wonder if the solution lay with more goods or fewer demons.

from the perspective of an educated member of a wealthy society, the sort of person who might read or write an article such as this. What is 'enough', for you or for me?

The answer to that question, apparently such an ordinary one, turns out to be surprisingly elusive. I shall explore various complexities in the concept which contribute to that elusiveness. Further difficulties with the concept derive from common human frailty. Modern societies, perhaps particularly the richer ones, are especially ill-equipped to grasp the concept, viewing it as they do through various distorting lenses. Let us begin, though, with a simple point: 'enough' implies a purpose.

3.2 Context and Purpose

'What is enough?' Only a philosopher would ask precisely that question. If someone says to you out of the blue, 'Have you got enough?', you wonder, 'Enough of what?' The question, 'Is there enough?' can be understood only by specifying (at least implicitly) enough of *what*, *in what circumstances* and *for what purpose*.[6] We ask, 'Have you had enough lunch?' and we imply: now, for the purposes of nourishing you and making you comfortable. A mother feeding her children regularly might also wonder about the overall balance of nourishment: are there enough vitamins, enough protein, in the meals? Enough, that is, to keep these children healthy. We can only answer such questions by making them specific, which means both relating them to a context and identifying the purpose of the question. Since we are material and biological beings, there will always be relevant limits to identify. It is when we ignore or disguise what is concrete and purposeful that we can be tempted by the madness of maximising.

Indeed, the choice of means and the amount of resources required are themselves shaped by the context and ordered to their goal. A mother in China might think of rice, one in France of bread or potatoes. There is then, a certain interchangeability in our answer: 'Well, I have enough protein if we use the bacon, but if not, I'll add some cheese.' This interchangeability is indefinite but not unlimited: there will still be an appropriate amount for the substituted cheese, while swapping the bacon for candyfloss would not do the job. Meals provide a simple example, of course: in the wider world we are often dealing with complex systems where the relation between different elements is not fully understood. We scarcely understand, for example, the role that many millions of different organisms play in something as essential to our lives as topsoil. We do know, though, that here too there are limits: these organisms need to function in balance.

Topsoil might stand as an image of many of the complex material systems among which we live. Our material world is made up of a indefinitely vast number of limited things which, when it works well (in its parts and as a whole), are in dynamic

[6] I assume here the point well-argued by the Skidelskys in their book that we cannot determine what is enough without a rich picture of what counts as a good life.

equilibrium. This means that you need a complex variety of things to make it work; that the relation between these things is at least as important as the quantity; and that you can always, and usually easily, have too much of any one material thing.[7] By contrast, there often are things of which you *cannot*, in a specific contexts, have *too little*: one pinch of arsenic in your wine is one pinch too many.

For these reasons and others, the concept of enough has a certain fuzziness and elasticity. Indeed, to ignore this would also lead to a kind of madness, calculating the food we need to the nearest calory, or its equivalent in other areas of life: 'vagueness is not necessarily a failing in an enquiry that is by nature vague' (Skidelsky and Skidelsky 2021, 167). That truth takes nothing from the reality of the limits of enough or from the fact that there are times when our desires clearly push beyond these limits. All we need is for enough to be a concept sufficiently firm and tight, like good elastic, to shape wise action.

3.3 What Is Too Little?

We say to children: 'Have you had enough?' or 'Stop that, that's quite enough!' These two ways of speaking remind us of an ambiguity in English of the word: 'enough' means both 'not too little' and 'not too much'. Consequently, we have two questions to ask: 'What is too little?' and 'What is too much?'

We normally approach the question of too little by thinking rather about the minimum needs of individuals and families. Less than what you need is too little. Nature sets our basic needs, so that these are relatively easy to determine: we need enough food (maybe around 2000 calories a day, balanced among various specifiable types of nutrient), we need shelter, companionship, the freedom to have a family and so on. Any list of basic needs or capabilities will refer to such goods, and although there is some cultural variation (healthy food and safe shelter will be different in different contexts), the list is pretty much the same for everyone.[8]

After that, there is room for greater variation. A second class of needs are inescapably personal in their shape, precisely because of their concreteness. You and I both need a worthwhile occupation, but you are a pianist and I am a plumber. You need a piano in a way that I do not, while I need screwdrivers and wrenches that are not essentials for you. I might enjoy playing the piano and you might enjoy fixing radiators, but in neither case will the tools for this count as needs. Or you might argue that we all need some hobbies. If so, then maybe my piano counts as a need and so do your tools, but neither of us need the artist's easel we ponder in moments of fantasy: for the time available for hobbies cannot be unlimited. This personal

---

[7] There are *immaterial* goods, of course, that you cannot have too much of, such as charity and peace; that at least is a standard theological claim, which St Thomas uses to explain why the theological virtues, unlike the cardinal virtues, which relate to this life, do not relate to a mean (*Summa Theologiae* 1.2.64.4).

[8] See Braybrooke (1987), especially ch. 2.

dimension of needs will also be shaped by our particular physiology, gifts and talents, our personal history, our family situation, religious practice and the place we live in, as well as by our work. Thus what is 'enough' for different people will vary not so much in amount, for we are talking of things that are not commensurable, but in content. As for amount, there will be some fuzziness and elasticity about 'enough', but also effective limits: our family may, arguably, need two cars given the commitments required by our genuine needs, but we would be exaggerating to say that we need six.

The lower limit of enough does not have to be set to Puritanical levels. Indeed, we might argue that a little comfort and pleasure, especially in social contexts, is important to a balanced life. A remark of St Thomas Aquinas' is so delightfully unexpected that I have to check it from time to time to make sure I have not dreamed it. Drunkenness did have an opposite, he said, a vice of not enjoying wine enough, but it is so rare it does not have a name.[9]

Thirdly, our needs are shaped by our societies.[10] This is true in obvious practical ways: if there is no public transport and no work within walking distance, I need a bicycle or car to be able to work. It is also true in subtler ways, connected with our need for recognition and respect, and for smooth social relations. If wearing scruffy but serviceable clothes on a specific occasion will mean either that I am mocked or that I insult someone else, there is a real sense in which I need something smart to wear. Again, such societally shaped needs have real limits, but an element of fuzziness and elasticity.

At this point, you might object: but surely there is too much elasticity here to be useful. In one cultural context, my 'smart' clothes might be a simple white robe that will last me for a lifetime. In another it might be a new outfit every month. Are 'societal needs' not simply an excuse for the rich to justify having more? The right answer seems to be 'Yes and No'. Mary, here and now, might need to drive to work, but it is a weakness of her society that she can neither find employment nearer home nor find a bus to take her to workplace. Similarly with the goods of esteem: while the needs for respect and courtesy are true human needs, and are inevitably socially shaped, at the same time, social practices in some societies are such that what counts as respect and courtesy are shaped by excess, and call for reform. 'Consumption ... could be seen as an act of discovering one's needs, one's values, even self-formation,' writes Agnieszka Wincewicz-Price (2021, 134) in the course of arguing that reasonable choices require the moral development of individual human agents. The same point can be made for the societies of which such agents are part.

[9] *Summa Theologiae* 2.2.150.1 ad 1.

[10] Miller (2012) provides a thoughtful account of the relative and objective dimensions of societal needs.

3.4 What Is Too Much?

What, then, about the upper limit for 'enough'? When can we say, 'Enough is enough?' There are strong religious, philosophical, and indeed medical traditions which hold that our own well-being sets an upper limit. St Thomas, for example, appealed here to virtues related to *temperantia*, which he described as follows: 'It is the role of temperateness, primarily and strictly speaking, to moderate the desires for the delights of touch' - in which he includes taste - 'and then other desires.'[11] A little later he adds, 'temperateness takes the needs of this life as a rule by which to use pleasurable things, so that it makes use of them just as much as the needs of this life demand.'[12] He stood in a long tradition, going back at least to Plato, Aristotle and the Stoics, and running like the letters on a stick of rock through Christian and other major religious traditions, which has held that virtues are essential to our true happiness.

The Skidelskys took a related but distinct tack, arguing that the pressures of consumerism bind us to a competitive treadmill that takes away our freedom. By limiting our need to earn, we are liberated to enjoy the good life. It is interesting that our official medicine is moving back (despite the commercial pharmaceutical pressures to do otherwise) to emphasising the values of limit in our health: not only the physical limits of food, drink, drugs and sleep, which affect our physical health, but also the limits needed by our minds and emotions, that are disturbed by unbalanced work, addictive obsesssions or anxiety-creating competition for status.

There is, however, a second, distinct route to identifying upper limits, by reflecting not on our own needs, but on the needs of wider society, or indeed of the whole world. To put the point in terms of the virtues: temperateness turns out, in our present context at least, to be more tightly related to justice than philosophers have always noticed.[13] Or perhaps one might say: the traditional teaching of the unity of the virtues is starting to make very detailed sense in respect of these two virtues, as we reflect on our current social and ecological challenges.

If a few people have too much of something, it can cause harm to others either socially or ecologically, and this is true at the local, regional, national and global levels. It has become commonplace to notice the global dimension of this claim, basic for example, to Kate Raworth's well-known *Doughnut Economics*, which argues that we need an economy that exists in the space between the limits of natural resources and the decent minimum needed by every person on earth. The inner ring of Raworth's doughnut, the decent minimum needed by the poor, grounds a *social* upper limit to the use of resources by the rich. The outer ring of the doughnut grounds a similar *ecological* limit. The latter depends on the increasingly widely accepted premises that (i) there are biological, geological and ecological limits to our planet's resources that we, as a human race, are over-stepping or close to

[11] *Summa Theologiae* 2.2.141.4 ad 1.

[12] *Summa Theologiae* 2.2.141.6.

[13] See Atkins (2003).

breaching; and that (ii) nearly all the use of material goods by people living in wealthy countries (at least) has some damaging impact on the wider environment and possibly an unjust impact on the lives of others.

Whether or not you accept the details of Raworth's arguments, her fundamental principles seem to follow directly from a basic idea of fairness. Any argument for justifying the protection of my own access to the goods that meet my needs is also an argument for justifying that same protection for others. Therefore if I take so much from a limited pool (of both goods and 'pollution sinks') that others have their basic needs compromised, I am acting unfairly. How, though, does this fairness work? Are we all to have exactly the same? Here we fall back on our previous discussion of the different levels of need. It makes sense to argue that we should all have more or less the same (again, the search for precision would be a sign of irrationality) in the sense that we should all have access to goods that satisfy our natural, personal and societal needs. Once again, if some cultures or societies have defined their needs in such a way that there is not enough to go around, they need, in justice, to reform themselves.

It is equally important to notice the ways in which justice, fairness and social well-being can set an upper limit to 'enough' at the level of local communities, regions or nations. To take a concrete example, David Wiggins' lifelong interest in understanding and promoting a philosophical understanding of need was triggered by a very practical question: how to explain what was wrong about a proposal to build a series of motorways being built in the north of London that would involve demolishing 20,000 homes (Wiggins 2005, 26 ff). The specific lives of actual families were about to be harmed in a range of very tangible and identifiable ways. Yet the abstract potential for money and time to be saved by relatively well-off motorists being able to travel faster to work was allowed to override this. An argument that began with social justice, might conclude that the indefinite group of commuters might need to set limits to their desires for wealth and leisure.

The ecological and social impacts on shared goods of the local use of resources affect the lives of ordinary people at least as much as their global equivalent. The rich who own multiple, underused, properties in areas with limited housing mean that the poorly paid cannot afford a home there; the parents who drive their children to school mean that no children who walk are as safe as they once were; if all of us choose to picnic every week at the local beauty spot, none of us are likely to enjoy it nearly so much. Moreover, there is nothing new about this problem at the local level. Traditional practices of the governance of local common resources, simple and familiar things such as fishing licenses, are responses to the local impacts of such collective excess.

One aspect of what I have called 'collective' excess is that actions which individually and in isolation may be entirely innocent can become cumulatively damaging. The pollution from a handful of cars driving past a school may quickly disappear; if there are several thousand, the numbers of children with asthma will increase. As the damage that we human beings inflict on our various environments continues to increase, the upper limit of 'enough' for each person, for a large and indefinite range of specific choices, will be lowered.

It is perhaps worth saying specifically that the excesses of the relatively wealthy harm the rich as well as the poor. Even if the poor are more immediately, directly and frequently hurt by ecological pressures or climate change, the rich are hardly unaffected by large-scale disasters such as flooding. The same point often holds also for the smaller, more local, questions. The by-pass that destroys the homes of the underprivileged to speed up the well-off commuters becomes, with the passing of the years, 'a car park' (to use the description one often hears of the M25). The butterflies destroyed by pesticides are less available on country walks even for millionaires. The infectious diseases that spread among paupers excluded by a health system are unlikely to check bank accounts before extending their range.

Whether we ask 'What is too little?' or 'What is too much?', whether our concerns are social justice or environmental harm, whether we begin with the individual, the community or the whole planet, in every instance the nature of 'enough' turns out to be not only shaped by society, but irreducibly relational. Our individual needs include the need for affective relationships. Our personal needs are determined in part by how we relate to others, in our work, at home, in our leisure time. Our social needs are structured both by the ways in which our society allows or enables us to fulfil more basic needs, and by the customs of courtesy and respect. Finally, the limit of 'too much' is overstepped not only when we fail ourselves through intemperateness, but also when we fail others through injustice. Indeed, we can only understand what might count as taking more than our fair share by considering ourselves in relation to our own communities and societies as well as to the rest of the world.

3.5 The Need for Judgement

Few readers of this article will be living on the breadline. The live question for most of us, in our daily lives, is not, 'Have I got too little?', but rather, 'What count as using too much, for me, in this context, now?' Can the argument so far give a basis for specific answers? It will be clear that there can be no easy checklist for deciding what is enough for each of us and no algorithm for calculating it. I have already discussed the elasticity of 'enough'. There are several further elements that would also make general guidance very difficult, and possibly of little use. First, the concreteness of the question means that we need to ask 'What is enough?' not only for a very large, and indeterminitely large, number of objects and activities. Arguably, we need to have internalised the question so that we are implicitly asking it of ourselves pretty much all the time. We will therefore need to ask it also for an indefinite and very large number of specific situations. In most of these situations there will be some obscurity and some uncertainty, since every object we consider using or consuming is embedded within a complex system: I cannot know, for example, whether in my own case eating chocolate might lead to diabetes, and if so exactly how many chocolates I can safely eat. I am unlikely to know which potentially harmful chemicals were used to grow the food I buy, and even if I do, I cannot be certain of their exact impact. Finally, we will need to deal with the familiar problems of incommensurability: whether or not to use the car to get to the nearest organic grocer's.

'Ten thousand difficulties do not make a doubt' (Newman 2011, [1864]). We should not slip lazily from the truth that our judgements about 'enough' are necessarily fallible and imprecise into the false claim that we can know nothing about its limits. Recognising unquestionable examples of too little or too much - the starving child, the alcoholic - is a basic skill of ordinary good sense, which all of us possess to some degree. However, the complexities of understanding that I have discussed do mean that we will not find a pseudo-scientific shortcut - an exceptionless checklist or an algorithm - to avoid the hard work of continuous judgement.[14]

On the personal level, more useful than rigid rules will be the relevant virtues. Practical wisdom, the disposition that enables us to make wise judgements, deals, as we need, with particular cases in all their complexity. It will be assisted by rules of thumb, but alert to the exception and to the need to apply rules appropriately. In this area, it will be informed by other virtues, especially those of temperateness[15] and of justice. Virtues are not mere acts of will, and cannot suddenly be switched on. They engage our whole personalities, conscious and subconscious, emotions, moods, calculation, reflection and values, and they grow out of our life histories. Importantly, they are nurtured and shaped by our cultures.

This is one reason why we need to develop not only individual virtues, but the good customs that function as the virtues of a healthy society.[16] Good customs will have the further benefit of reshaping the content of both our personal and our societal needs in the direction of genuine sufficiency rather than excess. In this context, general guidelines can be valuable (although they can only cover small areas of life): an example would be government advice about the appropriate temperature of different kinds of workplaces. The application of such guidelines, however, requires neither blind rule-following nor surly acquiescence, but an understanding of and goodwill towards their underlying purpose. In other words, good customs and personal virtues are mutually interdependent.

It is time to make explicit what I have been implying in most of my discussion: that nearly every one in the wealthier parts of the world, and almost certainly everyone reading this (not least its author), is more likely to be erring on the side of 'too

[14]A comment of Malcolm Schofield's on the description of the best constitution in *Cicero's Republic* 2.57 is pertinent here: 'The reiteration of "sufficient" is particularly indicative. It implies that how exactly such matters are to be determined will be a task for judgement, in the light of circumstances as assessed from a vantage point of practical experience, custom, and the actual realities of class and power, not of theory alone. In other words, a proper theory of the best constitution cannot remain a matter of "pure" theory, or a precise formula valid for all time, but must grant a crucial role to experience and judgement' (Cicero 2021, 81–82).

[15]Following Herbert McCabe, I prefer 'temperateness' to 'temperance'; the latter word is coloured by its associations with the suppression rather than the moderation of desire, and that commonly in the narrow context of alcoholic drinks!

[16]Cf. Blum (1998).

much' than 'not enough'.[17] To avoid digressing, we can leave aside the question of greenhouse gases. A host of other considerations, from the political - With which powerfully corrupt state or individuals do we collude to secure our fuel? What are the working conditions of those who mine our precious metals? - to the statistical - What percentage of invertebrates have been lost in Europe in the last 35 years? How much plastic is there in the sea? - to personal experience - What volume of waste does my own institution discard every week? How much cleaner has the air been during Lockdown? How much trash do I find half-buried on every quiet country walk? - combine to point to our excesses of thoughtless consumption and the careless discarding of waste that is its near-inevitable consequence. Such excess is built into the fabric of our society. It will be helpful to analyse this more precisely.

3.6 Temptations to Excess[18]

Our human nature, personal situation and society determine our needs. Each of these, in different ways, can also push us to excess. The temptations of our basic human nature - greed for amounts and varieties of food, predatory sexual behaviour - are, of course, ever-present, and (as recent protest movements have made clear) more dangerous when we ignore their existence. Given our inherent tendency to see the world through self-centred eyes, it is very rare for the well off to underestimate their needs, while most of us are very good at exaggerating them.[19] That same tendency becomes more tempting and more dangerous when it comes to personal needs: for here it is easy to contrast ourselves with others and persuade ourselves that our special situation 'needs' more: 'Of course a pianist has to have two pianos! How would they know? They are not pianists!' Conversely, we are likely to underestimate what others need: 'Well, they are used working hard, aren't they?'

---

[17] Carbon Footprints offer one way of measuring 'enough' for part of our lives; I doubt that anyone living in Britain, according to these, is using no more than their share of what is available for the planet; Berners-Lee (2019) offers a wealth of practical suggestions; MacKinnon's *The Day the World Stops Shopping* (2021) imagines how we might respond positively to a sudden decrease in 25% of our overall consumption, which he argues is the sort of figure that might make a serious impact on global warming. Less attention has been paid to what might be a fair share of products that damage ecology in other ways, such as non-durable plastic or inorganic pesticides. David Wiggins (2005, n.32), discussing pesticides and the precautionary principle asks: 'If we can bring about so much in seventy years, what shall we have done in a hundred and seventy?'. The whole long footnote is pertinent and sobering.

[18] The Skidelskys (2013, 33–42) provide an excellent discussion of 'insatiability'.

[19] Cf. St Francis de Sales: 'Hélas! Philotée, jamais personne ne confessera qu'il soit avare; chacun désavoue cette bassesse d'ame: on s'excuse sur le nombre des enfants, sur la prudence qui exige qu'on prenne les moyens de s'établir: jamais on n'en a trop. Il se trouve toujours quelque bon motif d'en avoir davantage; et même les plus avares, non-seulement n'avouent pas qu'ils le soient, mais encore en conscience ils ne pensent pas l'être: non, ils n'y songent pas; car l'avarice est une fièvre qui tient du prodige.' Thanks to Edward Hadas for this citation.

Societal pressures are likely to push us still further into redefining our excesses as our needs. 'There are huge numbers of people struggling against contentment' (Atkins 2014). The list of (apparent) goods that the Skidelskys identify in their discussion of insatiability are, as they note, all to some extent socially structured: stimulating experiences, positional goods, leisure goods, 'bandwagon' goods, 'snob' goods. We seek such goods as a means to either status or simple respect. The difference between the two is crucial. Status is intrinsically competitive: I want to be distinguished by being better than others.[20] Respect is cooperative: I want to share the marks of belonging to a group of mutually respected members. (The difference is beautifully illustrated in the film 'The Help', a fictional story based on the lives of the black nannies who cared for the children of wealthy white families in Jackson, Mississipi, in the 1960s. The black women were portrayed as seeking, and giving each other, mutual respect, the white women as mostly motivated by status.) Status is something we need to gain; respect is something that we have unless we forfeit it. Respect is not dependent on superior wealth; status is often bound up with 'conspicuous consumption'. Competitive status is, arguably, a false good; respect, as Aquinas argued of the closely related *fama* or 'reputation', 'is the most important of the exterior goods' (Atkins 2005).

There are two implications of this for reforming social customs. First, we should value the provision of goods that secure respect (which is not intrinsically insatiable), but be cautious of the desire for competitive goods of status. Secondly, we should be alert to the possibility that our society's interpretation of respect itself could be reformed in ways that allow us to live more lightly on the planet without sacrificing a genuine human good.

The practical shaping of our needs by society is arguably more significant even than the emotional. Only recently, for example, have we begun to attend (and even then too slowly and patchily) to the ways in which the design of a city can enable its participants to manage well with less travel. For decades, cheap oil had allowed, even forced, us to live in ever-increasing suburban sprawls. In practice, those of us who try to live simply encounter social limitations on our personal temperateness at every turn: when we try to buy without plastic, or to recycle or to avoid driving; when we need education for our children or healthcare for our parents; when the local bank or the local pub are forced to close. Health and safety regulations, built-in obsolescence, gadgets that cannot be repaired or separated for recycling; goods that can only be ordered on Amazon: in a thousand small ways, the structures and customs of our society compel us to consume more than our fair share.

A final motivation to excess might be legacy. We want to secure our children's future, and our children's children's, and so on, so we invest for high returns in ways that damage the environment, or else are nervous about what we might see as costly measures to reduce ecological damage. This creates what we might call the paradox of legacy: by accumulating to secure our own descendants' wealth, we make it less

[20] The chapter headings of Sandel's (2020) are telling: they include 'Winners and Losers', 'The Rhetoric of Rising', 'Credentialism: the Last Acceptable Prejudice', 'Success Ethics' and (on the elite universities) 'The Sorting Machine'.

likely that they will have a future at all. It is interesting here to note that well-off parents who think about legacy in concrete terms might invest in ways that really do benefit their descendants, e.g. by planting a forest on an estate or caring for a family home. Those, however, who think in abstract terms of amassing money to leave to their heirs, risk leaving them little else.

3.7 The Temptations That Come from Numbers

As Aquinas' miser reminds us, a particular type of temptation to excess comes from money, with its potential for increasing to infinity. 'Capitalism enlarges insatiability by increasingly "monetizing" the economy,' note the Skidelskys (2013, 41) who point out that (a) pricing things makes them 'enter the sphere of relational competition'; and (b) capitalism 'inflames the love of money for its own sake'. Underlying these shrewd points is the nature of money as numerical. It is this quality which gives it its peculiar power to distort our sense of 'enough', in at least five ways.

Firstly, 'relational competition'. Not only can I now add up my motley collection of possessions - a town house, two cars four tables and five computers - and say that it is more valuable than yours - a caravan, a hundred acres of woodland, two horses and a set of hand tools - but I can add up the possessions or the income of my firm or my institution or my company and compare them with that of yours. Given the fallen nature of human beings, numbering slides inevitably into value-laden ranking and competition for status.[21] The ranking, however, is an illusion, since the initial 'pricing' was an arbitrary act. It makes no sense to ask, out of context, 'Is an apple worth more than an orange?' Its illusory status, however, does not deprive it of its power to encourage competition and conflict rather than cooperation and peace.[22]

Secondly, 'the love of money for its own sake', a love which is of its essence unlimitable. 'No one ever has enough of you,' says Chremylus to Plutus, the god of money, in Aristophanes' play *Wealth*.[23] We are back to the madness of the maximising miser, whose endless desire for more is made possible only by the numerical nature of money. Once again, though, a society focused on money makes us collective and not just individual maximisers: the folly of focusing on GDP 'growth', irrespective of whether the exchanges it reflects were beneficial or harmful, is comparable to the madness of the miser writ large. For the fact that such growth is is reported in measures of money obscures the actual goods and services involved. One result of this is that the natural limits of both ecosystems and human beings are

[21] The numbers need not stand for money for the same disastrous effect to occur - league tables for schools and hospitals work similarly. Such tables in effect turn the genuine good of respect into the pseudo-good of status.

[22] Such competitiveness exists at the national as well as the personal level, and with potentially disastrous effects: 'Growth became a matter of national pride. It was important to win the "race" with the other rich countries,' Bannerjee and Duflo (2020, 236), on the 1980s.

[23] Quoted by the Skidelskys (2013, 76).

likely to be overridden in the search for abstract profits, driven by business interests and encouraged (or at least not discouraged) by governments with an eye on the figures. The consequences are countless, from slave labour to the Californian wine industry poisoning ground water through irrigation of a crop that is ecologically unsuited to the region.[24] In other words, GDP growth gives an illusory impression of being potentially unlimited, which drives social and ecological harm.

Thirdly, numerical abstractions disguise the very concreteness that enables us to answer our questions about enough. However much money we have, we cannot know in the abstract if we have 'enough', because what we need enough of is a myriad of specific things in their right context. Many of the most precious of these things cannot, or should not, be priced. Others have a price that bears no relation to their value. More fundamentally, we do not even begin to quantify until we have already done the most important work of identifying what is valuable enough for us to want to quantify it. Some things are incomparably more precious in one place than in another (a polar bear in the wild or in a zoo). For other things, whether we have enough depends on goals or means to goals that might be modifiable. Numbers are irredeemably abstract; 'enough' is irreducibly concrete. Numbers, in abstraction from context, can never tell us if we have enough.[25]

A fourth, related, distortion created by the numerical nature of money is false substitutability. As James Atkins (2020) put it with trenchant humour, in arguing that offsetting is not sufficient to protect biodiversity: 'An oak tree in Leamington Spa cannot be replaced by a larch tree in Malmö. Equating the two would be like saying: "If your Granny in Glasgow passes away, it's OK - there's a kid just been born in Shanghai."' Specifically, evaluation by quantifying cannot protect precious or irreplaceable things. This point becomes more urgent with the increasing disparities between the very wealthy and the rest: no matter how you price an irreplaceable natural or artistic treasure, the billionaire will have the power to purchase or destroy it at will.

Finally, the immaterial quality of money makes it infinitely easy to accumulate: the space Midas had to store his gold was limited. One of the consequences of this is that we have been able to save enormous amounts of money to secure (as we imagine) the future against the eventualities of old age. 'The United Kingdom, Switzerland, Australia, Iceland and the Netherlands all have pension assets worth

[24] The wine example is discussed in Ko and Busselato (2021), ch. 2.

[25] Consequently, 'The most important question we can usefully answer in rich countries is not how to make them grow even richer, but how to improve the quality of life of their average citizen' (Bannerjee and Duflo 2020, 166). The Skidelskys argue for a *general* consumption tax (2013, 204-207) to counter competitive consumption, arguing that 'in a dynamic economy the prohibition or taxation of particular goods is ineffectual, as well as arbitrary, since individuals determined to show off their wealth can always find alternative ways of doing so.' This seems to me to miss the point that different ways of spending money have very different impacts, socially and environmentally.

more than the size of their economies,' write Ko and Busselato (2021, 31). They argue powerfully that the pressure to provide large returns for these investments is one of the biggest single drivers of ecological and social harm. The paradox is that our illusory desire for financial security is undermining our ability to recognise the natural limits that might keep us safe.

3.8 How Can We Counter Excess?

The Skidelskys advocate a kind of cheerful reasonableness in urging us to measure 'enough' by our true well-being and thus make our lives better by working less. Their strategy could perhaps be effective on its own if we were all truly rational - rational, that is, in the traditional sense of being motivated simply by what is truly good and worthwhile. The sad truth is that our unreasonableness lies not in our failure to maximise 'utility' or preferences, but in the selfish lens which distorts our understanding, individual and collective, of what we actually need. This has been compounded over decades by the way we have structured our society on the availability of excess. As the Skidelskys themselves acknowledge, while avoiding the implications of the point, 'the luxuries acquired since [1974] may, even if they have added nothing to our real well-being, be painful to forgo' (2013, 179). That is why their strategy, valuable as it is, seems to me to need to be supplemented by a sense of 'counter-practices', as it were, aimed at restoring the virtues and good customs that we need: an asceticism, perhaps, to complement their moderation.

The first thing we will need is a determined, focused, consistent and collective commitment to change, despite the sacrifices this will demand of us. For we will need to take tough decisions as well as easy ones - to cut down on holidays abroad as well as on hours of work; not just to swap to LED lighting, but also to turn down the heating and eat much less meat. We will need to relearn the habits of integrating such choices into a sustained way into our lifestyles. This will be far easier if these choices are seen as collective not individual, as part of a renewal of our culture. We can be encouraged in this by sub-groups within our society who can show by their own lives that it is possible to live happily with less. By attending to such groups, we can subtly reshape our understanding of respect so that it becomes a downward rather than upward pressure on consumption. It is clear that the churches and other religious communities could play a powerful role here.[26]

---

[26] I focus here on the voluntary choices of individual, families and groups within civil society. I offer some reflections on how these might relate to political choices in Atkins (2022).

3.9 Integral Ecology and Joy in Enough

'Most climate radicals are also passionate haters of greed and luxury, people who in previous ages might have been Cromwells or Savaronolas,' comment the Skidelskys, in a rare moment of intemperate rhetoric. To illustrate this, they quote George Monbiot saying of his campaign that, 'Strangest of all, it is a campaign not just against other people, but also against ourselves' (2013, 131).

Who is right: Monbiot or the Skidelskys? My answer would be 'Both'. Our flawed human nature means that sometimes in order to act for ourselves we need to act against ourselves; sometimes, we need to accept austerity in order to attain happiness. As the Skidelskys themselves note, 'Joy is paradoxically congruent with suffering (2013, 118). More to the point, it is congruent with the purposeful and demanding challenges that often bring joy (for joy is always a side-effect and a gift, never a direct achievement). Think of the Olympic medallist or the mountaineer, of the parents cooking and cleaning for their children, of the gardener shifting manure to fertilise her crops. That is why Pope Francis gives the sub-title 'Joy and Peace' to a section of the chapter on 'Ecological Education and Spirituality' in *Laudato Si'*, describing Christian spirituality as 'capable of deep enjoyment free of the obsession with consumption.' He continues, 'A constant flood of new consumer goods can baffle the heart and prevent us from cherishing each thing and each moment .... Such sobriety, when lived freely and consciously, is liberating' (Pope Francis 2015, 222–223). It is not easy; it goes against the grain of our misshapen natures and cultures; ultimately, however, it is liberating.[27]

A second key idea from *Laudato Si'* suggests how at a communal level too self-discipline can lead to greater joy. 'Integral ecology' is the idea that our ecological, social, economic and personal systems of well-being are interconnected. Consequently, the efforts we make to reshape our societies so as to be able to consume less will in fact make us happier. This is partly because effective communal systems reduce the total cost and efforts required by individuals to achieve the same goals: where public transport works well, pretty well everyone benefits. Secondly, participating in the activities of flourishing local communities gives us pleasure and joy (no one could accuse, for example, Rob Hopkins, founder of Transitions Towns, of being a killjoy).[28] Thirdly, it turns out regularly to be the case that acting with respect for nature in one area has multiple benefits in another: walking or cycling to

[27] For a fuller discussion see Atkins (2003). Gill (1983, 138) makes the converse point: 'For, don't you see, in the Leisure State, people won't really *love* the 'good things' they will enjoy in such plenty. They won't love them in the sense that they will see them and use them as *holy* things, things in which and by which God is manifest. In reality they will despise everything. Things will be made only for passing enjoyment, to be scrapped when no longer enjoyable .... It is all a great illusion'.

[28] See his delightful book, *From What Is to What If: Unleashing the Power of the Imagination* (2021), which is full of examples of joy-filled simpler living. MacKinnon's (2021) equally creative and hopeful *The Day the World Stops Shopping* (see n. 23) is subtitled *How Ending Consumerism Gives us a Better Life and a Greener World.*

work improves mental and physical health, as does growing some of one's own food; reducing working hours strengthens family life; cutting down on commuting increases safety, air quality and leisure time and reduces noise and stress. This seems to be true, at least, of a profit-driven post-industrial society which has lost the courage to identify and articulate true human goods.

A final point is that many of the things we most need and want are not in limited supply, as St Augustine was the first to make explicit. Peace is not like bread, he pointed out, as the more you share it, the more you have.[29] The Skidelskys list of basic goods offers a good example: health, personality, friendship, security and harmony with nature are all clearly or arguably non-competitive. Indeed, even material goods can often benefit us more when we share them (think of the contrasting ways in which we use the words 'share' and 'divide'). For this reason, the supposed 'scarcity' that is assumed as fundamental by many economists is not fixed, and may be irrelevant to, or even reverse the truth about, much of what we value most deeply.

To argue this is not to pretend that it will be easy or painless to deal with the multiple crises that are likely to face us. Many hard decisions will need to be made, and many of these will involve balancing competing goods or the avoidance of competing harms. It is likely that many of us will in fact be forced to tighten our belts, whether we do so willingly or not. If this happens, it will happen whether or not we are 'passionate haters of greed and luxury'. However, insofar as we have learnt to find our happiness in a materially simpler life, we will be better prepared to be grateful for and enjoy, and not simply to suffer, what life may offer us.

3.10 Work for Good Economists

In the world in which the discipline of economics was invented, many human beings were short of basic material goods. It made sense to concentrate on ways of increasing production and trade, while economic 'growth', measured in numerical terms, arguably provided a useful shorthand for this. Our current material problems are caused more by destructive or toxic methods of production and excessive volumes of extraction and waste, compounded by inequalities of access to goods, than by an absolute shortage of the goods needed for safe and healthy lives. It is arguable that economic models and economic policies developed for an earlier age, because they have continued to focus on growth in production and trade, have been a necessary condition of the frenetic and inflamed consumerism of the society in which we now live. Could a reformed economics play a role in soothing the inflammation and restoring society to good health? I suggest that this might be possible, insofar as economists themselves are able to practise humility, caution and attentiveness.

My argument has focused on what is enough for an individual, and concluded that each must answer that question repeatedly in his or her own context, as a

[29] See *Sermon* 357.2.

continuous exercise of attentive judgement. At the same time, the way in which that question can be answered is shaped and constrained by the society in which each of us lives. Insofar as the collective ethos of that society is shaped by economics, it would be important that economists are aware of the ways in which their own attitudes and proposals might encourage or discourage a shared spirit of moderation. They would also need to be attentive to the pervasive human weaknesses which make us more likely to err on the side of excess.

I have argued that economists should be particularly careful about the way in which their language can mislead others ('rational') or cloak facts ('growth' of what exactly?). They would benefit especially from a heightened awareness of the limitations and dangers of quantification itself, of the ways in which abstract measurement can change or obscure what is measured, and fail to capture what is of human importance.

Our individual decisions about what is enough are vast in number, concretely situated and part of manifold, complex, relational and interrelated systems. This means that large-scale generalisations or global policies intending to encourage moderation are more likely to harm than help. This is where economics needs to be cautious, humble and experimental, attending to local differences and continually checking the effects of changes in policy.[30] The distinction is important here between negative and positive policies, between the removal of specific harms, which might be clearly necessary or valuable, and the speedy spreading of certain good practices, which could well be counter-productive on a massive scale.

Above all, perhaps, economists need to remember the richer context of multiple human purposes, not only material, but also emotional, social, and spiritual, in which economic decisions are made. They might imagine themselves, perhaps, as providing not a grand design for politics, but rather a modest kit of tools that can help guide us towards 'enough', as tape measures and screwdrivers are useful for a carpenter crafting a complex and intricate piece of furniture.

3.11 Back to the Question

What, then, is 'enough'? The more concrete the context, the easier that question is to answer. When we try to add up all our 'enoughs' and ask, 'What is enough consumption - for me, for my society?', the question becomes harder. I have suggested at least that the answer must be 'Significantly less than what we use now'. *Solvitur ambulando*, Latin tags goes: learn as you go! If we begin, then, to move decisively in the right direction, as individuals, as networks and communities, and as societies, we will have chance of resolving the question as we make our way. The interplay

[30] Bannerjee and Duflo (2020), provides a model of examples of such cautious, attentive, research, including a wealth of examples in their comprehensive overview.

between our individual, communal and political efforts could then create a virtuous circle that would make it easier as we progressed.

'Enough' has both an upper and a lower limit. The topic of consumption, in the context of a wealthy society, has led me to focus on the upper limit. In another context, the urgent question would be about providing for basic needs. This begs a third question: 'How can we be confident that the upper limit is higher than the lower?' How, in other words, can we be sure that if we who are rich learn to live more wisely, more justly and more temperately, that even then there will be enough to go round, while at the same time allowing the continued flourishing of the natural world which sustains us? Humanly speaking, it seems to me, we cannot be certain: there are too many imponderables. It is, however, the most solid hope that we have.

Some eco-pessimists believe that we are already doomed. Some techno-optimists assume that technology will wave a magic wand and produce a solution that costs the general public nothing. If we are to avoid disaster, we will need appropriate technology, as we will need humble economics. Neither, though, will suffice without the virtues of moderation, practised individually and communally. Beyond that, we can only trust and hope.

References

Atkins, Margaret. 2003. Temperateness, justice and chocolate. *Priests and People*, October, online at http://jerichotree.com/2015/08/10/living-simply-the-contemporary-relevance-of-the-virtue-of-temperance/.

Atkins, E. M. 2005. trans. *Thomas Aquinas: Disputed Questions on the Virtues: Fraternal Correction*, article 2, Response, ed. E. M. Atkins and Thomas Williams. Cambridge: Cambridge University Press.

Atkins, James. 2014. Pelicans, sufficiency and fear of the future. *The Bustard*, https://www.thebustard.com/2014/05/26/pelicans-sufficiency-and-fear-of-the-future/.

———. 2020. Some limitations in pricing nature. *The Bustard.* https://www.thebustard.com/2020/10/13/some-limitations-in-pricing-nature/.

Atkins, Margaret. 2022. The 'Undergrowth Movement' and the Virtues of Leadership. In *Rethinking Leadership for a Green World*, ed. Andrew Taylor. London: Routledge.

Bannerjee, A., and E. Duflo. 2020. *Good Economics for Hard Times: Better Answers to Our Biggest Problems*, 236. London: Penguin.

Berners-Lee, M. 2019. *There Is No Planet B*. Cambridge: Cambridge University Press.

Blum, Lawrence. 1998. Chapter 14: Community and virtue. In *How Should One Live? Essays on the Virtues*, ed. Roger Crisp. Oxford: Oxford University Press.

Braybrooke, David. 1987. *Meeting Needs*. Princeton University Press: Princeton.

Cicero. 2021. *The Republic*. Oxford: Oxford University Press.

Dietz, R., and D. O'Neill. 2013. *Enough is Enough: Building a Sustainable Economy in a World of Finite Resources*. London: Routledge.

Galbraith, J.K. 1958. *The Affluent Society*. Boston: MA, Houghton Mifflin.

Gill, Eric. 1983. *Holy Tradition of Working*. London: Golgonooza Press.

Hadas, E. 2021. *Counsels of Imperfection: Thinking Through Catholic Social Teaching*. Washington: Catholic University of America Press.

Hopkins, Rob. 2021. *From What Is to What If: Unleashing the Power of the Imagination*. Chelsea Green Publishing Co.

Ko, David, and Richard Busselato. 2021. *The Unsustainable Truth: How Investing for the Future is Destroying the Planet and What to Do about It*. Fritton: Panoma Press.
MacKinnon, J.B. 2021. *The Day the World Stops Shopping*. London: Bodley Head.
Miller, David. 2012. Grounding human rights. *Critical Review of International Social and Political Philosophy* 15 (4): 402–427.
New Shorter Oxford English Dictionary. 1993. Vol. II., Oxford.
Newman, John Henry. 2011. *Apologia Pro Vita Sua*, Chapter 5. Cambridge: Cambridge University Press.
Pope Francis. 2015. *Laudato Si': Encyclical Letter on Care for Our Common Home*. Vatican City: LEV.
Sandel, Michael. 2020. *The Tyranny of Merit: What's Become of the Common Good?* London: Penguin.
Skidelsky, R., and E. Skidelsky. 2013. *How Much is Enough? Money and the Good Life*. London: Penguin.
St Francis de Sales. 2015. *Introduction à la Vie Dévote*, in 'De la pauvreté d'esprit au milieu des richesses', Ch XIV, online at https://www.gutenberg.org/cache/epub/53540/pg53540-images.html (pp. 242–243). Thanks to Edward Hadas for this citation.
Wiggins, David. 2005. An idea we cannot do without. In *The Philosophy of Need*, ed. Soran Reader. Cambridge: Cambridge University Press.
Wincewicz-Price, A. 2021. Economic choice revisited: lessons from pre-modern thinkers. In *Words, Objects and Events in Economics: The Making of Economic Theory*, ed. Peter Róna, László Zsolnai Agnieszka Wincewicz-Price, online at (2021_Book_WordsObjectsAndEventsInEconomi.pdf (oapen.org)), ch. 8.

Chapter 4
Buddhism and Right Consumption

László Zsolnai

Abstract The ultimate goal of Buddhist life is to reach enlightenment and put an end to suffering. From this perspective, the goal of human life can be defined as inner development – that is, ethical and spiritual growth that requires only a minimum level of material consumption (food, clothes, shelter, education, and medicine). The paper argues that Buddhism requires to simplifying and reorienting desires through meditation, self-reflection, and social dialogue and to developing "right consumption" patterns. Right consumption can be understood as conscious consumption that is (i) wise (it supports the genuine well-being of individuals), (ii) non-violent (does not involve hurting other sentient beings), and (iii) compassionate (it helps others to satisfy their needs).

4.1 Introduction

Unmoderated consumption may destroy one's own well-being, the well-being of other (human and non human) beings, and the life prospects of future beings.

Overconsumption: the present consumption patterns of advanced Western economies produce welfare maladies, global inequality, and ecological overshot.

The paper investigates which form of consumption is consistent with Buddhist values. The preliminary conclusion is that Buddhism requires the de-growth of many material aspects of consumption, and the growth of many non-material parts of it. For the development of human and non-human sentient beings, we need consumption practices in which actors avoid vices such as greed, hatred, and ignorance, and exercise the virtues of generosity, non-violence, compassion, contentment, wisdom, and mindfulness.

L. Zsolnai (✉)
Business Ethics Center, Corvinus Institute for Advanced Studies, Corvinus University of Budapest, Budapest, Hungary

P. Róna et al. (eds.), *Homo Curator: Towards the Ethics of Consumption*, Virtues and Economics 8, https://doi.org/10.1007/978-3-031-51700-6_4

4.2 Human Development from a Buddhist Perspective

The central tenets of Buddhism are concerned with the suffering that stems from ageing, sickness, death, and the craving for objects of pleasure. The ultimate goal of Buddhism is to put an end to the suffering that is part of everyone's life (SN 56.11).

The central teaching of the Buddha and early Buddhism is the *Four Noble Truths* (SN 56.11). The first of these asserts that the processes of body and mind and one's lived experiences are unsatisfactory, frustrating, and produce suffering. The second asserts that this situation is caused by *tanha,* which is craving, or the desire for pleasurable objects, which lays one open to frustration and disappointment. The Third Noble Truth asserts that this situation can be transcended by the cessation of craving and its associated causes, such as attachment, hatred, and ignorance. The Fourth Noble Truth asserts that the final state of Nirvana can be reached by leading a life that accords with the Middle Way, consisting of the Noble Eightfold Path (Harvey 2000).

The *Noble Eightfold Path* is the Middle Way of practice that leads to the cessation of suffering. It has eight elements: (1) right view or understanding, (2) right resolve, (3) right speech, (4) right action, (5) right livelihood, (6) right effort, (7) right mindfulness, and (8) right concentration (SN 56.11). The eightfold path should not be interpreted as a stepwise process in which each component leads to another; rather, all eight paths are interrelated and should be practiced simultaneously.

The Buddha awarded central importance to the need to ensure that basic necessities are available to everyone, as each human requires enough food, clothes, shelter, and medicine (MN 33). In the case of monastics, these necessities are sufficient for leading a life that can foster inner development. Most lay people, however, see these four requisites as the basis on which more material wealth and comfort may be built. While householders may seem to require more material goods than monks, the fact remains that all of life's basic needs can be met by the four requisites (Payutto 1994).

The "right livelihood" of the Noble Eightfold Path suggests that one's means of livelihood should not be dishonest or cause suffering to other sentient beings. Because of this, the Buddha prohibited his followers from indulging in trading in weapons, animals, meat, alcoholic drinks, or poison. Furthermore, he asserted that the occupations of slaughterer, hunter, and fisherman, are not appropriate for the householder who strives to lead a noble life (AN 5.177).

In modern times, Buddhist Economics as a field of study began with British economist E.F. Schumacher's well-known essay "Buddhist Economics," first published in 1966 and later republished in his best-selling book *Small Is Beautiful* (Schumacher 1973). He foresaw the problems associated with an excessive focus on growth of income, especially overtime and dwindling resources. Schumacher argues that the Buddhist requirement of "Right Livelihood" means that there is a Buddhist economics whose goal is the purification of character and liberation. Schumacher bases Buddhist economics on the central values of simplicity and non-violence, and argues that the optimal pattern of consumption should involve maximizing well-being and minimizing resource use. Schumacher concludes that the Buddhist approach to economics represents a middle way between the modern growth-focused economy and traditional practices that may lead to economic stagnation.

More recent contributions to Buddhist economics include, in chronological order, works by Zsolnai and Ims (2006), the Dalai Lama and van den Muyzenberg (2009), Zsolnai (2011), Giorgino (2014), Tideman (2016), Magnuson (2016), and Brown (2017). These works systemically address the problems of business, environmental protection, social well-being, and economic performance in the contemporary economic context, and present Buddhist economics as an alternative to the materialistic and individualistic Western mindset as applied to the individual-, the business-, and the national level.

The ultimate goal of a Buddhist's life is to reach enlightenment and put an end to suffering. For this reason, the goal of human life can be defined as *inner development* – that is, ethical and spiritual growth that requires only a minimum level of material comfort (food, clothes, shelter, education, and medicine).

4.3 Right Consumption

Buddhism recognizes two different kinds of wanting: (1) *tanha*, the desire for pleasure objects; and (2) *chanda*, the desire for well-being. Tanha is based on ignorance, while chanda is based on wisdom and intelligent reflection. Tanha could be called wanting to have or to obtain, while chanda is the desire for that which is right and skillful. As the objective of chanda is truth and goodness, chanda leads to action, as opposed to tanha, the seeking of objects that pander to self-interest. For example, people who are driven by tanha will seek to satisfy the blind craving for sensual pleasure, but when guided by chanda, desires are directed to realizing well-being (Payutto 1994).

Payutto (1994) stresses that consumption and other economic activities are means of promoting the well-being of individuals, society, and the environment. Right consumption is the use of goods and services to achieve true well-being. Wrong consumption is the use of goods and services to satisfy the desire for pleasing sensations, or ego-gratification.

Buddhism suggests simplifying our desires, rather than multiplying them. Above the minimum level of material comfort, which includes having enough food, clothing, shelter, and medicine, it is wise to reduce one's desires. Wanting less may create substantial benefits for individuals, for the community, and for nature. Avoiding the consumption of certain goods and services makes sense, as this may be one way to preserve or to increase one's true well-being (Zsolnai 2007).

Buddhism recommends conscious consumption, and has a direct focus on changing one's preferences through meditation, reflection, analysis, autosuggestion, and the like. French economist *Serge-Christophe Kolm* (1985) developed a formal model for treating consumption and meditation in a combined form.

In a simplified form, the model is as follows: Let "u" represent one's *well-being* (or *sukkha*). Let "c" and "tm" represent consumption and meditation, respectively. These variables are linked by the relation u = u (c, tm).

The acquisition of goods (for consumption) takes time, because labor is required to produce them, or money is required to buy them. Let this length of time be "ta." The quantity of c is an increasing dependent variable of this, so c = c(ta).

We then have u = u [c(ta), tm]. Time should be divided between meditation and working for consumption. What is the optimal allocation of time between these two activities? According to Buddhism, the optimum solution is engaging in some meditation to lessen the desire for consumption and to be satisfied with less, but also in some consumption and the requirement to work that this entails. This is the "Middle Way." In economic terms, this means "the marginal productivity of labor involved in producing consumption is equal to the marginal efficacy of the meditation involved in economizing upon consumption without altering satisfaction" (Kolm 1985, 240–242).

Right consumption is conscious consumption, which can be characterized by the following attributes: (i) it is *wise* (it serves one's true well-being), (ii) it is *non-violent* (it does not hurt other sentient beings), and (iii) it is *compassionate* (it helps others to satisfy their needs). Vegan food, decreasing the water footprint, eco-housing, ethical clothing, preventive and natural medicine, ecological literacy, sustainable energy, human-scale transportation, fair trade, and ethical and sustainable banking are good directions to right consumption.

4.4 Conclusion

Buddhism requires simplifying and reorienting desires through meditation, self reflection, and social dialogue for developing "right consumption" practices. Buddhism suggests that we should directly evaluate and compare the well-being of people in relation to their quality of life – a proposition that matches with the capabilities approach of Amartya Sen (1999). In this approach, it is understood that people require the basic goods and services considered essential for their well-being, and that their quality of life is based upon their ability to achieve a meaningful life, including nurturing the human spirit. Income is only one element of the quality of life, and economic performance should no longer be evaluated according to how fast average national income grows.

References

Brown, C. 2017. *Buddhist Economics: An Enlightened Approach to the Dismal Science*. New York, London, Oxford, New Delhi, Sydney: Bloomsbury Press.

Dalai Lama, H., and L. van den Muyzenberg. 2009. *The Leader's Way: Business, Buddhism and Happiness in an Interconnected World*. Broadway Books.

Giorgino, V., ed. 2014. *The Pursuit of Happiness and the Traditions of Wisdom*. Springer.
Harvey, P. 2000. *An Introduction to Buddhist Ethics. Foundations, Values and Issues*. Cambridge: Cambridge University Press.
Kolm, S.-C. 1985. The Buddhist theory of 'no-self'. In *The Multiple Self*, ed. Jon Elster, 233–265. Cambridge: Cambridge University Press.
Magnuson, J. 2016. *From Greed to Wellbeing. A Buddhist Approach to Resolving Our Economic and Financial Crises*. University of Bristol: Policy Press.
Payutto, P.A. 1994. *Buddhist Economics: A Middle Way for the Market Place*. Bangkok: Buddhadhamma Foundation.
Schumacher, E.F. 1973. *Small Is Beautiful. Economics as if People Mattered*. London: Blond and Briggs, Ltd.
Sen, A. 1999. *Development as Freedom*. New York: Oxford University Press.
Tideman, S. 2016. *Business as an Instrument for Societal Change: In Conversation with the Dalai Lama*. Greenleaf Publishing.
Zsolnai, L. 2007. Western economics versus Buddhist economics. *Society and Economy* 29 (2): 145–153.
———., ed. 2011. *Ethical Principles and Economic Transformation – A Buddhist Approach*. Springer.
Zsolnai, L., and K.J. Ims, eds. 2006. *Business within Limits: Deep Ecology and Buddhist Economics*. Oxford: Peter Lang.

References from the Pali Canon

AN 5.177 2017. *Vanijja Sutta*. Translated by Bhikkhu Sujato: Trades. https://suttacentral.net/an5.177/en/sujato. Accessed on 28 July 2017.
MN 33 2017. *Maha-gopalaka Sutta*. Translated by Bhikkhu Sujato: The Longer Discourse on the Cowherd. https://suttacentral.net/mn33/en/sujato. Accessed on 28 July 2017.
SN 56.11 2017. *Dhammacakkappavattana Sutta*. Translated by Bhikkhu Sujato: Rolling Forth the Wheel of Dhamma. https://suttacentral.net/sn56.11/en/sujato. Accessed on 28 July 2017.

Chapter 5
Good Consumption in the Perspective of Thomistic Personalism

Laura Baritz

Abstract A large number of scholars and people of good will endeavour to reduce the scope and threat of the problems of environmental degradation and overconsumption. The aim of this paper is to complement these efforts with a theological and personalist (Thomistic) viewpoint. This perspective offers an important normative framework to explain why we need a concept of good consumption and how to put in in practice.

The logic of good consumption advanced in this paper is based on some key ideas of Thomas Aquinas regarding the good and its different categories. It also touches on another important topic of the Thomistic literature, namely virtues, understood here as intrinsic inclinations of persons. Building on the concepts of the good and virtues, a vision of consumption that is good, moderate, just, magnanimous and prudent and therefore environment-friendly and sustainable is suggested.

It is understood here that preservation of our world requires a moral effort and moral order.

The claim of this paper is that if we attune our reasoning and order of values to the perspective found in Thomas Aquinas's teaching, (Aquinas 1934) we, humans, could exercise a healthy, modest, human-centred consumption, in other words, *good* consumption, one that is based on real needs and could create the conditions for sustainable development. The arguments that follow are based on the understanding that consumption is a shared concept of the human value (ethical) order, and predominant economic order (Baritz 2014, 10). Going a step further, it can be stated that human value order is a building block of an economic order in so far as the human person has priority over the economic structure, that is, the human comes

---

L. Baritz (✉)
Sapientia Szerzetesi Hittudományi Főiskola, Budapest, Hungary
e-mail: laura.baritz@domonkosnoverek.hu

P. Róna et al. (eds.), *Homo Curator: Towards the Ethics of Consumption*, Virtues and Economics 8, https://doi.org/10.1007/978-3-031-51700-6_5

before the structure. This latter idea finds its expression in a number of theories. One of them is so-called self-determination theory (SDT) which originated in the humanistic psychology in the works of Richard M. Ryan and Edward L. Deci (Ryan and Deci 2000). It says that the ultimate decisive factor in human behaviour is the human person him/herself and his/her intrinsic motivation.

Theological interpretation of a similar thought can be found in Saint John Paul II's apostolic exhortation "Reconciliation and Penance" (John Paul II 1984), where the pope discusses the idea of structures of sin and of the ultimate specific responsibility of the person regarding the individual deeds within the structure. Albeit sin spreads in a structure, individual responsibility for sin never goes away. When a person works in a corrupt environment and commits corruption that might be influenced by his/her environment, the structure of corruption does not exempt him/her from his/her individual deed.

Both self-determination theory and the concept of structures of sin can be contrasted with behaviourist theories that claim the supervenience of the structure, where the environment can overcome the human person, can absorb his/her personality. Group pressure theories, and the writings of Aronson, Allport, or Luhman are examples of this approach. Behaviourist influences are clear in mainstream consumption theories, especially in such areas as marketing, advertising, social media and PR activities, where the pressure on the consumer is thought powerful enough to change the behaviour of the individual.

The theme of responsibility which forms the core of the structures of sin theory, leads us to another key determinant and indeed the crown of human values, namely, the notion of freedom. Saint Augustine and Saint Thomas would see structures of sin as diminishing our freedom, and would maintain that grace is needed to liberate us. In Christian theology freedom reflects the fact that the person is created in the image of God. The Godlikeness present in the gift of freedom provides the basis for the ultimate argument as to whether the structure or the person should be given precedence. The structure can never take away the inherent freedom of the person (though it can limit his/her social and political liberty). It is an inseparable part of his/her person. Various examples of people in jail and confinement, who managed to preserve their freedom, free will and mental health, albeit they were captured by a sinful, closed structure testify to this. Edith Stein, Father Olofsson Placid, Viktor Frankl or Saint Maximilan Kolbe are just some of the best known names.

These preliminary thoughts serve as a background to a more detailed analysis of consumption seen as part of the economic structure. If we want to arrive at a healthy, moderate, and human-friendly way of life that can lead us to sustainability of the world's different dimensions, we must begin our discourse with the person and with the human value order.

In order to analyse the Thomistic views on consumption, more thoroughly it will help to first look at what Thomist scholars say about needs, and what important conceptual distinctions they make between different categories of needs, for this will later determine the understanding of consumption developed in this essay.

5.1 Towards Good Consumption: Real and Apparent Good, Real and Apparent Need

Consumption and needs, as we experience them and reflect on them, cannot be separated from their subjects and goals, and their normative assessment of whether the subject and goal of our consumption and our need is good or bad. Do they fulfil us, perfect us or harm us? Both Thomas and Aristotle, who inspired most of Thomistic thought, and Thomist scholars after them distinguished between concepts of real good and apparent good. Ralph McInerny (1997, 13) explains the gist of this distinction in his volume "Ethica Thomistica":

> *Aristotle needs some criterion whereby he can distinguish between real and apparent goods. How will he find one? His procedure is roughly this. If any action is undertaken with an end in view, with an eye to some good, what is sought as good is taken to be perfective of the agent. That is, the not-doing or not-having is less perfective than the doing or having. One seeks what one does not have and seeks it because having it is preferable, is the completion of a capacity, the fulfilment of a need. Whatever a human person does or seeks is done or sought under this broad assumption. But not everything so sought is really perfective of the agent. Thus, Aristotle proceeds on the assumption that knowledge of the kind of agent we are will provide a criterion for distinguishing among the things we seek those that are truly perfective of us from those that are not. Hence the traditional talk of real and apparent goods.*

Thus, Aristotle locates an important criterion that distinguishes between real and apparent good in "knowledge of nature". This knowledge, as it will become apparent in further discussion, is a prerequisite for distinguishing between real and apparent need, which in turn informs real and apparent, or put differently, good and distorted consumption. Knowledge is the deciding factor behind whether the good or need in question perfects and fulfils us or not.

Still, knowledge is not the ultimate factor that gives a final reason for distinguishing between real good and apparent good. In their ground-breaking book *Managing as if faith mattered*, Helen Alford and Michael Naughton (Alford and Naughton 2001) address this question, identifying the concepts of *the good* and *human nature* behind the Aristotelian term *knowledge*, as the final decisive factor in distinguishing the real good from the apparent good.

They write as follows:

> *"The distinction between real and apparent goods concerns the good as the object of judgement, the good under the scrutiny of truth."* And: *"...we can say that the ends that are most fundamental to our good are in harmony with our natural inclinations. For this reason, real joy is a token that we have hit on the good"* (Alford and Naughton 2001, 62–63)

Real good and apparent good can therefore be better distinguished from one another when we clarify the meaning of the concepts of good and of human nature (natural inclinations), in the context of happiness (or joy as the writers refer to it).

In order to better understand the Thomistic understanding of the good itself and a good life, of the human person and values, and how all these relate to a proper, sustainable consumption, we need to take a closer look at his ideas of human nature and natural inclinations of the human person, natural law, the defining features of the good (its universality, perfection, objectivity and hierarchical structure), the analogical connection between different types of goods, the difference between pleasure and happiness, and finally human relations.

These will serve as building blocks of a new approach to consumption.

5.2 Natural Inclinations and Human Nature

Thomas Aquinas grounds his moral teaching in the concept of natural inclinations. The human person is free when pursuing his/her natural inclinations, not in acting against them. The main constitutive element of human nature is reason, which is understood as the activity of the intellect as it moves from one truth to another. Thus, all enjoyments that correspond to reason, and are thus worthy of the human person are natural for human beings. This is why it is natural to find joy in contemplating the truth and practicing the virtues. Thomas remarks, that the key virtues correspond to the natural inclinations and to the good (S.Th. I.-II. q.63., a.1.). Furthermore, natural inclinations constitute a spiritual spontaneity, they are at the root of the will. Free acts and virtues, therefore, are at the basis of morality, as well. Thomas calls them the instincts of reason *(instinctus rationis)* (Pinckaers 1995, 412). The deepest instinct of the reason is the rational inclination to the good and justice. Thomas goes further in explaining the origin of these inclinations, saying that they are *"instinctus Spiritus Sancti"*, the instincts of the Holy Spirit (S.Th. I.-II. q.68., a.1.). The inclination to happiness and to spirituality makes us capable of overcoming all restrictions and orients us toward perfect freedom. Inclination to spirituality is an inward inclination that makes us free.

Cicero begins his reflections on the meaning of inclinations by indicating that they are natural endeavours to protect our life and body against harmful things and to look for all things necessary for life, like food, shelter, etc. The natural inclinations further all these things. Inclinations are relatives of human desires, as well; it is on the level of inclinations, where the famous natural desire of contemplating God occurs, upon which the desire of truth and happiness is centred. Cicero's thoughts point to a good consumption, as well, a kind of consumption that is connected to human inclinations, that originates from them, that is simply natural and harmonious with virtues. A natural human desire indicates a natural way of consumption, that fulfils the real necessities of life.

Based on the role of reason and freedom in the nature of inclinations, Thomas distinguishes five main types of inclinations of the human person that correspond to different parts human nature. Human nature naturally seeks (inclines to) the good unless turned otherwise by sin or habit. The other four are the inclination to preserve one's own being, to preserve human species, the inclination to know the truth about God, and the inclination to live in society (S.Th. I.-II. q.94., a.2.) The theory of inclinations brings us to a much larger question that deals with human nature more thoroughly and is at the heart of Thomistic thought: natural law.

5.3 Natural Law as the Substratum of Good Consumption

The concept of natural law was invented by the Stoics. Thomas Aquinas inherited their interest in different types of law and took it further. After he worked out his own concept of natural law, it became the tradition of civil humanism, and indeed of civil economy (Bruni and Zamagni 2007). The doctrine of natural law directed human reasoning until the end of the Middle Ages which marked a breach with the classical understanding of metaphysics as the natural world was becoming the key concern of thinkers. Still, Declaration of Independence in the United States in 1776 was written in the spirit of natural law, and in 1948, when formulating the Universal Declaration of Human Rights, philosopher Jacques Maritain proposed natural law as its theoretical foundation, but without success. Since then, its spirit is cultivated by Aristotelian and Thomistic philosophical schools and by Catholic Thomistic theology.

The reference text defining Aquinas's concept of natural law reads as follows:

> *every agent acts for an end under the aspect of good. Consequently, the first principle of practical reason is one founded on the notion of good, viz. that "good is that which all things seek after." Hence this is the first precept of law, that "good is to be done and pursued, and evil is to be avoided." All other precepts of the natural law are based upon this: so that whatever the practical reason naturally apprehends as man's good (or evil) belongs to the precepts of the natural law as something to be done or avoided. Since, however, good has the nature of an end, and evil, the nature of a contrary, hence it is that all those things to which man has a natural inclination, are naturally apprehended by reason as being good, and consequently as objects of pursuit, and their contraries as evil, and objects of avoidance. Wherefore according to the order of natural inclinations, is the order of the precepts of the natural law. Because in man there is first of all an inclination to good in accordance with the nature which he has in common with all substances: inasmuch as every substance seeks the preservation of its own being, according to its nature.* (S. Th., I-II., q. 94., a. 2.)

In other words, right reason recognizes the eternal law (lex aeterna) which is the utmost fundamental divine law in the operation of the cosmos and in the human person, and which rules the order of cosmos. To put it shortly, this is nothing else than the eternal law of God's wisdom. The twin love commandments are in a sense the most obvious and basic commandments of the natural law. As Saint John states in 1Jn 4:16b.: *"God is love, and whoever lives in love, lives in God and God lives in him."* The recognized norms of this law constitute the natural law itself, that is, "*the natural law is nothing else than the rational creature's participation in the eternal law.*" (S.Th. I-II., q 91., a.2.) The basic precept of the Natural Law is *"to do good and avoid evil"* and the innate habit of the human mind to be directed by this principle is called *synderesis*. This basic "structuring" of the intellect goes with the will's basic dynamic towards the good.

The doctrine of natural law and its spirit have been referred to by various scholars in a number of disciplines. Suffice it to mention here psychology, where Aristotelian trends, like humanistic psychology and SDT maintain the spirit of the natural law. Carl Rogers, famous humanistic psychologist thus writes about his professional experience as psychotherapist: *"the person is good by his/her essence, he/she is the bearer of positive values and possibilities."* (Tringer 1992, 9.)

With this we have arrived at the notion of good which is examined in more detail below.

5.4 Why Is Being Good?

In Thomism, the ultimate point about the good, has a metaphysical and ontological grounding, as does morality. Thomas Aquinas takes up Plato's metaphysical position on existence *("Being is good, and the bad is the deficit of the being")* (Nyíri [1973], pp. 70.), saying: *"Now in things, each one has so much good as it has being: since good and being are convertible" [...] So that as much as he has of being, so much has he of goodness" [...] "Evil acts in virtue of deficient goodness."* (S.Th. I.-II. q. 18., a.1.) Similar thoughts can be found in more recent theology and metaphysics that draw on that tradition. A widely used Hungarian handbook on metaphysics says: *"Beings are good by participation. Each thing is good only in so far as it is a kind of likeness and a sharer of the Supreme Good, whose goodness is represented in it in a lesser degree (of a hierarchical order) than in the Perfect Good (i.e., it has a lesser, not as perfect existence). The most perfect being and good is God."* (Turay 1984, 125.) The metaphysical argument can be summarised as follows:

> In metaphysics we speak of three kinds of goodness: 1. The existential goodness, when a thing is good simply because it exists. A rusty piece of iron counts as good, too, from the point of view of its existence. 2. The physical goodness, when a thing is good because it corresponds to its own essence. From this point of view, the rusty piece of iron is not good, because the essence of a piece of iron is to be found in clean iron without rust. 3. The third type of goodness refers to the natural moral law: an act is good in so far as it corresponds to the natural moral law. (Turgonyi 1993, 99.)

C.S. Lewis noted that among the fundamental laws moving the world, the natural moral law is the only one which can be violated by free will (C.S. Lewis, I/I.). And a Hungarian philosopher, Gábor Czakó, adds that this violation does not happen without consequences. With regard to freedom it should be emphasized that: *"Morally right behavior is not the result of divine despotism; it is good by its nature."* (Baritz 2014, 47–48.)

Having spoken briefly about the good in relation to freedom, we can now examine the question of the good as it was understood by the classics and is now used by some contemporary authors who borrow from them.

5.5 From Goodness to Good Consumption

Neither Thomas nor Aristotle give a definition of the good because they see in it one of the chief ideas that precede other ideas and cannot therefore be defined by them. They say that grasping it is a unique experience, nothing can explain the good, it is a substantial reality. In modern philosophical terms, it is a primitive. If we want to understand it, we must stay satisfied with describing it by its effects. Since the good actuates human inclinations, its usual description refers to this. Actuating power manifests itself through the actuated object, therefore Aristotle says in his *Nicomachean Ethics* that the good is what each person strives for. Going further, based on the classic authors, we can say that the good is defined here by the appetite, by the attraction and by the love aroused by it. The good is something that is lovable, that is desirable. It attracts every being. The person is there to capture the good and transform it into moral good by his/her deeds. Such is the known, loved and wanted good. The most frequently used connotations of the good are "love" and "desire" ("appetite") which are realized in their fullness in the human person who is a spiritual being. In this context we can state that the good is what every person desires, what causes love and appetite in each person, and what each of us desires in his or her will.

From the above arguments we can derive a claim that the good is universal. Since each person desires the good, it is found in everyone and exceeds the limits of other desires. In the deepest part of each person's being we can always find an inclination toward the good, same as toward the truth, that is always there and unavoidable even when a person engages in evil-doing or lies.

Another key feature of the good is that it is perfect. Each person strives for the perfection and fullness of the good, which also means perfection of freedom.

The objectivity of the good, manifests itself in the fact that it is goal oriented, there is a desire to achieve it. Human acts originate from it. The will of the human person strives for an end in which it finds rest. Thomas says in S.Th. I.-II. q.1., a.1. that every human act necessarily happens in order to achieve a goal. It is the rational being's feature that he/she strives for a goal, that the moral order is governed by goal orientation. The goals are ordered hierarchically and there is an ultimate end above them.

What we have learned so far about the good sheds a clearer light on the meaning of related concepts of *real good* and *apparent good*. What should be noted in particular is that apparent good belongs to the category of good within the realm of subjectivity. In his work *Moral Theory, a non-consequentialist approach* David Oderberg, a Thomist, explains that the bad is the lack of the thing that would be needed for personal fulfilment. The bad can be chosen freely and willingly, but *"it is impossible to choose the bad because it is bad. We choose the bad because the chosen thing brings us subjectively something good that is real or apparent. All knowingly bad acts are chosen because of some good, genuine or phoney, that the person tries to obtain.*" (Oderberg 2005, 40) The genuine good, as we saw earlier, is inherent in the essence of things, of the rusty piece of iron. In order to achieve it we need to understand the hierarchical order of the good in its different forms. This is what we turn to in the next section.

5.6 Hierarchy of Goods as a Guiding Rule of Good Consumption

To know what counts as a goal and what counts as a tool in our life is very important. This distinction can change paradigms and transform various parts of life. As Alford and Naughton note: "A person, who would like to light a cigarette because of pleasure or against weariness or obesity, misunderstands the goal and the tool of his/her fulfilment." (Alford and Naughton 2001, 61) Aristotle and Thomas Aquinas recognized this matter, and, when speaking of the hierarchy of goods, they began their message with this categorization.

In his book *De Anima* (*On the Soul*) Aristotle sets up a hierarchical order between the body and the soul, stating that the soul has primacy over the body and that the body is the tool of the soul (Book II. Part 4) Going further, in his *Nicomachean ethics* he extends the categorization of the goods, adding the category of "external goods" to bodily and spiritual goods. These are none others than the material goods themselves. They serve as tools or instruments, they are useful insofar as they exist for the sake of something else. He puts money and the economy in the same category (NE 1096a Book1, Chap. 5). In his *Politics* he also explains that these external goods must be used "*soberly, with temperance*" "*…external goods have a limit, like any other instrument, and all things useful are of such a nature that where there is too much of them they must either do harm, or at any rate be of no use, to their possessors…*" (Book 7, Part 1, 1323b) We find in this sentence the first clear insight into how good consumption can be defined in the Aristotelian-Thomistic paradigm. External, or material goods have limits, when used in the extreme they become harmful and lose their usefulness, therefore they need to be used soberly and with temperance. Curiously enough, this sounds very much like the stipulations of sustainable development activists some 2000 years later.

Another important feature of external goods is that they are positioned on the lowest level of the hierarchy of goods, as they serve the goods of the body and of the soul. When we add that money and its accumulation (Thomas calls acquisition of money "*pecuniativa*") are even below the level of material goods, we realize how the logic of the classic scholars is harmonious with the gospel. Consumption that does not fulfil the requirements of the good and is not natural in Thomistic terms, regards money and its accumulation as the pinnacle of the hierarchy of goods, and instead of considering them as tools, it sees them as possible usurpers of the role of the ultimate good. In contrast, Aristotle and Thomas Aquinas state that money and profit are merely tools and not goals, as Thomas indicates: "*Those, therefore, that abound in what is strictly speaking necessary for life are richer than those that abound in mere money"* (Jarrett 2007, 154). In other words, consumption of natural things necessary for life better approaches good consumption, in a Thomistic sense, than consumption oriented to money making. Contemporary literature of sustainable development offers direct links between Thomism and ecological economics.

An important question that arises here is: How do we live out this logic in the real world? The commonly exercised approach to the hierarchy of values is in direct opposition to Aquinas' proposition. People strive for money as the most valuable objective that enables their living. The Thomistic way which sees money as a tool located at the bottom of the hierarchy of values could be discovered by those who can live virtuously, accepting the moral rules, who have arrived at the fullness of their humanity. These persons could act in the society as yeast, affecting their environment. The power of a good deed is effective as Saint John Paul II explains in his theory of the structure of virtue and philosopher, Elizabeth Leseur (1918) noticed decades before him. The structure of virtues means that all those persons who already have obtained a particular level of morality, are connected, and it is their duty to enrich their environment through their good example. They set an example in their families, or workplace, they can preach, give presentations, lead missions, but the most effective way to act virtuously is in everyday situations. For, as a contemporary economic psychologist R.H. Frank states, "Good behavior is contagious" (Frank 2004, xii.) And he grounds this claim on numerous empirical research and experiments.

In the way consumption is exercised today, the hierarchy of goods and of values have been turned upside down. In the *"treadmill of materialism"* (Kasser 2002), the supreme values in the consumer's logic are the material values that represent identity, self-esteem, sense of belonging, providing false fulfillment and content for these psychological needs. In the Thomistic paradigm, identity and self-esteem would be defined by moral and ethical concepts. Originally conceptualized by Aristotle, the hierarchy of goods has been used and expanded by contemporary authors.

Hungarian philosopher, Béla Weissmahr (1978), calls it an *"objective value order"*, stressing the role of the moral good that is at the top of the hierarchy of goods and has precedence over the other goods, values. He says that moral value is not merely a value among the others, but it is the preciousness of the behavior of the person and of her actions. It is in fact the inclination of the person who acts in line with the logic of the objective value order. (Weissmahr 1978, 82–83). Max Scheler also speaks of value hierarchy. In his book about values, he mentions "higher ranked" and "lower ranked" values along with spiritual and moral values, and values that connect to the holy (Scheler 1973, 86–111) Finally, contemporary economists and mathematicians engage with the hierarchy of goods and values in their research: Arjo Klamer (2002) and Milton Rokeach (1973) both categorize goods and values according to their instrumental or goal-oriented features.

In an attempt to summarize the hierarchy of goods as conceived of by the antient Greek philosophers, we can draw a scale, where material goods are at the bottom, with dead material, with money and money accumulation at the lowest level, followed by vegetative and sensitive values, then the intellectual values, with their humanistic reference and finally come moral values. According to Aristotle's statement the whole structure points in the direction of the ultimate value, the ultimate good, which is none other than the contemplation of truth. According to Thomas and the Christian authors, the ultimate goal of the hierarchy of goods is God himself, the "Visio Beatifica" (Beatific Vision) contemplating the face of Good in the eternal life. When we look at the hierarchy of goods from the point of view of values, we can see that each level has an added value, the upper levels get richer and richer as we progress, until we arrive at morality as the ultimate goal.

Thomas Aquinas draws on the logic of the hierarchy of goods, but he extends it with a deeper layer of analysis to which we now turn.

5.7 Analogous Connection of the Goods: The Key to Good Consumption

In S.Th. I. q.5., a.6. Thomas describes characteristics and mutual relations of three categories of the good: useful good, pleasant good and moral (virtuous) good. These categories help him sketch a world order that would be desirable for a sustainable, happy life, where consumption would realize the good we have talked about.

> *"For everything is good so far as it is desirable, and is a term of the movement of the appetite" [...] "Thus, in the movement of the appetite, the thing desired that terminates the movement of the appetite relatively, as a means by which something tends towards another, is called the useful; but that sought after as the last thing absolutely terminating the movement of the appetite, as a thing toward which for its own sake the appetite tends, is called the virtuous; for the virtuous is that which is desired for its own sake; but that which terminates the movement of the appetite in the form of rest in the thing desired is called the pleasant." [...] "Now those things are called pleasing which have no other formality under which they are desirable expect the pleasant, being sometimes hurtful and contrary to the virtue. Whereas the useful applies to such as have nothing desirable in themselves, but are desired only as helpful to something further, as the taking of bitter medicine; while the virtuous is predicated of such as are desirable in themselves."* (S.Th. I. q.5., a.6.)

Thomas calls all these categories good since they all represent goodness and are good in a way described above. Thomas links the three categories of good by what is called an analogous connection. This mode of reasoning recognizes some characteristics that the items in question have in common, but at the same time acknowledges each item's own essential features. To illustrate this let us draw an analogous connection between an apple, a face, and a pen. The element they all share could be that they are red: red apple, red color of the face, a pen filled with red ink. Still, each of them preserves its own distinct character; the apple is food, the face is part of the body, and the pen is a writing tool.

Thomas follows the same pattern concerning the goods. Each of them, the useful, the pleasant and the moral good is good. This is their shared essence, in what they resemble each other. But the unique characteristic of the useful good is that it is a *tool*, it serves the other goods. A useful good is not good by itself, it is good only inasmuch as it furthers the goodness of other goods. Thomas's example of a useful good is bitter medicine (S.Th. I. q.5.,a.6.) It is not good in itself, alone, but only when it serves the health and life of others. Useful goods for Thomas are the material goods, elements of the material world. The material part of our world is at the lowest level of the value hierarchy. They represent values that are instrumental to the promotion of and help the other parts of the world, the immaterial ones. Present-day consumerism with its idolatrous treatment of the material goods which receive precedence over all the other goods is in direct contrast to the Thomistic hierarchy of goods. Material goods have become the ultimate goals, and the virtues (the moral goods) serve as tools to realize the material goals. This is well captured in Kotler's *Marketing management* (Kotler and Lane 2019) or a remarkable study from Turkey, *Luxury consumption* by Hümeyra Ashm Bilge (2015), as well as Colin Campbell's *Wants and Needs, Consumption and Consumer Society, the Craft Consumer and Other Essays* (2021) all of which provide rich studies characterizing consumption in the modern world..

Overconsumption and wasteful consumption that mark our time illustrates a reversed ranking of goods. In that they defy the Thomistic order in which the moral values determine the place and content of the material world.

The second category, pleasant good carries a similarly important message. The special characteristic of the pleasant good is that it is a companion. It accompanies the useful good with positive properties, like fresh fruit or a comfortable pair of shoes, but it can also partner with the moral (virtuous) good, usually causing joy or delight when the person accomplishes a morally good deed. "To do good is good" sounded a commercial advertising charity outside one of Catholic churches in Hungary.

The moral good is the most important one among the three. Its unique property is that it has priority over all other, it is the first and highest among them and is desirable for its own sake.

As Thomas says *"Goodness is not divided into these three as something univocal to be predicated equally of them all, but as something analogical to be predicated of them according to priority and posteriority. Hence it is predicated chiefly of the virtuous, then of the pleasant, and lastly of the useful."* (S.Th. I. q.5., a.6.)

5.8 The Fruits of Good Consumption: Happiness and Pleasure

According to Aristotle, pleasure is an elementary part of happiness. However, as he adds immediately, that pleasure is nothing more than an associate, subordinate to the conditions of morality, to virtues. As such it cannot be the final good. This approach opposes Epicurus whose definition of happiness was that its goal is to seek pleasure and avoid pain. According to Epicurus then, seeking pleasure is the goal in itself rather than an associate of seeking happiness as Aristotle had it. For Aristotle and others (e.g. Cicero[1]) pleasure cannot be a goal in itself since it does not have a moral value, and its place in the human value structure is to accompany moral values. The opposite insights that were at the origins of hedonistic and eudaimonistic philosophies continue to inform human thinking and behavior today. They help us understand the important distinction between the goals and tools that are necessary to attain the goal. When we miss what the goal of our happiness is, we miss what the goodness of our consumption should consist in as well, since we then tend to consume what we take as pleasurable and amusing, and what brings profit, without realizing that ultimately they will neither be useful nor virtuous for us. When we fail to understand the hierarchy of goods, we end up missing the moral, virtuous step which dictates our true goals and preferences. Virtuousness makes consumption happier than amusement, and provides more fulfilment and perfection for the person than mere delight.

Thomas goes further in his understanding of happiness. He says that the moral good is not always associated with pleasure and enjoyment. Pleasure does not always accompany the virtuous, or moral good. Joy may go along a moral good, but not every moral good is enjoyable. He thinks here for example of martyrdom, of sacrifice, of an action that embodies moral or virtuous conduct, but is not pleasant.

> *Many people act and they must act for the sake of pleasure, but they can never act for pleasure alone. Pleasure can never be an ultimate end. Hedonism has got the role of a sign, it indicates, but does not embody the 'good'. Thomas delineated his principle of 'Principle of delight', (delectation principle) hut he rejects the 'delight only' principle.* (Williams 1974, 290)

The above distinctions are helpful in distinguishing between good and bad consumption: one that promotes sustainability and personal fulfilment or one that destroys the world and the human person as a result of misunderstanding human nature and the nature and order of the created world.

What then is the correct meaning of happiness according to the Thomistic philosophy? Aquinas's and Aristotle's take on happiness, as opposed to hedonistic and the epicurean way, is captured in the concept of eudaimonia which interestingly enough is supported by many psychologists and philosophers today. For Aristotle, eudaimonia involves three components that makes a person happy: fulfilment, personal relationships and spiritual life.

Fulfilment can be found in realizing one's noble goals, which increases the person's sense of self-worth and helps him/her approach perfection. In the process she/he becomes virtuous and rich in moral values. According to some psychological researchers (Szondy 2010), this type of happiness, based on reason and goal setting, provides a higher degree of happiness than hedonism with its state of delight as an end.

Furthermore, the core message of Thomistic personalism is that human person can only find fulfilment through a relationship with another person. This is a

[1] Cf. Cicero: De Finibus Bonorum et Malorum

consequence of natural law, the fifth inclination of the person directed toward living in society, as Thomas stated. He maintains that personal connections are crucial to happiness. Personalist thinkers who draw on Aristotle and Thomas distinguish levels and categories of relationships with others. When two persons are on an equal level, they esteem their human dignity and they love each other for the values found in the other (intrinsic-value), we speak of an I-YOU connection (Buber 1937) or moral friendship (Aristotle) or *amor amititiae* (Pinckaers 1995). However, there is also a type of relation that is expressed in what is called *amor conscupistentiae,* which means that I appreciate the other person only insofar as he or she may prove useful to me (I-IT connection). Martin Buber describes the incompleteness of the I-IT connection very vividly. He puts it as follows: I put my own interests ahead of theirs and wish to fulfil myself through using them, as tools to fulfill my own subjective interest. As Thomas states, this is a partial connection only, where the goal of the personal connection is misunderstood and misused.

For Aristotle the so-called friendship of utility involves mutual help among free citizens and friendship of pleasure, one that brings about a pleasant state, e.g. drinking with companions who enjoy each other's company. The I-YOU connection is understood as a friendship of true worth that is realized between people who recognize and cherish each other's goodness and share noble ideals.

In the case of an I-YOU connection we speak of *reciprocity* (Bruni and Zamagni 2007), a reciprocal connection, where both partners are able to give nobly, magnanimously, and gratuitously, thus establishing "conditional unconditionality". Conditional unconditionality means that the parties can give unconditionally, without waiting for any compensation and the condition of reciprocity is that they both can act the same way. The contemporary economic literature calls this type of persons *"Homo reciprocans"*, in contrast to *"Homo economicus"*, the utilitarian human image. When we think of consumption, we should pay particular attention to "relational goods" that embody all those material and immaterial goods that are involved in establishing a blossoming human relation. Good consumption in the Thomistic perspective leads to a market full of Homo reciprocanses, a business culture of reciprocity with magnanimousness and gratuity, and the world overflowing with relational goods rather than with consumer goods, many of which are unnecessary and harmful (see Zamagni's paper in this volume).

Spiritual life is naturally included in the constitutive parts of happiness as a consequence of the hierarchy of values in which the soul is placed above the body and the external goods.

5.9 Defining Good Consumption in the Thomistic and Personalist Perspective

The above reflections addressed select notions, categories, and insights of Thomistic philosophy regarding the human being and the natural order. The concepts of human nature, natural law, the good itself, and the hierarchical order of the world and human life in it together define an ideal system in which everything has its own naturally ordained place, and where human persons live in peace and happiness. This is the world which functions according to the laws set by God, that is the Divine laws that Thomas described thoroughly in the Summa and in his other works. He also wrote, however, about sin, greed, avarice, and all deviations that remove us from the good. We also remember from Cicero that the bad "is the deficit of the being," and *"All knowingly bad acts are chosen because of some good, genuine or phoney, that the person tries to obtain.*" (Oderberg 2005, 40) So the good is the basis for the operation of the world, and all the deviations we observe today are unnatural and the result of the lack of the basic good. When the good is the first idea that defines the way the world operates, the constitutive parts of the world (including the economy and consumption) are good, as well, under the conditions of the good delineated by Thomas. So what can we learn from all this about good consumption?

Good consumption requires virtue. For Thomas virtues are natural human inclinations, for the *"Morally right behavior is not the result of divine despotism; it is good by its nature."* (Baritz 2014, 47–48.) Thus good consumption can be found in the nature of a good person who by her good nature behaves well or virtuously nearly automatically in all spheres of life, including consumption. Just as was mentioned earlier that *"The more virtue ethical is the value order of the person, the more likely is he/she involved in creation of an ethical (three dimensional) economic order…"* (Baritz 2014, 10), so, adapting that statement slightly, we can say that the value order of the person which is based on virtue will also lead the person to an ethical consumption.

In their 2001 book *Managing as if faith mattered* Alford and Naughton provide a number of examples of how different virtues connect to different areas of economic life and are thus conducive to their goodness in contributing to human fulfilling and economic life that realize the common good. In the area of job design they talk about prudence and subsidiarity in operations; in the area of just wages they mention justice and the subjective dimension of work; in reference to corporate ownership they highlight temperance and common use in finance; with regard to marketing communication and product development they stress solidarity and courage (Alford and Naughton 2001, vii–viii.). Their work is just one illustration of how emphasising the role of virtues in various areas of the economy make them human centred and bring out what can be good in them.

With regard to good consumption it is particularly important to look closer at the virtues of justice, temperance, prudence and fortitude. The virtue of justice promotes the exercise of just distribution in which everyone gets his/her own that he/she needs. Just distribution means that nobody should remain homeless or starving, since everyone gets what they need. This is an ideal to which a just state should aspire with its infrastructural, legal and political power. In his book *Development as Freedom*, Amartya Sen discusses some characteristics of a just state, where special importance is given to the notion of equity and equitable treatment of the people by the state. Putting an end to malaria in India is mentioned as one of the equitable deeds of the state towards the inhabitants (Sen 1999).

Just distribution contributes to the overcoming of poverty as well. Still, not only justice but also sympathy are needed to help the poor. As the example of Mother Theresa has shown, mental and spiritual help driven by love, is even more important for human fulfilment than material support. And that is in line with the above discussed hierarchy of values.

The virtue of justice helps foster good consumption by practices of just marketing, just advertising, just commercials, or just sales activity. If the virtue of justice meaningfully informed the consumption structure, it could reduce the 10–90 social gap and the difference between the highest and lowest consumption levels could be much less. The virtue of justice also helps a more just and more modest resource distribution, which brings us to another virtue, that of temperance.

If temperance were taken seriously in our consumption behaviour, it would significantly decrease the quantity of consumed goods and we could stop overconsumption and waste, reducing consumption to the necessary quantities that for the consumption of real goods that meet real needs rather than the apparent ones. With temperance we could focus more on the immaterial elements of consumption and less so on the material ones, thus easing the environment from the strain and decreasing the ecological footprint. Relational goods could be obtained through the virtue of temperance, as well, since it is creativity, good will, kindness, and self-denial that are necessary to establish a good relationship with the other person within the society, which in turn promote the common good part of which is good consumption. In the literature devoted to environmental protection and global warming the virtue of temperance takes a special place and is called frugality. Temperance is a universal virtue for those concerned with the environment ranging from the use of energy saving bulbs, automatically switches of lights, scrapings actions by supermarket and selectively collected garbage in the households.

Virtue of prudence helps to structure and rank consumption goods. Prudence orders the goods in the value hierarchy and distinguishes the material from the immaterial ones. It finds the right place for the relational goods. Prudence, as the principal virtue, has an important role in all stages of consumption. One cannot be temperate, just or powerful without the virtue of prudence.

Finally, the virtue of fortitude is responsible for supporting the whole structure of virtues. Fortitude encompasses the virtues of magnanimity, generosity and gratuitous giving, when the person can surrender his/her own subjective self-interest and forgo it for the sake of the other. As such it helps form human relations in which a person's self-interest includes the interest of others, so that cooperation can be established between those who have similar approach. This way a win-win situation is formed with both parties benefiting from it. This pattern of human cooperation could foster an environmentally friendly consumption which would benefit both the environment and the human person. Self-interest rightly understood and virtue-driven would in this case include the interest of the environment . If this could become a dominant pattern of human relations, sustainability would be easier to attain.

The above reflections can be traced back to and substantiated with our initial hypothesis, namely, that human value order comes before the economic system, and determines it as its ultimate cause, bearing in mind that the impact of the system on the human value order is also substantial. If the value order of the person in her consumption decisions and behaviour does not tend toward the fulfilment of human nature, or towards the good, the systemic aides of consumption, e.g. infrastructure, health care, education, architecture, even art might become corrupt and subvert good inclinations and pursuits. Greedy behaviour can spoil and corrupt the best designed structure, the most effective technology and highest-level processes. While it is true that a virtuous and just human being alone cannot solve the problem of thirst without the necessary infrastructure, our point here is that the infrastructure without sufficient moral grounding might also be used against the well-being of the human.

The fact that we need morals and virtues in the world is obvious. It is obvious, too, that there are virtuous and good people around. The structures of sin coexist with the structures of virtues. When the structures of virtue is embraced by people in the higher political and economic levels, a substantial change might occur in the whole society. In order to influence the spreading of virtues we need the help of the media, culture, education, and faith which is the most intrinsic catalyst in obtaining the virtues, especially by way of personal conversion. In the process of conversion virtues become intrinsic motivators and defining part of personality. As it is the case in all areas of human life so it is with regard to consumption: the key is in the hands of virtuous individuals who are called to spread the virtuous way to others (for "good behaviour is contagious").

5.10 Concluding Thoughts

The above theoretical and abstract reasoning could be criticized for having close to none real capacity to affect thought, behaviour and actions of consumerist societies. For how could a society that ceased to operate in the virtue-driven paradigm and is comfortably and mindlessly persisting in the hedonistic habits be reoriented so radically in the spirit of temperance, justice and prudence? One answer is education. In the past decade or two we have seen a revival of Thomistic virtue ethics programmes in universities around the world. The Angelicum, the Pontifical University of Saint Thomas, in Rome, the University of Saint Thomas, Minnesota, USA, the Sophia University Institute, Loppiano, Italy, and the Sapientia College in Budapest all teach economics and other social sciences on the basis of the Social Teaching of the Church which is very much Thomistic in its spirit. The founders of the Sapientia program attach great value to the teaching of "human centred" economics in which the human person is the subject, the basis and the goal of the economic processes. Since the person is considered the centre and not the tool of economy, we must conduct a thorough-going study of what the person is and what her environment is like in order to better approach the multidisciplinary problems that society, the economy and, indeed the natural world face today. We acknowledge that the human person consists of body and soul, and therefore deeper knowledge of the soul in needed as much as of the body to better understand what it is to be human. These in turn can be learned with the help of theology and philosophy which – contrary to popular and mainstream sentiment – are rich sources of insights for economic questions, too. The program at Sapientia is organised in three blocks of subjects: theology/philosophy, social sciences and economics. This is a profound change in the way economics is taught and our hope is that those students who studied in this and similar programs will be the ambassadors of an economic order that is integrated into a human order. Without this paradigmatic shift, pro-environmental policies of de-growth and systemic reduction of consumption are bound to fail to accomplish the goal of sustainable growth, for they miss the ultimate goal of human flourishing that has been developed here in the analysis of good consumption.

Bibliography

Alford, H.J., and M.J. Naughton. 2001. *Managing as If Faith Mattered. Christian Social Principles in the Modern Organization*. Notre Dame: University of Notre Dame Press.

Aquinas, Thomas. 1934. *The "Summa Theologica."* Trans. Fathers of the English Dominican Province. London: Burns Oates and Washbourne Ltd.

Aristotle n.d.-a *On the Soul*. http://classics.mit.edu/Aristotle/soul.2.ii.html

——— n.d.-b *Nicomachean Ethics*. http://virtuescience.com/nicomachean-ethics.html

——— n.d.-c *Politics*. http://classics.mit.edu/Aristotle/politics.html

Baritz, S.T. 2014. *Three-Dimensional Economy. Is It Possible to Manage in Virtue Ethical Paradigm?* (PhD dissertation). Budapest: Corvinus University of Budapest.

Bruni, L., and S. Zamagni. 2007. *Civil Economy, Efficiency, Equity, Public Happiness*. Bern: Peter Lang.

Buber, M. 1937. *I and Thou*. Trans. R. G. Smith. Edinburgh: T&T Clark.

Cambridge Dictionary. n.d.. https://dictionary.cambridge.org/dictionary/english/

Campbell, C. 2021. *Wants and Needs, Consumption and Consumer Society, The Craft Consumer and Other Essays*. Berlin: Springer Nature.

Cicero, M.T. n.d. *De Finibus Bonorum et Malorum* https://en.wikipedia.org/wiki/De_finibus_bonorum_et_malorum

Frank, R.H. 2004. *What Price the Moral High Ground? Ethical Dilemmas in Competitive Environments*. Princeton: Princeton University Press.

Hümeyra Ashm Bilge. 2015. Luxury consumption: Literature review. *Khazar Journal of Humanities and Social Sciences* 18 (1): 35–55.

Jarrett, B.O.P. 2007. *Social Theories of the Middle Ages, 1200–1500*. San Rafael: Archive.

John Paul II 1984. *Reconciliation and Penance*. Apostolic exhortation. http://www.vatican.va/holy_father/john_paul_ii/apost_exhortations/documents/hf_jp-ii_exh_02121984_reconciliatio-et-paenitentia_en.html

Kasser, T. 2002. *The High Price of Materialism, A Bradford Book*. Cambridge: MIT Press.

Klamer, Arjo. 2002. Accounting for social and cultural values. *De Economist* 150 (4): 453–473.

Kotler, P.T., and K. Lane. 2019. *Marketing management*. Pearson Education Limited.

Leseur, E. 1918. Journal et pensées de chaque jour. Paris, pp. 31.

Lewis, C.S. n.d. Keresztény vagyok! [*I am a Christian*!] Pázmány Péter Elektronikus Könyvtár, http://www.piar.hu/pazmany/konyvek/cslmch01.txt

McInerny, R. 1997. *Ethica Thomistica, The Moral Philosophy of Thomas Aquinas*. Washington: The Catholic University of America Press.

Nyíri, T. (1973) *A filozófiai gondolkodás fejlődése* [Development of Philosophical Thinking]. Budapest: Szent István Társulat.

Oderberg, D.S. 2005. *Moral Theory, a Non-consequentialist Approach*. Malden: Blackwell Publishing.
Pinckaers, S.O.P. 1995. *The Sources of Christian Ethics*. Edinburgh: T&T Clark.
Rokeach, M. 1973. *The Nature of Human Values*. New York: The Free Press.
Ryan, R.M., and E.L. Deci. 2000. Self determination theory and the facilitation of intrinsic motivation, social development, and well-being. *American Psychologist* 55 (1): 68–78.
Scheler, M. 1973. *Formalism in Ethics and Non-Formal Ethics of Values*. Evanston: Northwestern University Press.
Sen, A.K. 1999. *Development as Freedom*. New York: Anchor Books.
Szondy, M. (2010) *A boldogság tudománya, fejezetek a pozitív pszichológiából* [Science of Happiness, Chapters from the Positive Psychology]. Budapest: Jaffa Kiadó.
Tringer, L. 1992. *A gyógyító beszélgetés* [Healing Conversation], Semmelweis Orvostudományi Egyetem Képzéskutató. Budapest: Oktatástechnológiai és Dokumentációs Központ.
Turay, A. (1984) *Lételmélet* [Theory of Being]. Debrecen, Katolikus Hittudományi Főiskolai Jegyzetek.
Turgonyi, Z. (1993) *A filozófia alapjai* [Foundations of Philosophy]. Budapest: Egyházfórum Alapítvány.
Weissmahr, B. (1978) *Bevezetés az ismeretelméletbe* [Introduction into the Epistemology]. Roma: Tipografia Dario Detti.
Williams, C.O.P. 1974. The hedonism of Aquinas. *The Thomist* 38: 257–290.

Part II
Is Mainstream Economics to Blame?

Chapter 6
Political Economy, Moral Reasoning, and Global Warming

David C. Rose

Abstract Many worry that global warming may produce dire consequences not just for humankind, but for many other living organisms on the planet. This has raised concerns about the desirability of the political and economic policies that brought us to this point in history, a period of markedly higher levels of consumption that produce higher levels of CO_2. That, in turn, has raised new concerns about the ideologies and theoretical paradigms upon which such political and economic policies are based. Many now call for a rejection of free market economies to make room for more centrally planned economic systems. Even the idea of *Homo Economicus* – the primary actor in the modern free market economy – is under fire in favor of a new conceptualization of the primary actor: *Homo Curator*. This essay explains why these changes are both unnecessary and dangerous. I argue they are unnecessary by showing: (1) *Homo Economicus* and excessive consumption are not the root of the problem, and (2) how the theory of market failure already gives us proven means to address problems like global warming. I argue that abandoning *Homo Economicus* and the free market economy is dangerous because it will inevitably lead to a world that is far less likely to support individual and collective human flourishing; one that poorer, less free, and less respectful of the sanctity of the individual.

6.1 Introduction

Does the reigning economic paradigm, through the behavior of *Homo Economicus* in the context of the free market economy, encourage excessive consumption that is producing excessive CO_2? If so, does it follow that we should we begin looking for a new primary actor and economic system – a new economic paradigm?

D. C. Rose (✉)
University of Missouri-St. Louis, St Louis, MO, USA
e-mail: rose@umsl.edu

P. Róna et al. (eds.), *Homo Curator: Towards the Ethics of Consumption*, Virtues and Economics 8, https://doi.org/10.1007/978-3-031-51700-6_6

Calls for such drastic changes without first identifying superior alternatives would normally be viewed as foolish, but not if the present course guarantees disaster. One does not quibble about which way to turn a runaway stagecoach if it is about to head over a cliff. Are things now so dire that we are morally required to replace *Homo Economicus* with something like *Homo Curator* and to replace the free market economy with something that involves greater central planning?

This paper argues against such an endeavor for three reasons.

First, the role played by *Homo Economicus* in economic theory is largely misunderstood. *Homo Economicus* is not inconsistent with the kind of tastes that might reduce aggregate consumption so as to slow global warming due to the production of CO_2. The genius of the modeling metaphor we call *Homo Economicus* is that it avoids discussion of the tastes that drive individual behavior toward specific ends. It focuses, instead, on the instrumental means of behavior.

Second, thinking of *Homo Curator* as a substitute for *Homo Economicus* implicitly assumes a particular kind of *Curator*, one best described as "early *Curator*." Early *Curator* centrally planned and directed economic activity in the small group social contexts of our ancestors. But the mass flourishing we take for granted today is a product of very large free market economies that can only be regulated through decentralized planning. There should be no illusions: resurrecting early *Curator* to replace decentralized planning will result in a poorer and less free society.

Third, the theory of market failure provides guidance for how a modern version of *Homo Curator* already addresses problems like excessive levels of CO_2 production within the context of a free market economy animated by individuals whose behavior is well modeled by *Homo Economicus*. Whereas early *Curator* substitutes for the free market economy, modern *Curator* uses the theory of market failure to complement it. In so doing it addresses the problem of global warming in a way that is consistent with maximizing social welfare, broadly construed.

6.2 *Homo Economicus* in the Context of Political Economy

The basic idea of *Homo Economicus* goes back at least as far as J.S. Mill in his discussion of how human behavior should be considered in the study of political economy (Mill 1848). *Homo Economicus* is normally taken as a reference to the phrase "economic man." Note that neither the locution *Homo Economicus* nor *economic man* was used by Mill. Indeed, *Economic man* was actually coined by his critics (Persky 1995).

Mill's characterization of human behavior was a descriptive and therefore positive analytic exercise, not a normative one. Moreover, even before complex mathematical models of the economy existed, Mill understood the futility of trying to provide a descriptive account for the full range of human behavior when the goal is the study of political economy. *Homo Economicus* (hereafter simply *Economicus*) should likewise be viewed as pertaining only to the parts of human behavior that are most likely relevant to the study of political economy.[1]

What makes the metaphor of *Economicus* so useful is not the tastes that parameterize the utility functions of individuals. Quite the opposite. The tastes that determine what individuals seek as ends are taken as given so as to focus on the instrumental means of economic behavior. An important byproduct of this is that it allows the model to be applicable to societies filled with different kinds of persons. In doing so it provides a way to model the behavior of individuals across different societies, and even within societies, that tolerate and perhaps even encourage diversity and individuality.

Much behavior is habitual and/or pattern-imitative in nature and therefore largely unthinking, like driving on the right side of the road or holding a door open for the next person. Such behavior largely comports with what Kahneman (2011) calls System 1 thinking. Such thinking is fast, intuitive, and sometimes driven by emotion.[2]

But decision making as it relates to political economy is normally taken to be consciously purposeful. To put a variable in an individual's utility function in the context of standard economic analysis therefore implicitly assumes that decision-making as it relates to that variable is purpose-driven. As such it enlists our ability to think carefully – rationally – about the best course of action. This largely comports with what Kahneman (2011) calls System 2 thinking.

The more purposeful thinking is, the more it will strive to account for tradeoffs arising from some actions producing more benefit to the individual than others. This raises the question of how competing courses of action are balanced against one another in such thinking. The answer provided by modern economic theory is that one thinks and acts in a manner that is expected to achieve the greatest level of welfare as measured by the individual's own utility function.[3]

Maximizing such a utility function subject to material constraints accounts for the tradeoffs involved in such thinking. The utility function assigns values to the benefit of actions *as if* individuals were consciously considering these internalized valuations. The constraint function accounts for the external costs associated with taking actions. The mathematics of constrained optimization results in the former netting out the latter so as to ensure decision making results in the highest possible net benefit arising from available resources.[4]

---

[1] All that is relevant to the study of political economy cannot be known fully *ex ante*. Behavioral and experimental economics tries to address failings of the current paradigm by identifying relevant factors that have, heretofore, been overlooked or that only recently became relevant.

[2] Frank (1987, 1988) has argued that part of the reason why we have emotions is precisely to override careful, deliberative, rational thinking in contexts where it can produce worse outcomes for the individual or the group.

[3] See Boland (1981, 1982) on the futility of criticizing the maximization assumption.

[4] Milton Friedman (1953) illustrated the plausibility of "as if" modeling through the example of trying to predict how an expert billiards player would line-up shots. Even if the player had no schooling in mathematics, our use of such mathematical tools would do a good job predicting the player's behavior, so it is sensible to model the player's behavior with such mathematics even though the player might not even be capable of explicitly employing it.

The more one behaves *as if* one is solving such a constrained optimization problem, the more one does not waste happiness because: (1) the opportunity cost of happiness not experienced from actions not taken is accounted for by the utility function, and (2) the opportunity cost of material resources is accounted for in the constraint functions. Careful reckoning of benefits and costs of competing ends across varying circumstances produces consistently better outcomes than when behavior is locked-in by the "if-then" protocols of habitual or pattern-imitative behavior that comports with Kahneman's System 1.[5] This is why in modern economics the concept of rationality is often equated with the maximization hypothesis.

The maximization of utility is therefore best thought of as a description of how individuals make purposeful decisions to best promote their welfare by considering opportunity costs as fully as possible. Although highly critical of what she believes to be excessive emphasis on this approach in economics, Deirdre McCloskey has nevertheless given us a simple way to convey the basic idea: *Max-U*.[6]

Behavior being driven by utility maximization makes a great deal of sense in evolutionary terms. It provides a mechanism for balancing the survival benefits of competing actions so as to avoid waste. Obviously, any trait that supports modes of thinking that leads to a better chance of survival by not wasting resources is likely to be reinforced by natural selection.

Because maximization considers things that go beyond the *if* antecedent in "if-then" genetic or cultural coding, it should normally produce better outcomes. The more cognitive horsepower a species or individual within a species has, the more often this difference will be substantial, and can therefore significantly improve the likelihood of survival. Over time natural selection likely came to be affected by which kinds of decisions were made. Decisions that directly or indirectly increased the reproductive success of one's own children were then reinforced vis-à-vis traits that led to such decisions.[7]

Wouldn't the evolution of such traits simply produce more nuanced "if-then" encoding which would still suppress the benefits of thinking carefully

[5] See Rose (2019b) for an account of how System I style behavioral protocols emerge as described by Adam Smith (1982 [1759]). As markets develop, however, group norms that provide the foundation for System I style protocols falter thereby forcing ever more behavior to be mediated in System II fashion, that is, through rational thinking.

[6] McCloskey (2006, 2010) has argued, correctly in my view, that *Max-U* mostly operationalizes the single virtue of prudence. Therefore, those who think *Max-U* fully captures the totality of human behavior, even the totality of economic behavior, are revealing a poor understanding of human history, the role of ethics, the rise of virtues, and the importance of institutions on understanding economic phenomena. See also Rose (2011, 2016).

[7] Note that the more important it is that behavioral responses comport with "if-then" encoding, the stronger tastes that give rise to the feeling we call happiness will be. Consider how miserable a crying infant makes us, and how happier we become when we are able to offer the needed comfort. In such cases there are low returns to creativity relative to the costs from a lack of consistency.

before acting? Perhaps it would in a world devoid of uncertainty.[8] But in a world of genuine uncertainty the answer would be no if traits only drive behavior in vague directions. When behavior is vaguely driven rather than precisely scripted, one is given impetus to think carefully about how to tailor decisions to make the most of specific circumstances.

This is quite different from searching for the right "then" to go with the observed "if." Consciously careful – rational – thinking gets put to work. To what end? To maximize our chances of feeling happier, of course. But the feeling we call happiness is largely a mirage, a mechanism for getting us to do what we need to do to survive and successfully reproduce.

When traits lead to behavior that results in greater resource waste and therefore lower rates of survival, such behavioral traits are not reinforced. When traits lead to behavior that results in less waste (the flipside of optimization) and therefore higher rates of survival, such traits are reinforced. As our intellectual horsepower increased to make us better potential maximizers, traits that support conscious efforts to betterment therefore also grew stronger.

At the same time, when the maximization of utility for a given set of taste parameters results in greater resource waste and therefore lower rates of survival, such tastes are not reinforced. But when the maximization of utility for a given set of taste parameters results in less waste and therefore higher rates of survival, such tastes are reinforced.

One might object that many of the things we like, and would therefore be valued in our utility functions, have nothing to do with survival. But where did desire for the attributes that make a thing desirable come from? I cannot think of anything that makes me happier that cannot be understood as an amalgam of tastes that exists because of more fundamental needs for survival.

Candy makes me happy, but it is not necessary for survival. But a strong taste for sugar led my ancestors to crave eating fruit which is important for a species that cannot synthesize vitamin C. Those who created candy did so because they thought they could make others happy by doing so. But in reality, they were simply exploiting tastes that exist to solve a vitamin C problem.

Max-U therefore functions as a proxy for maximizing the probability of survival albeit a few steps removed. Words like happiness or utiles are inventions we use to provide a framework for describing how our behavior is ultimately guided, without our knowledge, in directions that have resulted in prior evolutionary success.

Some find that economic models that feature *Max-U* are objectionable because they don't believe that people are perfectly rational. But people need not be perfectly rational for *Max-U* to provide a good model of behavior any more than Friedman's expert billiards player needs to have earned an A grade in trigonometry.

[8] Frank Knight (1921) distinguished between risk and uncertainty in an important way. The effects of random variables whose probability distributions were known can often be ameliorated by insurance markets. But the effects of random variables with unknown probability distributions, for example the effect of the emergence of an unforeseen new technology, leave economic actors with no way to convert variance into known costs, *ex ante*.

The rationality assumption can be viewed as a general director, like using moss on trees to find north. This is inferior to using a compass, but it does eliminate South, West, and East.

I submit that rationality is a matter of degree and that there are no species that are categorically irrational because that would be antithetical to natural selection. There are, however, species that possess so little intellectual horsepower that they appear to us to be poor at rational thinking. Humans have the most intellectual horsepower, so we behave in ways that are more rational than other species, but that doesn't mean those other species are irrational. A mouse that cannot solve a very difficult maze is not being irrational because he is still doing the best he can, it's just that his best isn't very good compared to a human.

In teaching, some economists will say at the outset that "we assume individuals are selfish." Most understand that this is an act of pedagogy, of keeping the story simple (only two goods, no interpersonal utility effects, etc.). But what is really needed is not selfishness but the assumption that individuals take actions *as if* they are maximizing their own utility. It just so happens that a great deal of boring but important behavior, like choosing which can of green beans to buy, is well-modeled in this way.

In reality *Max-U* is in no way a model of selfish behavior since the model easily accommodates selfless behavior through interpersonal utility. Most of us have the welfare of others in our own utility functions and there is nothing unusual or irrational about this because we sincerely care about their welfare, too.[9]

6.2.1 Curator *Is Not Inconsistent with* Economicus

If *Curator* is proposed to replace *Economicus* out of a desire to get individuals to consume less to save the planet, then *Curator* is about tastes, not maximization. The maximization associated with *Economicus* is about the instrumental means of behavior, not its ends. In the formulation of *Economicus* tastes are taken as given, so they exert their influence on decision making upstream of rational calculation (tastes affect the terms of rational calculation, not how it is conducted).

There is nothing about *Economicus* that cannot accommodate very strong positive or negative tastes of any sort. There is nothing irrational about having tastes, for example, that conform to a desire to be ascetic for its own sake or for the sake of the planet, and there is no need to have such tastes actuated through an irrational (non-maximizing) actor. Similarly, there is nothing irrational or contrary to *Economicus* about someone who possesses tastes that would lead him or her to die for a loved one, for the planet, or for a political cause.

[9] Part of the problem might be a bit of the modeling tail wagging the theoretical dog. In most cases, interpersonal utility effects are very difficult to build into a model that can produce an easy to analyze closed-form solution. But this is a problem with convenient mathematical modeling and subsequent analysis, not with the theory itself.

The call for *Economicus* to be replaced by *Curator* therefore commits a kind of category error. *Economicus* is a positive analytic description of the instrumental means of a subset of behavior, while *Curator* is a normative analytic endorsement for specific kinds of tastes. There is no reason why such tastes cannot be pursued in the context of *Economicus*.

Is it not true that even the most public spirited and selfless person should not want resources wasted? But that is what happens when behavior is inefficient because people aren't behaving "as if" they are maximizing an index that effectively minimizes waste. If behavior is not driven by rationality, what is the competing model? With the exception of some details that pertain to mathematical tractability, *Max-U* really just comes down to the execution of rational choice. If one does not like the choices made by *Economicus* through *Max-U*, then either the tastes need to be changed, the constraints need to be changed, or rationality needs to be abandoned.

6.2.2 Excessive Consumption

Consider a multiperiod world in which the children of period t are the adults of period $t + 1$. The adults of any given period cultivate the tastes of their children so when they become adults their behavior is guided in ways that are good for their individual children because they are good for the group within which they will live.

My teachers taught me to be concerned about the environment. My wife and I, and our children's teachers, inculcated those same tastes into our children. My children and their friends never litter not because they are irrational but because they have internalized tastes that results in such behavior making them feel so badly that littering is now irrational. Because of this, they long ago got out of the habit of even considering littering as an open question. This allows their generation to live in a world where life is good in part because littering is rare.[10]

Nothing about this account conflicts with *Economicus*. The account above illustrates that the real story is about the tastes that define utility functions or factors that affect constraints. *Economicus* therefore does not automatically lead to excess consumption because selfishness or excessive emphasis on material consumption are not products of maximization, they are products of tastes.

Suppose I have a strong taste for asceticism. The more my behavior is well-described by a model in which behavior is driven *as if* I were maximizing my utility, the greater would be the manifestation of my personal ethic of ascetism relative to

[10] I submit that these tastes are effectively social capital because the social gains from behavior that results from them exceeds the private gains (Rose 2019b). Sometimes these private gains are actually negative in that selfish behavior produces a higher net payoff for the individual defector. As such no rational person would choose to have such tastes. This points to the power of culture because tastes that overcome the inexorable logic of the commons' dilemma will not be chosen by rational individuals (Rose 2019a).

material consumption. We could conceivably reduce consumption by urging existing adults to change their tastes or by trying to cultivate more ascetic tastes in young children, but that does not require abandoning *Economicus*.

6.3 *Homo Curator*

The earliest version of *Curator* has been with us from the beginning, well before the emergence of *Sapiens*, and still lives in our genes today. This early *Curator* provided active management of the group. One of early *Curator's* main concerns was taking care of individuals indirectly by directly taking care of the group within which they lived. This was necessary because in some cases individual behavior does not result in what's best for the group.

Before agriculture ended small group living for most humans, behavior was largely governed by conforming to social norms. Many anthropologists have documented this highly pattern-imitative behavior in small groups. The work of Boyd and Richerson (1985; Richerson and Boyd 2005) provided compelling models of such behavior that shed new light on why such behavior is highly efficient and therefore the traits that support it are evolutionarily prepotent. Rose (2019b) contrasted this early modality of small group behavior (*Max-C*) with *Max-U.*[11]

In that era market pricing did not exist. Orderliness arose from a combination of closely followed social norms and centrally planned direction. Early *Curators* can be thought of as the care takers for the group, likely a matriarch or patriarch. They coordinated activity because if everyone just did their own thing, the performance of the group would suffer. As long as there are social dilemmas that drive wedges between what is good for the individual and what is good for the group, there will be a need for *Curator.*[12]

This life was a very far thing from Adam Smith's invisible hand or F.A. Hayek's extended order.[13] Early *Curator* provided central planning. Since, for the vast majority of our evolutionary history, we lived in very small groups with no forms of money and no market pricing, predilections for providing and seeking such direction has every reason to be well-written in our genes. Groups that had little central

[11] *Max-C* is a reference to "maximize conformity" in Rose (2019b). The basic idea is that when a given circumstance presents itself, one first thinks of what one is supposed to do (*Max-C*) rather than how best to produce benefit to oneself (*Max-U*).

[12] The literature on social dilemmas is immense, but the common theme is the divergence between what is individually optimal and therefore individually rational and what is socially optimal. For a good general review see Kollock (1998).

[13] See Hayek (1945, 1988) and Smith (1981 [1776]). Note that Hayek was well aware of this tension between small and large group social organization. Smith (1982 [1759]) in his *Theory of Moral Sentiments*, provided a compelling model for how moral standards that guide behavior in a somewhat formulaic way to produce group harmony likely emerge in small group contexts. This is superior to genetically encoded behavior because it allows different groups of the same generation to create different guideposts for behavior that are adapted to different environments.

planning were far less efficient and if the vagaries of nature didn't end them, competing groups that were well directed did.

With the rise of agriculture human groups grew. This led to greater specialization which, in turn, led to more extensive exchange. After the emergence of money people began thinking in terms of money based prices. As markets thickened, pricing became increasingly parametric in nature, meaning that the market price was simply taken as given. Economic behavior was increasingly being mediated by impersonally determined market prices rather than through bilaterally negotiated transactions between individuals or direction from the top by *Curator*.

In some societies early *Curator* slowly lost control as decentralized planning facilitated by the price system emerged. Those societies within which that did not happen faltered compared to those within which it did. Although central planning was absolutely necessary for small groups, the local knowledge problem associated with specialized production and exchange made it increasingly unworkable with growing group size. At the same time, growing group size thickened both supply and demand and therefore made the price system work even better.

With the number of goods and the degree of specialization increasing, individuals increasingly found themselves needing to choose among alternatives with little guidance from learned social norms (Rose 2019b). They therefore increasingly found themselves benefitting from thinking carefully about how to make such decisions in a way that made them happiest. This led to increasing emphasis on *Max-U* over *Max-C*. That, in turn, led to the rise of greater individualism that is a hallmark of *Economicus*.

When certain cultural, ethical, and legal constraints were in place and strong support for the institutions of private property and contract enforcement also existed, the result was a largely self-regulating free market economy that did a good job taking care of society and the individuals who comprised it. This is because honest market competition amidst voluntary transacting with strong property rights and contract enforcement led to strong incentives to cooperate. This dramatically increased output per capita.

Unfortunately, it is only when a number of assumptions are met that this self-regulating free market economy strongly aligns individually rational actions with the common good. When these assumptions aren't met, it becomes increasingly important that society address these divergences because they reduce social welfare.

Slowly a new role for *Curator* emerged, which was to take care of society by addressing circumstances in which there was a significant divergence between what was individually rational and what was socially optimal. This shifted *Curator* from the role of central planner in small groups to that of using government power to address such shortcomings of the free market economy.

This modern form of *Curator* was increasingly dealing with problems arising from individual behavior that was increasingly well described by the metaphor of *Economicus* in the context of the free market economy. But in doing so modern *Curator* was substituting for neither *Economicus* nor the free market economy.

Modern *Curator* was, instead, complementing both, by alleviating the tendency of *Economicus* to undermine the free market economy through actions, like industrial pollution, that are individually rational but socially harmful. Note that the large and impersonal markets that produce so much human flourishing also make it hard for *Economicus* to perceive of some of the harms its behavior can cause. In my view the success of Western societies is due in large part to the evolution of a particularly effective relationship between *Economicus* and modern *Curator*.

Some societies experimented with putting a resurrected version of early *Curator* atop existing free market economies. But free market societies are nothing like the milieu within which the traits that support early *Curator* emerged. They are large, anonymous, and highly specialized, so knowledge is unfathomably localized in nature. After many of these experiments the lessons of history were clear: it has always resulted in spectacular failure in the form of reduced freedom and material deprivation.

The success of the free market system resulted in an increasing number of circumstances for which individual and collective interests diverge. Modern *Curator* recognizes this problem and takes steps to correct it. But modern *Curator* does not do this by reforming *Economicus*, inculcating new tastes, replacing the free market economy, or otherwise replacing the reigning economic paradigm. Modern *Curator* does this best by employing the theory of market failure.

6.4 The Theory of Market Failure

In one of the most important papers ever written in economics, Arrow and Debreu (1954) demonstrated the existence of an efficient competitive market equilibrium under very general conditions. The theory of market failure essentially describes problems that arise when that proof's assumptions are not satisfied.[14] It also provides guidance for how to nullify these effects, thereby realigning individually rational behavior with socially optimal behavior. This allows such problems to be addressed without undermining the free market economy, *Economicus*, or individual freedom.

The most prominent parts of this theory involve externalities (positive or negative spillover effects resulting from production or consumption) and public goods (goods that will likely be underproduced by the private sector). The first rigorous analysis of externalities dates back to Pigou (1920) and the first rigorous analysis of public goods dates back to Samuelson (1954).

At first the theory of market failure was met with great enthusiasm. But it was soon the object of growing skepticism from a variety of economists, most notably Ronald Coase and James Buchanan.

[14] It should be stressed that the theory of market failure applies to a very broad set of problems, such as the provision of military defense from external threats, the provision of policing and justice, the provision of a variety of public goods like roads, parks, libraries, schools, the provision of social insurance to provide social safety nets and, of most pertinence to the issue of global warming, addressing problems arising from consumption and production externalities.

Coase did not argue that market failure problems do not exist. His goal was to clarify the precise nature of the problem in the case of externalities (Coase 1960). He argued that the crux of the problem was mostly the existence of transaction costs that get in the way of bargaining that naturally takes us to efficient outcomes. Support for Coase's position takes the form of various ways in which externality effects have been handled privately (lighthouses that are privately provided, for example). But this just means that in some cases transaction costs are so low that government intervention is unecessary.

James Buchanan and Gordon Tullock introduced the idea of government failure. They argued that before undertaking government remedies to market failure problems, the expected cost of government intervention needs to be shown to be lower than the social harm arising from such problems. Others have noted that the concept of market failure is often abused to expand the role of government far more than warranted by the theory. A good review of this and other objections to the theory of market failure can be found in Cowan (1988).

None of these criticisms object to the concept of market failure *per se*, they instead point out its limitations and the ease of its abuse. Rare, of course, is the theory for which all the required assumptions are perfectly met. I know of no compelling argument against employing the theory of market failure to launch one's thinking about what might be causing adverse outcomes in free market economies. While it is useful to understand the limitations of the theory of market failure, to reject it outright would constitute a perfection fallacy.

In small societies early *Curator* used a combination of judgment, empathy, and sympathy, applied to intimate knowledge of every individual in the group, to conduct central planning. In many cases this held the group together and, apparently, produced enough success to avert destruction or absorption by other groups, and thereby supported successful replication of genes that gave rise to traits that supported the activities of early *Curator*.[15]

But if Dunbar's number ($\approx$ 150) is any indication, the smartest person to have ever lived could not do this well even for a large neighborhood (Dunbar 1992, 1993). For groups of tens of thousands or more, the required processing of the utility tradeoffs would be far beyond any *Curator's* cognitive horsepower. As groups grew beyond Dunbar's number it became increasingly necessary for early *Curator* to begin abandoning efforts to achieve joint utility maximization over a coalition of individuals and to increasingly make decisions solely for the good of the group *per se*.

This need not have been a conscious decision. Those whose decision-making was a little more skewed toward thinking in terms of the group rather than trying to promote the welfare of each individual in the group were more likely to have surviving groups. Whether early *Curator* understood this or not was irrelevant because the

[15] This is basically an argument for the evolution of traits that arise from group-level selection. Although not considered a terribly controversial concept initially, by the mid twentieth century it was increasingly dismissed as being an unnecessary distraction. But eventually new worked pushed back on this view by providing more precise mechanisms for how multi-level selection might actually work (Wilson and Sober 1994). See also Wilson (2015).

former role simply became impossible. Choices that used up resources to achieve impossible tasks came at the expense of resources that could have strengthened the group relative to other groups.

Overtime this produced ever more focus on making decisions for the good of the group. While there remained the well-known tradeoff within the group arising from individually evolved traits that supported individual welfare at the expense of the group, this was increasingly offset by collective decision making at the top that focused on promoting the survival of the group.

Because of the power of gains from specialization through finer division of labor, keeping groups small and manageable as coalitions of individuals was never really an option except where the environmental conditions (e.g., the Amazon jungle) invited very little competition by other humans. On most of the planet human groups would have to get larger or face destruction or absorption by larger groups. This meant that a shift to decision making that was more focused on the group than on the individuals that comprised it was inevitable. Natural selection would then favor traits that supported such decision making.

Curator "looks after" things. The closer "looking after" was to "maximizing," the more likely the group in question would prevail over other groups for whom "looking after" was less vigorously pursued and singularly focused. Evolutionary pressure therefore led to *Curator* behavior that increasingly looked more like maximization than merely "looking after."

Because of this, individuals became increasingly responsible for looking out for their own welfare and the welfare of their immediate families within the group and it became increasingly morally respectable for them to do so. This further clarified *Curator's* role. *Curator* maximized the welfare of the group as a whole while individuals maximized their own welfare as well as the welfare of those close to the individual. Indeed, the latter contributed to the former by shifting the responsibility for the individuals who comprise the group to the individuals themselves so *Curator* could focus on the group, rather than each and every individual in the group.

What are the implications of *Curator* maximizing the welfare of the group? As a matter of pure mathematical logic, maximization can only be clearly achieved with respect to a single dimension. We can maximize height or weight, for example, but what does it mean to maximize a sample according to physical size, which is a construct that conflates several dimensions? It follows that to maximize the group's welfare, some kind of single dimension index or measure of group welfare is needed.

In economics this was provided by the social welfare function. The social welfare function allowed the use of optimization which meant that group level decisions were being made in a way that comported with rationality because it allowed for decision making to be conducted as if something was being maximized.

This was a brilliant achievement, but after Kenneth Arrow's demonstration of the shortcomings of the idea of a social welfare function, enthusiasm for theoretical work based on the analysis of social welfare functions largely disappeared (Arrow 1950). But by making full use of Pareto's conception of efficiency, some economists figured out how to use the idea of social welfare without needing specific social welfare functions to devise policy solutions.

The modern theory of market failure therefore doesn't work by maximizing an explicit social welfare function. It works by removing that which drives a wedge between individually rational behavior and socially optimal behavior. Removing such wedges realigns individually rational behavior with the common good. Where society ends up can then be presumed to be socially preferable even without having a specific social welfare function to check to see if it is now actually being maximized.

Arrow and Debreu (1954) and others identified the assumptions that must be met for a free market economy to automatically produce a stable equilibrium of input and output prices that induces a Pareto efficient pattern of resource allocation. This demonstrated in formal terms that individually rational behavior was not inconsistent with the maximization of economic efficiency.[16] What was individually rational was socially optimal.

But when these assumptions are not met we can no longer presume that *laissez faire* will take us where we want to go. The free market fails to maximize social welfare even by the Pareto criteria.

This frames the debate over market interventions in a sensible way. Economists need not make an affirmative case for the free market economy since that case has already been made. The only way forward for a would-be interventionist is to identify which of the Arrow-Debreu proof's assumptions are violated. At that point, the debate can ensue about whether such assumptions are indeed violated and, if so, whether the benefits of rectification would likely exceed the costs.

The theory of market failure recognizes the problems that such unsatisfied assumptions present to the free market economy. It then explores how they might be rectified to return the individual actions of *Economicus* to alignment with best promoting the common good.

The most obvious example of how this works involves the basic framework of Pigou, which is to recognize that the existence of a negative production externality (which violates the assumption of no externalities) implies that social supply lies above private supply, so private markets produce an outcome in excess of what is socially optimal. This can be addressed with an excise tax that has the effect of lifting private supply up to the social supply curve, effectively internalizing the adverse effect of the externality into individual behavior.

Note that in Pigou's remedy, no attempt is made to change anyone's tastes or tell anyone what to do – both of which would obviously raise a variety of ethical concerns. Instead, all that is required is that people not get away with paying less than what the full cost their actions impose on society. This seems eminently fair and ethical.

[16] I say "not inconsistent with economic efficiency" because Pareto efficiency, which allows us to get around not having a social welfare function, is not equivalent to economic efficiency. Pareto optimality is only a necessary condition for economic efficiency in that it eliminates allocations that cannot possibly be economically efficient.

This is a very rough introduction to just one of the basic ideas of the theory of market failure. But even if the direst predictions about global warming are true, the basic problem it presents differs only in degree from the generic problem of industrial pollution. The crux of the man-made part of global warming is that burning fossil fuels produces a negative production externality in the form of CO2 which is not being adequately accounted for in the rational utility maximizing decisions of individuals and the organizations they create.

Applying this theory to problems like global warming allows modern *Curator* to do what she *should* always do, which is deal with problems that are not well addressed in the private sector.

So rather than overturn the reigning economic paradigm or the free market economy, modern *Curator* should look to the theory of market failure for guidance as to how to align individual behavior with behavior that is socially optimal.

Direct management of the physical and social environment has always been, and will always be, of paramount importance to human social behavior. It is necessary for survival in the small group social contexts of life where we do most of our actual living. Our marriages, families, small firms, and small communities will always require some degree of direct management.[17]

But across a large society the flow of resources for production and consumption through market based transactions does not require direct management. The spontaneous order of the market automatically solves the deepest problem associated with the large group settings required to achieve the gains from specialization identified by Smith – what Hayek (1945) called the local knowledge problem.

Replacing market pricing with central direction can undermine this spontaneous order to the point of destruction, and thereby destroy much of what was made possible by it. Misguided attempts to do so is the terrible story of the twentieth century.

A better approach is to leave *Economicus* unmolested and retain the free market economy, but complement both with modern *Curator*, who addresses problems that arise from individually rational decision making in the contexts of large groups. Modern *Curator* need not be a noble and wise king who wields power to run society. The theory of market failure shows precisely how to rectify these problems in the context of free market economies without needing to coerce or even presuming to coax individual behavior.

6.5 Concluding Remarks

The backlash against the theory of market failure from some free market advocates would seem to undermine my arguments. But which is worse: a remedy that, if improperly applied or abused, can undermine the free market economy, or a

[17] This notion is consistent with one of the most influential papers ever written in economics, yet another one by Ronald Coase (1937). He argued that firms exist because the transactions undertaken by them are, apparently, more costly to achieve over markets than under direct management.

remedy that calls for the abandonment of the free market economy altogether? Ironically, it may be the theory of market failure that saves the free market economy from those who view its abandonment as necessary to save the environment.

Many environmentalists, economists, and policy makers have known for some time that the best way to reduce CO_2 is through policies that are very similar to those that have already reduced other forms of air pollution with great success. Given this, why raise the question of whether we are morally required to replace the reigning economic paradigm?

There is nothing inherently bad or wrong about global warming. We are concerned about it because of the harm it might do. If there is a moral issue here it is therefore fundamentally consequentialist in nature.

Suppose when the theory of market failure is correctly applied that humans, acting as described by *Economicus* in the context of a free market economy, will then act in a manner that produces the best possible social outcome. In such a case, does not the morally consequentialist nature of the problem of global warming imply that nothing else is morally required?

It is believed by some that *Economicus* is suspect more generally because such behavior is rooted in rational maximization. But it is hard to imagine a better world arising out of the diminution of rational behavior. Maximization is, after all, the flipside of the minimization of waste, which would seem to be highly prized by those concerned about overusing the planet's resources.

There is nothing about rational maximization that does not allow ascetic or selfless values that strongly emphasize the collective welfare over the self. The more effectively an individual with such values and tastes engages in rational maximization, the more fully ascetic and selfless the behavior of such a person will be.

Does this mean we should try to solve the global warming problem by changing tastes so we can preserve rationally directed decision making? Not quite. Whose tastes should we modify? Who should do the modifying? How should they be modified? What ethical issues would this raise? On what moral authority would any of this occur?

Since an individual's tastes are an important part of what makes a person an individual in a society rather than a bee in a beehive, does not such changing of tastes threaten diversity and individualism? There is no clear path to modifying tastes to address the problem of global warming by reducing consumption, let alone one that does not raise obvious ethical issues. Luckily employing the theory of market failure does not require such intrusion into freedom or free thinking.

Replacing the free market economy with a system that involves more direct management of the economy is also problematic. But given Arrow and Debreu's (1954) theorem and proof, and given that the remedies already devised from the theory of market failure are rooted in social welfare maximization, the best such central planning could do is approach, from beneath, what the theory of market failure already accomplishes.

Perhaps calls for the replacement of *Economicus* and the free market system are better explained by the existence of principled disapproval of each. Some appear to believe that we shouldn't be maximizing our individual utility because of the mistaken belief that doing so is inherently selfish or that we shouldn't support the free market economy because it inevitably produces unjust outcomes because of this selfishness.

But the metaphor of *Economicus* animated by *Max-U* is not inherently selfish, it is inherently rational. Selfishness depends on the tastes in the utility function. The most effective rational maximizer in the world can also be the most selfless person in the world. Surely the world would not have been a better place if Mother Theresa had just been a little less rational.

Throwing out *Economicus* and *Max-U* is therefore basically throwing out rationality. Even throwing the baby out with the bathwater makes more sense because used bathwater is of no value, but *Economicus* and the free market economy have, in fact, produced mass flourishing.

Perhaps what is really going on is moral disapproval of the individualistic ethic associated with *Economicus* relative to the communitarianism of early *Curator* because of the latter's concern for the group first and the individual second. This seems, on its face, to be less selfish, and to many "less selfish" seems self-evidently morally superior. This is an ancient and powerful view.

Calls for a new economic paradigm, therefore, might be an exercise in the delegitimization of the individual as the primary unit of analysis in political economy. But that implies that the value of individuals is derived from their group membership, not from each and every one of them being precious ends in themselves. This comports with the increasing influence of identity politics which is contributing to increasingly rancorous and dangerous tribalism.

One wonders if the rejection of individuality is part of a broader rejection of Western systems of political economy. But this is a path to the kind of pervasive tyranny that arose after the emergence of large scale agriculture. It was those very Western systems of political economy that increasingly displaced tyrannical government over time to produce the modern world we now take for granted (Ferguson, 2012).

In western systems, especially in the American constitutional republic, the objective of government is not to advance the interests of the group as early *Curator* is wont to do. It is, instead, to put the government in service to individuals rather than the other way around.[18] This includes enlisting modern *Curator* to employ the theory of market failure to address problems like global warming in a way that does not erode the individualism exemplified by, or the free market systems made possible by, *Homo Economicus*.

---

[18] This sentiment was immortalized in the last line of Abraham Lincoln's Gettysburg address, where he referred to America as nation with "… government of the people, by the people, for the people…"

References

Arrow, Kenneth J. 1950. A difficulty in the concept of social welfare. *Journal of Political Economy* 58 (4): 328–346.

Arrow, Kenneth J., and Gerard Debreu. 1954. Existence of an equilibrium for a competitive economy. *Econometrica* 22 (3): 265–290.

Boland, Lawrence A. 1981. On the futility of criticizing the neoclassical maximization hypothesis. *American Economic Review* 71 (5): 1031–1036.

———. 1982. *The Foundations of Economic Method*. London: George Allen & Unwin.

Boyd, Robert, and Peter J. Richerson. 1985. *Culture and the Evolutionary Process*, 1985. Chicago: University of Chicago Press.

Coase, Ronald H. 1937. The nature of the firm. *Economica* 4 (16): 386–405.

———. 1960. The problem of social cost. *Journal of Law & Economics* 3: 1–44.

Cowan, Tyler. 1988. *A Theory of Market Failure*. Fairfax: George Mason University Press.

Dunbar, R.I.M. 1992. Neocortex size as a constraint on group size in primates. *Journal of Human Evolution* 22: 469–493.

———. 1993. Coevolution of neocortical size, group size and language in humans. *Behavioral and Brain Sciences* 16 (4): 681–735.

Ferguson, Niall. 2012. *Civilization: The West and the Rest*. London: Penguin Publishing Group.

Frank, Robert H. 1987. If homo Economicus could choose his own utility function, would he want one with a conscience? *American Economic Review* 77 (4): 593–604.

———. 1988. *Passions Within Reason: The Strategic Role of Emotions*. New York: W.W. Norton.

Friedman, Milton. 1953. The methodology of positive economics. In *Essays in Positive Economics*, 3–43. Chicago: University of Chicago Press.

Hayek, F.A. 1945. The use of knowledge in society. *American Economic Review* 35 (4): 519–530.

———. 1988. *The Fatal Conceit: The Errors of Socialism*. Chicago: University of Chicago Press.

Kahneman, Daniel. 2011. *Thinking, Fast and Slow*. New York: Farrar, Straus and Giroux.

Knight, Frank H. 1921. *Risk, Uncertainty, and Profit*. Boston: Hart, Schaffner & Marx; Houghton Mifflin Company.

Kollock, Peter. 1998. Social dilemmas: The anatomy of cooperation. *Annual Review of Sociology* 24: 183–214.

McCloskey, Deirdre N. 2006. *The Bourgeois Virtues: Ethics for an Age of Commerce*. 1st ed. Chicago: University of Chicago Press.

———. 2010. *Bourgeois Dignity: Why Economics Can't Explain the Modern World*. Chicago: University of Chicago Press.

Mill, John Stuart. 1848. *Principles of Political Economy*. London: John W. Parker.

Persky, Joseph. 1995. Retrospectives: The ethology of Homo Economicus. *The Journal of Economic Perspectives* 9 (2): 221–231.

Pigou, Arthur C. 1920. *The Economics of Welfare*. Macmillan and Company.

Richerson, Peter J., and Robert Boyd. 2005. *Not by Genes Alone*. Chicago: University of Chicago Press.

Rose, David C. 2011. *The Moral Foundation of Economic Behavior*. New York: Oxford University Press.

———. 2016. Virtues as social capital. In *Economics and the Virtues*, ed. Mark D. White and Jennifer Baker, 202–216. New York: Oxford University Press.

———. 2019a. *Why Culture Matters Most*. New York: Oxford University Press.

———. 2019b. On the evolution of ethics, rationality, and economic behavior. In *The Oxford Handbook of Ethics and Economics*, ed. Mark D. White, 160–178. New York: Oxford University Press.

Samuelson, Paul A. 1954. A pure theory of public expenditure. *Review of Economics and Statistics* 36 (4): 387–389.

Smith, Adam 1981 [1776]. *An Inquiry into the Nature and Causes of the Wealth of Nations*. Edited by R.H. Campbell and A.S. Skinner. Indianapolis: Liberty Fund Press.

———. 1982 [1759]. *The Theory of Moral Sentiments*. Edited by D.D. Raphael and A.L. Macfie. Indianapolis: Liberty Fund Press.

Wilson, David Sloan. 2015. *Does Altruism Exist? Culture, Genes and the Welfare of Others*. New Haven: Yale University Press.

Wilson, David Sloan, and Elliott Sober. 1994. Reintroducing group selection to the human behavioral sciences. *Behavioral and Brain Sciences* 17 (4): 585–654.

Chapter 7
A Critical Approach to Critiquing Economics

Geoffrey Brennan and Hayden Wilkinson

Abstract The critique of mainstream economics and its damaging role in bringing about the ecological is based on a number of misconceptions: about the relation between economic inquiry and economic phenomena; about exact use and understanding of homo economicus within economics; and about the usefulness of some economic tools in addressing some of the harms that economic science is accused of causing. There is nonetheless scope for improvements to be made to the discipline, particularly in the area of normative considerations which are usually understood all too narrowly. Overall, however, despite some objections, we argue that economic discipline equips us in useful tools to combat the harms that humanity and our habitat are suffering.

7.1 Introduction

According to some critics, economics has a lot to answer for. It is alleged that this 'purported science' has inflicted 'apocalyptic damage' on humanity and its habitat, as well as profoundly redefined who we are as human beings. So say the organisers of this volume, as well as contributors to earlier volumes in this same series (e.g., Róna 2017a, p. 4; Lépineux and Rosé 2017, p. 255). Given these charges, you might conclude that we ought to radically overhaul or abandon economics as a field of inquiry, at least in its current form. You might think we would be better off without economics.

It is true that serious damage has been done to our natural world during the time that economics has existed as an academic discipline. On the ecological front, 680 different vertebrate species have been driven extinct by human activity (IPBES 2019, 11), and wild populations of vertebrates have been cut by 60% since just 1970 (Grooten and Almond 2018). And on the climate front, humanity's greenhouse gas

G. Brennan · H. Wilkinson (✉)
University of Oxford, Oxford, UK
e-mail: hayden.wilkinson@philosophy.ox.ac.uk

P. Róna et al. (eds.), *Homo Curator: Towards the Ethics of Consumption*, Virtues and Economics 8, https://doi.org/10.1007/978-3-031-51700-6_7

emissions have driven atmospheric concentrations of carbon dioxide to their highest point in 800,000 years (Lüthi et al. 2008), putting the Earth on track for a likely rise in average atmospheric temperature by 3 °C compared to pre-industrial levels (Olhoff and Christensen 2019).

On an even more apocalyptic level, some human activities present risks of future damage to the natural environment so severe that humanity may not survive them. To the best of our current knowledge, greenhouse gas emissions in a business-as-usual scenario have some probability of increasing the average atmospheric temperature by more than 10 °C (Weitzman 2011 suggests a 1% chance, but that may well be optimistic; see also Olson et al. 2012; Tomassini et al. 2007; Schwartz 2012), which would lead to much of the Earth's surface being uninhabitable. Meanwhile, nuclear weapons, if used in even a small-scale conflict, pose a risk of rapid and long-lasting changes to global temperatures that would disrupt agriculture on a global scale (Mills et al. 2014).

But are any of these harms causally attributable to economics as a field of intellectual inquiry? We think not. Should economists as a group be blamed for these phenomena? Again, we think not. And ought we do away with or radically overhaul the methods of economic inquiry? This depends on what aspects of the economic method are under scrutiny and just how radical the changes recommended are. The organisers of this volume propose that orthodox economic models be rewritten to replace homo economicus—a hypothetical agent who frequently appears in those models—with a more benevolent homo curator. So here our discussion will focus largely on this proposal and on the accompanying critiques of homo economicus. As we see it, this critique stems from several dubious claims, most notably concerning the criteria that ought to be used for evaluating scientific models.

For the most part, we defend mainstream economics against its critics. In fact, we suspect that several elements of the critique arise only from misconceptions: about how economic inquiry relates to economic phenomena (see Sect. 7.2); about how exactly homo economicus is used and understood within economics (see Sect. 7.3); and about the usefulness of the tools economics provides us in addressing some of the those same harms for which economics is thought to be responsible (see Sect. 7.5). In Sect. 7.4, we also briefly examine the role of normative considerations in mainstream economics and attempt to distinguish problems with the moral assumptions made by economists and the value of their empirical analysis.

Despite our objections to some elements of the critique, we certainly agree that economics has its failings. For instance, some of the experimental findings of economics fail to replicate (Camerer et al. 2016)—although as it turns out, fewer than for many other scientific disciplines (see Open Science Collaboration 2015). As well, many of the models used by mainstream economics have been shown to rest on assumptions that are demonstrably false; but whether these are necessary abstractions or fatal flaws is a matter of dispute. Recent work in behavioural economics provides one example, though how damaging such demonstrations are to the general economic project is debatable. More worrying, we think, is that economists are prone to use an implausibly narrow account of human motivations (see Sect. 7.3); and adopt a similarly narrow conception of what matters morally (see Sect. 7.4).

There is scope for improvements to be made to the discipline. But we must take care not to throw out the baby with the bathwater. And the basic methods and core findings of economics are a great deal more than mere bathwater.

7.2 Economic Inquiry and Economic Phenomena

Take the claim that "Economics has done great harm to humanity and its habitat". This could be interpreted in either of (at least) two ways, depending on what we take 'economics' to mean. Here are two possible meanings of the term (adapted from Robbins 1932, p. 15).

1. Economic phenomena: phenomena that arise as a result of agents pursuing their ends via scarce means that have alternative uses.
2. Economic inquiry: the study of agents' behaviour when pursuing ends via scarce means that have alternative uses.

It should be uncontroversial that economic phenomena are often causally responsible for harmful effects. For instance, in the absence of inexpensive alternatives, many humans buy petroleum and burn it in combustion engines to achieve the end of reaching their destinations in a timely manner. Poachers hunt endangered animals to sell their pelts and raise an income, with the end of feeding themselves. And weapons manufacturers design and build delivery systems for nuclear weapons to sell to governments and deliver a profit to the firms' shareholders. All of these situations involve agents pursuing their ends under conditions of scarcity, buying or selling goods, and having deleterious effects on the world around them. Indeed, each of these situations constitute a collective action problem—a class of problems widely studied within economics (and to which we return in Sect. 7.5.)

But is economic inquiry also causally responsible for those effects? We think not.

Consider a setting in which not even a hint of formal economic inquiry is practiced, nor any economic theories widely accepted, nor any economists to espouse particular moral views. One such setting is ancient Greece in the early Mycenaean Age (ranging from 1100 to 600 BCE). In that setting, would the ancient Greeks have been free of all similar collective action problems? Of course not. For instance, hunters in ancient Greece faced a problem analogous to that of modern poachers: it was in each hunter's interest to hunt more than their fair share but, if everyone did so, the population of huntable game would quickly dwindle. And that problem got the better of the ancient Greek hunters, just as many collective action problems are getting the better of us today. For example, lions—which had been widespread in Southern Europe since the early Holocene—were eradicated in Greece, and elsewhere throughout the continent, by the collective action of those ancient hunters (Cohen 2010: pp. 68–9)., As well, during the Mycenaean Age, Greek farmers collectively cleared hundreds of millions of hectares of forest for grazing, resulting in disastrous soil erosion and the drying of many natural springs (Daly 1997: pp. 5–6). That outcome was almost certainly undesirable even from the point of view of the farmers themselves, taken as a whole; their judgment of the optimal extent of land clearing would have stopped well short of what actually occurred.

This all illustrates an obvious point: whether or not anyone engages in economic inquiry, (at least some of) the phenomena under study still arise. Even if no one studies collective action problems, failures of collective action still occur. If the ancient Greeks had access to combustion engines, modern hunting equipment, and missile technology—but somehow still no access to the findings of modern economics—we have no reason to think that they would fare any better than we have. The harms associated with those technologies would plausibly arise with or without the presence of economics as a scientific discipline. Given this, the claim that economic inquiry caused those harms seems unsustainable.

But perhaps those critics of economic inquiry mean something subtler by the claim that "economics has done great harm". Even though we have good reason to think that great harms would have occurred with or without economics, it may still be that economics has caused those harms to be worse than they otherwise would have been.

How might economics—a mere field of study—have exacerbated those harms?

7.2.1 Harms via Economic Technologies

Here is one possibility: the results of economic research might have provided insights that are key to some technology that agents have then used to do harm.

The story here would be similar to one that might be told of physics: findings in particle physics provided insights that were necessary for the development of nuclear weapons; such weapons were used to devastating effect in Hiroshima and Nagasaki and, ever since, have continued to pose risks of catastrophe. One might conclude from this that physics has done humanity a great harm.

But this would be a peculiar story to tell. It is certainly true that those exact harms would not have occurred had those findings in particle physics not been made, so research in particle physics was indeed a necessary condition for those harms to occur. But many events count as necessary conditions, without also counting as relevant causes. Nor does the presence of this causal relationship imply that the world would have been better overall had the necessary condition not been met. The first time a fish crawled onto land was necessary for every event of human history that has followed; but it is far from clear that the world would have been better had that fish stayed put. Nor does an event being a necessary pre-condition mean that agents involved in that event are morally blameworthy for all that occurs as a result. The physicists who made those early strides in particle physics, without knowledge of what their research would uncover nor of how it would be used, do not seem at all to blame for the harms inflicted with nuclear weapons. Nor does the mere fact of being involved in a long causal chain imply that, to prevent such and such harms, we ought to do away with the field of research. It would be bizarre to claim that, as a result of the harms of nuclear weapons, we should do away with the study of physics. Even putting aside the fact that that technology already exists, it is an unnecessarily costly course of action. It would be far less costly (and, we suspect, more feasible) to prohibit the use of physics' findings to build and deploy such destructive weapons. And similarly for economics: if economics has allowed the development of technologies that are now used to do harm, this need not imply that we should do away with further research in economics.

Besides, if we were to tell an analogous story of economics, what would those harmful technologies be? Examples of novel technologies that have arisen from economics include: Pigovian taxes, which impose costs on agents equal to the negative externalities of their actions; Vickrey auctions, which ensure that the prices of auctioned goods accurately reflect the bidders' private evaluations; the assorted 'nudges' identified by behavioural economics, which allow the behaviour of agents to be modified without significantly changing their material incentives; and assorted models of voting processes, some of which provide electoral outcomes more faithful to the electorate's preferences. And some of these technologies might be used to do harm. For instance, a faux-Pigovian tax might be implemented to reduce behaviours that are actually beneficial, such as recycling metals and paper products. Or Vickrey auctions might be used when bidders are poor and sellers rich, resulting in higher prices paid by those poor bidders. Or nudges might be used to encourage consumers to buy greater quantities of harmful goods. Any of these practices would clearly be harmful. But of these harmful uses, only the nudging of consumers to buy particular goods is remotely common. And we doubt that nudging is much implicated in the threat of apocalyptic harms to our environment and atmosphere.

Critics might respond that there is one economic technology that does great harm: the market (in particular goods). But this would be a mistake. Markets themselves are not an economic technology, so much as an economic phenomenon—markets existed in ancient Greece, and in certain goods much earlier. It is true that many economists, from Adam Smith onwards, have often been supportive of market systems. But whether and to what extent that attitude has been responsible for the role that markets play in most societies is unclear: it seems likely that markets would be a widespread phenomenon whether many economists approved of them or not. Moreover, the question of whether markets are harmful overall is debatable. More on this in Sect. 7.4 below.

7.2.2 *Harms via False Beliefs*

Here is another possibility of how a field of academic inquiry might harm the world: it produces false beliefs, perhaps no true knowledge at all, and thereby convinces agents to take unwise actions.

Róna (2017a, 2018) appears to pursue this line of attack, among others. He seems to advance the quite radical stance that economic inquiry has no predictive power whatsoever, at least when it comes to objective facts. How could this be? In his words:

> …economics, unlike the natural sciences, does not have an ontologically objective subject, because economic life, unlike matter, is the product of human intentionality. The objects of economics, such as 'employment', 'interest', 'money', 'utility', 'supply', or 'demand' … are objects of thought that come into being through language and perception that posits them as its objects. The tool-based language of modern economics, expressed in the form of models … constitutes the reality that is its object and does not represent some objective reality outside it … (Róna 2017a, p. 4).

As we interpret it, his basic argument goes something like this: the phenomena that economic inquiry interprets and predicts are subjective (in that they do not exist independently of any conscious awareness of them); and therefore the predictions of economic inquiry are subjective too (in that they are not true independently of any conscious awareness of them, nor perhaps independently of whether one adopts the `language of economics'). But this argument is neither deductively valid nor empirically sound.

For one thing, the intended meaning of 'subjective' differs between premise and conclusion—one is a property of phenomena while the other is a property of propositions.

Just because a property holds of a phenomenon, it doesn't mean that it (or a similar) property holds of propositions about the phenomenon. We can easily have phenomena be subjective (in the first sense) without propositions about those phenomena being subjective (in the second sense). For instance, for any subjective phenomenon X, the proposition that "X is subjective (in the first sense)" is surely objectively true. So is the proposition that "If X occurs, then X occurs", or even that "From the perspective of observer O, X occurred". Just because some phenomenon exists only subjectively, it does not follow that any and all propositions concerning that phenomenon are only subjectively true.

For yet another, the argument's sole premise seems clearly false–not all phenomena studied in economic inquiry are purely subjective. Economics concerns itself primarily with the behaviour of human agents, and whether a human agent behaves in one way or another is typically a matter of objective reality, regardless of whether the action was spurred by human intentions. Some number of ancient Greek hunters killing lions, or farmers chopping down a tree, is an objectively real phenomenon. So is that of some number of agents handing lion pelts to others and receiving such and such in return (whether physical currency that is exchanged for further goods, or further goods themselves), or of many agents doing so. Regardless of whether some external conscious observers are aware of it, the events will nonetheless have occurred (or not). That is a matter of objective reality.

Moreover, Róna's conclusion is demonstrably false—it is clearly true that the predictions of economics about such phenomena can be objectively true. Propositions stating whether hunters will hunt a given species to extinction would be objectively true or false. Likewise, predictions about how many lion pelts those hunters will give to other agents and what they get in exchange will be objectively true or false. We can even make objectively true claims about counterfactual situations such as how many lion pelts an agent would give away if the agent were to receive such and such goods or such and such amount of currency instead (as is predicted by models of supply and demand). So, at least for some of the predictions about economic phenomena that economics makes, the truth or falsity of those predictions is an objective matter.

Perhaps Róna has in mind a related argument in the same vicinity: all intentional human behaviour is 'subjective', in the sense that such behaviour is constituted by the agent's free choices; the free choices of human agents can go either way depending on those agents' intentions; if so, they cannot be accurately predicted; the predictions of economics are all about intentional human behaviour; and so those predictions cannot be accurate. As a result, in at least some sense, you might say that the predictions of economics do not describe objective reality. And this argument is deductively valid, at least. But it relies on a false premise—as it turns out, freely made choices can be predicted quite accurately. Experimental economics demonstrates again and again that, if you raise the cost of (particular kinds of) material goods, the amount of the good that an agent attempts to buy will fall. Likewise, roughly 60% of the findings of experimental economics replicate reliably for different groups of experimental subjects (Camerer et al. 2016). This is not a perfect record of accuracy, but economics is clearly having some success in describing objective reality—for comparison, if its findings were produced by random chance, only 5% would replicate.

7.2.3 *Harms via True, but Corrupting, Beliefs*

There is one further possibility of how economics has caused additional harm to the world, which we take to be the core worry of many proponents of the homo curator project: that the knowledge provided by economics somehow corrupts those who pursue and/or obtain it.

It may seem surprising that accurate empirical knowledge would have such a corrupting effect, but it is not impossible. There is certainly precedent. Consider the phenomenon by which almost everyone perceives their own positive qualities (including intelligence, appearance, charm, honesty, and even ability to drive) far more generously than others perceive them. Almost all of us exhibit this self-serving bias, as it is known in the psychology literature—except, it has been suggested, for the clinically depressed (see Taylor and Brown 1988). This is a situation in which accurate information may be harmful—learning that others find us less smart, less charming, less attractive, less moral, than we take ourselves to be may well imperil our mental well-being. Or consider another beneficial illusion: most people that, if they commit a crime, the chances of their being discovered are much higher than they in fact are. Criminologists assure us that that belief is widespread among non-offenders (Waldo and Chiricos 1972). And, plausibly, this is for the best, as disabusing people of the illusion could well lead to greater incidence of crime—indeed, criminals are far more optimistic about their chances of getting away with it (ibid.).

Could the findings of economics harm those who come to believe them? And, if so, how? Perhaps that knowledge makes its knowers more self-interested than the rest of us, or more concerned with material well-being. There is some evidence in favour of the claim: early undergraduate students of economics have been found to be less generous in ultimatum games (Carter and Irons 1991), threshold public goods games (Cadsby and Maynes 1998), and dictator games (Wang et al. 2011), and more likely to defect in prisoner's dilemmas than students in other disciplines (Frank et al. 1993). Interestingly, when the students in those studies were quizzed on their motivations for acting as they do, it was found that this difference in behaviour is not due to their having a lesser concern for fairness or justice than other students, but instead due to their having less confidence in other players' generosity (Gerlach 2017). And this is consistent with explanations other than that the economics students were more concerned with their own material well-being than others. For instance, those students may have had concerns identical to their peers, but those concerns may have included a desire for esteem—if one is in a community in which others are not especially benevolent, one loses relatively little esteem by failing to be benevolent (and so if one learned that one's peers were not very benevolent, it would make sense to be less benevolent oneself). And so the proliferation of accurate beliefs about how benevolent others are may lead to greater harms–in collective action problems beyond the classroom, those with a knowledge of economic findings may be less likely to cooperate and more likely to impose harms on others. Perhaps, in this way, economic inquiry contributes to the great harm that humanity has done to its habitat.

We will return to this possible critique of economics in the next section. But, for now, there are several reasons not to abandon the field of economics immediately. The first is that there is strong prima facie justification for a science to provide accurate findings on any given topic, as against suppressing lines of enquiry or actively promoting falsehoods. For economics in particular, it is particularly plausible that there is great benefit to be had by pursuing truth on matters such as how benevolent or self-interested human agents are. Without accurate beliefs here, economic policymakers might well falsely expect many collective action problems to resolve themselves spontaneously. And if accuracy is beneficial, it would take a great deal of justification to give us decisive reason not to pursue accuracy. The harm caused by accurate beliefs would have to be significant, and the evidence for that harm quite strong. It is notable that the critics we have cited provide no empirical evidence for such harm occurring, and no empirical evidence on the magnitude of the relevant effects.

7.3 Homo Economicus

For those same critics mentioned above, a key target of their critique is homo economicus: a characterisation of human agents that frequently appears in mainstream economic models. Of this model, Róna (2017b, p. 152) laments that:

Economic theory posits the utility maximizing agent as its paragon. It is widely thought that the root vice of modern economic theory is the construction of a homo economicus who is a grotesque mutilation of the biological human being, and that the way forward is its replacement with a better paragon.

Similar claims are made by Zamagni (2017), Ims (2017), Thompson (2017), Lépineux and Rosé (2017, p. 255), and Róna (2017a). They share a worry that, in assuming that humans resemble homo economicus, economics has profoundly redefined who we are as human beings, and that this redefinition is for the worse.

But what exactly is homo economicus? This hypothetical agent that populates economic models has two defining features:

(a) Agent Rationality: each agent has a consistent preference ordering over the possible outcomes of their actions, that can be represented by a utility function (or preference function) such that the agent chooses actions that maximise (expected) utility.
(b) Material Concern: the agent's material well-being (or full income in Becker's sense) exclusively (or predominantly) constitutes their utility(/preference) function.

A few points about homo economicus bear noting. The first is that their two characteristics are independent. An agent can satisfy Agent Rationality with any set of preferences over outcomes whatsoever (so long as those preferences are reflexive, transitive, and complete). And a utility function can be made up of any such preferences. Being rational in this sense, and maximising one's utility, does not imply that one satisfies the Material Concern condition. For instance, a saint might embrace a life of poverty if she believes that that is what God is calling her to do—that saint, too, would count as rational, and as a utility maximiser, in the above sense.

The second is that is that homo economicus is an extreme simplification of a realistic human agent. Human agents routinely fail to act in ways that are representable by utility functions: their preferences are often inconsistent, incomplete, or intransitive; they sometimes fail to choose what they claim to prefer; and they show computational shortcomings when comparing available actions. And most economists are well aware of this; few serious economists believes that typical human agents are perfect utility maximisers who care exclusively about their own material well-being. But the homo economicus construction is not designed to describe the motivations and abilities of individual human agents with perfect accuracy. (If it were, economic models would be far too complicated for practical use!) Instead, the goal of such models is typically to predict general tendencies, especially in the behaviour of large groups, and for this goal the simplifications of homo economicus often detract little from the model's predictive accuracy. For example, it might be that all individual agents have incomplete preferences. But, if we are predicting their choices among options over which they (or at least most of them) do have preferences, that incompleteness will not (greatly) affect the accuracy of the prediction. And it is not obviously problematic that economic models are inaccurate representations of reality—most scientific models are not perfectly accurate representations of the real world. For example, climate models routinely fail to represent air movement down to the finest possible grain; but that would be poor justification for dismissing the predictions they generate, or for abandoning climate science completely.

A third point that bears noting is that standard uses of homo economicus are purely descriptive, not prescriptive. Economic models are tools of prediction: they are frameworks by which we can input some variables and generate predictions of what effects changes in those variables will produce. In doing so, the models provide answers to questions of the form "How would the world turn out if these conditions held?" rather than any question of the form "How should the world turn out?". So what does it tell us if an economic model assumes that human agents resemble homo economicus? It tells us that many human agents behave like homo economicus in the relevant ways much of the time. But it says nothing at all about whether humans should behave like homo economicus; certainly not that homo economicus is some moral paragon. These two matters are entirely separate, and to conflate them is a mistake. Indeed any claim that economic inquiry is built on the normative proposition that humans should behave like homo economicus is mistaken: no economist thinks this as a general proposition—though some might think it true in some particular instances. We will say more about this in Sect. 7.4.

7.3.1 Corrupting Effects

If agents are rational in the terms that we understand the concept, we would expect that their beliefs would have some effect on their behaviour. And, as noted in the previous section, such beliefs can have effects whether they are true or false; and those effects may be desirable or undesirable, somewhat independently of their accuracy.

The aforementioned critics seem to have the following worry: that beliefs about human nature in particular have an effect not just on agent behaviour directly but also indirectly via effects on agent motivations. Roughly speaking, the thought is that if you think that a concern for material well-being is a predominant motivation in people in general, you are more likely to be motivated by such a concern yourself. (An analogous thought closer to traditional theological concerns might be that if you think humanity is basically sinful, it will induce you to become more sinful.) The distinction between direct and indirect effects here might be illustrated by appeal to the prisoner's dilemma. If you think others are less likely to cooperate in the game, that might make you less disposed to cooperate yourself: that is a direct effect. The indirect effect arises if the effects are mediated, not via the objective payoff structures, but via the other motives you might have to cooperate—e.g., the tendency to want to do your part in securing an outcome that is best for both (all) players.

On our reading, this is the sort of phenomenon that the critics have in mind when they lament that economics has "redefined who we are as human beings". They seem to worry that how we model human motivations has an effect on that which is modelled. When economists build their models, perhaps the exercise may alter the way in which the economists perceive themselves and, thereby, their motivations. And if the economists' views become widespread, the effects may extend to the general population. And so the general public too may be corrupted by the belief that humans resemble homo economicus with its concern for material well-being.

Do such effects occur and, if so, how widely? We do not know. Nor have we seen any compelling evidence of it from the critics who suggest that it does. On the face of it, we find it implausible that economists and their models have quite so extensive an influence (as flattering as it may be to economists to think they do!).

Suppose, for the sake of argument, that the effects are significant and deleterious. Should we then rewrite or abolish our economic models to prevent it? Here are two distinct reasons why you might think that, yes, those economic models should be rewritten or abolished.

1. A model changing our perception of human nature (or that nature itself) is itself objectionable, regardless of its consequences.
2. Such changes produce bad consequences–and in the case of particular concern here, consequences that are bad for the environment.

But, even if we accept that the appearance of homo economicus in economic models causes such changes, and that either or both of (1) and (2) hold, it need not follow that economics should be reformed in any way. Each of (1) and (2) would entail that there are moral reasons weighing in favour of changing the models, rather than epistemic ones. And it is far from clear that, in doing science, we ought to compose models and theories based on what will have the best effects, rather than on what is best justified on epistemic grounds. To be persuaded by this objection, one must accept this controversial normative claim, as well as accept the (severely unjustified) empirical claim that those ill effects do occur. We are unconvinced of both.

7.3.2 Replacing Homo Economicus

But the critique of homo economicus does not stop there. Some of the aforementioned critics advocate for replacing it in our economic models with a new breed of agent called, perhaps, homo curator. We gather that this new character would no longer satisfy Material Concern, but instead care only, or predominantly, about the well-being of others, the health of ecosystems, the long-term trajectory of the climate, and so on. But there is no suggestion that this character would depart from Agent Rationality—that their actions would be consistent with the motivations and dispositions ascribed to them.

Given the above, we see three possible justifications for this replacement, although it is unclear which of them its proponents have in mind. The first is that economic models have the corrupting effect described above, and that replacing homo economicus with homo curator will have beneficial effects. Instead of changing perceptions of human nature for the worse, we might take advantage of the same process to change them for the better. Those whose perceptions are so easily influenced might then aspire to the properties of this new character instead. They will have greater concern for the wellbeing of others and so on, and so might choose to perform fewer actions that harm the environment or those around them. We might thereby solve climate change and the various other problems described above, or so you might think. But we think this implausible. For one, as noted above, there is no compelling evidence that the adoption of one economic model rather than another would have such enormous effects. For another, agents must lose almost all concern for their own material well-being for this strategy to succeed. As we describe in Sect. 7.5 below, problems like climate change are collective action problems. They arise not from agents being indifferent to environmental harms, but instead because each harmful action is so strongly in the agent's interest. For agents to rationally choose not to commit such actions by a mere change of their preferences, they would need to have almost no concern for their own material well-being. And we do not think that changing economic models could have so extreme an effect on many real-world agents at all.

The second possible justification for substituting homo curator into our models is this: again, it will affect the motivations of real-world agents but, regardless of the ensuing consequences, it is intrinsically desirable for people to have such altruistic motivations. We find this justification dubious—it depends on other normative commitments, perhaps upheld by some versions of virtue ethics, but which are controversial. And such an effect must be weighed against other moral considerations. For instance, it seems plausible that economists (along with any sort of scientist) ought to strive for predictive accuracy. But here we would introduce inaccuracy into predictions in order to deceive the public and influence their motivations—it is far from clear that the modeller's reasons to pursue the truth are outweighed by the consideration that doing otherwise would have this benefit. As well, there are the concrete harms that such inaccuracy would likely impose—programs run by governments and charities are often guided by economic predictions and, if such predictions become less accurate, the benefits provided by those programs will be lessened. It is far from clear that the harms that would thereby be done to the beneficiaries of those programs would be outweighed by the benefit of making people more altruistically motivated.

A third possible justification is this: adopting the homo curator characterisation of agents would make economic models more accurate. But we think this clearly implausible. Real-world agents do care, at least significantly, about their own material well-being. It would be wishful thinking to pretend otherwise.

But we do think there is a valuable criticism of economics somewhere in the vicinity of the homo curator proposal, for reasons similar to that third justification. In building their models, economists do tend to house homo economicus in settings where they are inappropriate—not because they influence anyone's perception of human nature but because their presence leads to inaccurate predictions. In particular, the Material Concern characteristic often undermines predictive accuracy in certain key settings. For instance, in public choice theory, the assumption that voters can be modelled satisfactorily as concerned with their self-interest, is mistaken and seriously misleading—voting behaviour, more so than behaviour in many other settings, is driven largely by concern for others' well-being and by the desire to express one's convictions. To take another example, when modelling market exchange, economists often overlook the importance of trustworthiness norms. When modelling costly acts of discrimination, of malice, or of hatred, economists have previously overlooked the preferences that some agents have to harm others, regardless of their own material well-being (at least prior to the analysis of Becker 1971). And when modelling behaviour in a wide range of settings—including career decisions in academia, the arts, and sports—economists routinely overlook the important role played by social esteem in motivating behaviour (see Brennan and Pettit 2004).

In such settings, we think the Material Concern property of homo economicus should be relaxed. But Agent Rationality is still extremely useful—only with Agent Rationality can we draw out predictions of how agents will act to pursue their desires (predictions which, in the settings mentioned above, are startlingly accurate). That is one characteristic of homo economicus that we think old-fashioned economic models get right (at least for predictive purposes).

Our proposal may sound similar to that of homo curator—it involves rewriting the motivations of the characters who appear in (at least some) economic models to include concern for others' well-being (among various other things). But we do not seek to give our characters motivations beyond those of real human agents. We seek merely to make those characters such that they behave more like real human agents, and only in those select settings where homo economicus does not already do an adequate job. We seek predictive accuracy, not the deliberate manufacture of convenient falsehoods.

7.4 Normative Assumptions Within Economics

Our focus so far has largely been on the assumptions that economists make about human nature. But critics might be worried about certain other assumptions that economists make: namely, the rather narrow ethical presuppositions that economists tend to import. One such assumption is that material concerns weigh heavily, not in the context of modelling agent motivation but in evaluating overall outcomes. Another is that outcomes should be evaluated in terms of aggregate well-being, and that such well-being should be understood exclusively in terms of the satisfaction of preferences. These two features are related, because if (1) preference satisfaction has overwhelming normative significance and (2) most agents' preferences are dominated by concern for their own material well-being (as the homo economicus construction assumes), then the morally best outcomes will be those with the greatest aggregate of material well-being. Unsurprisingly then, economists tend to think that we morally ought to focus on promoting individual's material well-being.

What roles material well-being and preference satisfaction play in ethical assessments are normative, rather than descriptive, issues. And the typical economist's assumptions about these issues are controversial. Within moral philosophy, the view that well-being consists exclusively in the satisfaction of preferences is rare. And the view that not only is this true, but also that outcomes are properly evaluated according to their aggregate well-being, is even less common. Given this, we think it entirely appropriate to criticise many economists for assuming these positions without argument.

But it would be even more controversial to assume that human well-being matters not at all, and that we have no moral reason to promote it. A significant part of the case for avoiding climate catastrophe is that it would have disastrous consequences for human well-being. Some might think that these disastrous consequences do not exhaust the case for climate protection, but they are surely a major part. Along similar lines, it would be extremely controversial to assume that material well-being contributes little or nothing (whether intrinsically or instrumentally) to the morally relevant notion of human well-being. For example, suppose that the consequences of climate change were to change living conditions to match those of, say, 1776 (when The Wealth of Nations was first published). What would those changes look like? To catalogue a few:

(a) 90% fewer human lives would be enjoyed at any given time;
(b) Life expectancy would fall dramatically, after having risen by around 2 years every decade during the twentieth century in most developed countries;
(c) Infant mortality would skyrocket—two thirds of children would not live to the age of ten;
(d) Average income, as best we can measure it, would fall to about one tenth of present levels;
(e) 90% of the world's population would find themselves living in extreme poverty (up from roughly 10% at present), with a purchasing power equivalent to \$1.90 (in 2011 US dollars) per day (Bourguignon and Morrisson 2002).

Perhaps some commentators would regard the rise in material well-being enjoyed since 1776 as a morally irrelevant matter. But we think it an enormous moral improvement, and that a reversion to that previous state would be a catastrophe. In short, we think that economists are correct that material well-being matters morally to some extent (whether instrumentally or intrinsically); where they go wrong is in assuming that it is all that matters.

7.5 Averting Catastrophe

So far, for the most part, we have argued that the field of economics is not responsible for the harms that its critics have in mind. But not only is it not responsible; the findings of economics seem to be necessary to properly understand and feasibly solve many of the greatest problems faced by humanity.

Recall the setting of the Greeks of the early Mycenaean Age, without access to any of the findings of economics. As noted above, the ancient Greeks were already beset by various collective action problems: situations in which a group of individuals are each incentivised to act in a way that, collectively, brings about an outcome that is worse for each of them than another available outcome. Greek hunters were incentivised to hunt additional lions due to the profit they each stood to make but, collectively, they eradicated them, to the detriment of all hunters. And Greek farmers were incentivised to clear additional land to grow crops but, collectively, they cleared so much dense forest that the land became far less fertile. Had the ancient Greeks access to modern technology (but not economic knowledge), we suspect they would have fallen prey to same problems of overhunting, rampant carbon emissions, and nuclear arms competition that we have. With or without economic knowledge, such problems arise.

But only with modern economic knowledge can we understand and solve such problems (at least without imposing unnecessary burdens).

Suppose we attempted to tackle these problems without modern economic knowledge. To solve collective action problems without properly understanding their mechanics, we would most likely resort to the traditional, Hobbesian method: banning whichever behaviour is (collectively) causing harm, and then supporting that ban with the coercive force of the state. To prevent the harms of excess carbon emissions, such a strategy would likely involve the state simply banning the burning of fossil fuels.

But there are serious problems with this strategy. The first is that it requires a state with significant coercive power to be operating at the level at which the problem occurs. In the case of carbon emissions, it would require a global state. But this does not exist—there is no institution that can constrain the actions of all the world's people. Individual countries might sign up to agreements under which they will each enforce the ban within their own borders but, in the absence of any central enforcement powers, there is nothing to prevent countries failing to live up to such agreements even if they make them. And it seems that not many countries are likely to sign up to enforceable such agreements anyway—for most, doing so will not be in their interests of their citizenry. Such is the nature of collective action problems.

The second problem with this strategy is that it imposes burdens beyond what are needed to solve the problem. A complete halt in emissions rules out many activities that seem well worth the emissions they require, e.g., the transport of food and other essential supplies to those who need them, and even the manufacture of clean energy infrastructure such as wind turbines. It is hard to deny that the world would be better off if we continued to emit small amounts for sufficiently worthwhile purposes than if we ceased emitting entirely. The latter would lead to widespread starvation and plunge many into poverty, even in wealthy countries. But, if the state did allow carbon emissions for sufficiently worthwhile purposes, how would they determine what is sufficiently worthwhile? How should they allocate our carbon budget? For a state with no economic knowhow, determining this would be a challenging task; we suspect that such a state would be extremely unlikely to settle on an allocation anywhere near that which is optimal for its citizens' welfare.

The findings of economics offer us potential solutions to both problems, and strategies far superior to a Hobbesian ban.

One such solution is basic Pigovian taxation. When emitting greenhouse gases, by producing or consuming some kinds of goods or services, agents impose negative externalities: costs imposed on others that are not included in the market price of the good or service. This generates the collective action problem that individuals face with respect to their emissions–emitting imposes harm on others, but (the vast majority of) this harm is not felt by the emitter themselves, so that they are incentivised to nonetheless emit. Such collective action problems can often be addressed with a Pigovian tax: a tax on those harmful activities, equal in value to the external cost. (For greenhouse gas emissions, this external cost is estimated as being in the range of roughly US$54 to $417 per tonne of CO_2-equivalent emitted by the activity.) This raises the price for consumers of the good or service without raising the revenue of producers, leading to a drop in demand. And it can be shown that, if the tax rate is properly set, producers and consumers making their own decisions will naturally reach the optimal level of emissions—sufficiently worthwhile activities proceed, while less worthwhile activities are halted. As a result, the collective action problem is resolved at the least overall cost.

Another strategy is provision point mechanisms. If individual countries sign up to an agreement to reduce their emissions (perhaps by implementing a Pigovian tax on emissions), they are providing a public good (a non-excludable and non-rivalrous benefit). In deciding whether to sign up to such an agreement, those countries face a particular kind of collective action problem: a public goods dilemma. And so, even though a country signing up will benefit all (or at least most) other countries, it is in each individual country's interest to not sign up but to instead free-ride. Unsurprisingly, few countries voluntarily opt in to such agreements when the terms are strict. But studies in mechanism design offer a method for inducing agents to be more generous in providing public goods: namely, provision point mechanisms. They work like this: each agent (e.g., each country) is asked to commit to provide their share of the public good (e.g., reduce their carbon emissions by the required amount); if the number of agents who sign on is sufficient to provide the public good fully, then and only then are they required to provide their share; if the number is insufficient, then none are required to provide their share (Marks and Croson 1999). Or, instead of taking effect when a sufficient number of agents sign on, the mechanism might take effect only when all agents commit to providing their share. Under such a mechanism, it is in each agent's interest to sign on and in no one's interest to free ride. And such mechanisms have been demonstrated experimentally to be far more effective in bringing about the provision of public goods (ibid.). By implementing treaties which such a mechanism, we may have greater hope of resolving the international public goods dilemma over emission reductions.

For another lesson from economics that may help us in averting catastrophe, consider the way decisions are made by individual countries. In liberal democracies, it is far from clear that such nations act to pursue their national interest or the collective interests of their citizenry. If they did, we would perhaps have seen even less international consensus on emission reduction than what little we have seen. Instead, their decisions are largely driven by the expressed preferences of their electorate. And individual voters routinely vote against their own interests—even if they are extremely self-interested, each voter has such a minute chance of swaying an election result that their voting behaviour tends to instead be driven predominantly by a desire to express their judgements about what their government ought to do (see Brennan and Lomasky 1993). As a result, electorates do sometimes vote for ambitious emission reduction policies even when they themselves do not stand to benefit from them. This understanding of the phenomenon comes to us from economic analysis and, if accurate, raises potential strategies to solve international collective action problems such as that posed by carbon emissions. For instance, advocates of international emission reduction agreements should plausibly appeal to national electorates and, in doing so, frame the issue of emission reduction as a moral one rather than a matter of national or individual interests.

These are just some of the fruits of economic inquiry that may help us overcome the key challenges facing humanity today. We do not mean to claim that any of these will solve a problem like climate change in one fell swoop. But they are useful tools to have in our kit when combatting such problems. Without them—and without the findings of economics more broadly—our situation would be rather more hopeless. Even without these examples, that would be overwhelmingly plausible—it is generally much easier to solve a problem when one properly understands it. And that is true not only of the carbon in our atmosphere, pollutants in our waterways, and other physical problems, but also of the social forces that lead to such a situation. So we maintain not only that economics is not to blame for apocalyptic harms to humanity and our habitat, but that it is a crucial tool in combatting those harms.

References

Becker, Gary. 1971. *Economic Theory*, A. Knopf.

Bourguignon, François, and Christian Morrisson. 2002. Inequality among world citizens: 1820–1992. *American Economic Review* 92 (4): 727–744.

Brennan, and Lomasky L. 1993. *Democracy and Decision: The Pure Theory of Electoral Preference*. Cambridge/New York/Victoria: Cambridge University Press.

Brennan and Pettit. 2004. *The Economy of Esteem: An Essay on Civil and Political Society*. Oxford: Oxford University Press.

Cadsby, Charles Bram, and Elizabeth Maynes. 1998. Choosing between a socially efficient and free-riding equilibrium: Nurses versus economics and business students. *Journal of Economic Behavior & Organization* 37 (2): 183–192.

Camerer, Colin F., Anna Dreber, Eskil Forsell, Teck-Hua Ho, Jürgen Huber, Magnus Johannesson, Michael Kirchler, et al. 2016. Evaluating replicability of laboratory experiments in economics. *Science* 351 (6280): 1433–1436.

Carter, John R., and Michael D. Irons. 1991. Are economists different, and if so, why? *Journal of Economic Perspectives* 5 (2): 171–177.

Cohen, Ada. 2010. *Art in the Era of Alexander the Great: Paradigms of Manhood and Their Cultural Traditions*. Cambridge: Cambridge University Press.

Daly, Herman E. 1997. Georgescu-roegen versus solow/stiglitz. *Ecological Economics* 22 (3): 261–266.

Frank, Robert H., Thomas Gilovich, and Dennis T. Regan. 1993. Does studying economics inhibit cooperation? *Journal of Economic Perspectives* 7 (2): 159–171.

Gerlach, Philipp. 2017. The games economists play: Why economics students behave more selfishly than other students. *PloS one* 12 (9): e0183814.
Grooten, Monique, and Rosamunde E.A. Almond. 2018. *Living Planet Report 2018: Aiming Higher*. Gland: World Wildlife Fund.
Ims, Knut I. 2017. Happiness and Human Flourishing. In *Economics as a Moral Science*. Ed. Peter Rona and Zsolnai Laszlo, 79–93.
Intergovernmental Science-Policy Platform on Biodiversity and Ecosystem Services. 2019. Global assessment report on biodiversity and ecosystem services of the Intergovernmental Science-Policy Platform on Biodiversity and Ecosystem Services. ed. E. S. Brondizio, J. Settele, S. Díaz, and H. T. Ngo. IPBES secretariat, Bonn. https://www.ipbes.net/global-assessment
Lépineux, François, and Jean-Jacques Rosé. 2017. Transdisciplinarity governance and the common good. In *Economics as a Moral Science, Virtues and Economics 1*. Springer.
Lüthi, D., M. Le Floch, B. Bereiter, T. Blunier, J.-M. Barnola, U. Siegenthaler, D. Raynaud, J. Jouzel, H. Fischer, K. Kawamura, and T.F. Stocker. 2008. High-resolution carbon dioxide concentration record 650,000-800,000 years before present. *Nature* 453: 379–382. https://doi.org/10.1038/nature06949.
Marks, Melanie B., and Rachel T.A. Croson. 1999. The effect of incomplete information in a threshold public goods experiment. *Public Choice* 99 (1): 103–118.
Mills, Michael J., Owen B. Toon, Julia Lee-Taylor, and Alan Robock. 2014. Multidecadal global cooling and unprecedented ozone loss following a regional nuclear conflict. *Earth's Future* 2 (4): 161–176.
Olhoff, Anne, and John M. Christensen. 2019. *Emissions Gap Report 2019*. United Nations Environment Programme.
Olson, R., et al. 2012. A Climate Sensitivity Estimate Using Bayesian Fusion of Instrumental Observations and an Earth System Model. *Journal of Geophysical Research: Atmospheres* 117 (D4): 4103.
Open Science Collaboration. 2015. Estimating the reproducibility of psychological science. *Science* 349 (6251): 943.
Robbins, Lionel. 1932. *An Essay on the Nature and Significance of Economic Science*. London: Macmillan.
Róna, Peter. 2017a. Why economics is a moral science. In *Economics as a Moral Science*, Virtues and Economics 1, ed. P. Róna and L. Zsolnai. Springer.
———. 2017b. Ethics, economics and the corporation. In *Economics as a Moral Science, Virtues and Economics 1*, ed. P. Róna and L. Zsolnai. Springer.
———. 2018. Objects of nature and objects of thought. In *Economic Objects and the Objects of Economics*, Virtues and Economics 3, ed. P. Róna and L. Zsolnai. Springer.
Schwartz, S.E. 2012. Determination of Earth's transient and equilibrium climate sensitivities from observations over the twentieth century: Strong dependence on assumed forcing. *Surveys in Geophysics* 33: 745.
Taylor, S.E., and Brown, J.D. 1988. Illusion and Well-Being: A Social Psychological Perspective on Mental Health. *Psychological Bulletin* 103 (2): 193–210. https://doi.org/10.1037/0033-2909.103.2.193.
Thomson, Mike. 2017. Economic Wisdom for Managerial Decision-Making. In *Economics as a Moral Science*. Ed. Peter Rona and Zsolnai Laszlo, 199–211.
Tomassini, L., et al. 2007. Robust Bayesian uncertainty analysis of climate system properties using Markov chain Monte Carlo methods. *Journal of Climate* 20 (7): 1239.
Waldo, Gordon, and Theodore Chiricos. 1972. Perceived penal sanctions and self-reported criminality: A neglected approach to deterrence research. *Social Problems* 19: 522–540.
Wang, Long, Deepak Malhotra, and J. Keith Murnighan. 2011. Economics education and greed. *Academy of Management Learning & Education* 10 (4): 643–660.
Weitzman, Martin L. 2011. Fat-tailed uncertainty in the economics of catastrophic climate change. *Review of Environmental Economics and Policy* 5 (2): 275–292.
Zamagni, Stefano 2017. Economics as if Ethics Mattered. In *Economics as a Moral Science*. Ed. Peter Rona and Zsolnai Laszlo, 21–41. Cham: Springer. https://doi.org/10.1037/0033-2909.103.2.193.

Chapter 8
Response from Péter Róna

Péter Róna

Abstract The critical approach to critiquing economics taken by Geoffrey Brennan and Hayden Wilkinson is a valuable and interesting attempt to defend the methods developed by modern economics, not least against the challenges posed to them in this volume. The building blocks of this approach, however, rest on several inaccurate assumptions about economics as science, relation between economic phenomena and theory that describes them, objectivity of economic concepts, and descriptive rather then prescriptive character of economic tenets. The objective of this paper is twofold. Firstly, it identifies and clarifies the missing elements in the attempted defence of economics. Secondly, it enlarges upon the idea behind the Homo Curator project which is to re-establish the connection between economic theory and the material as well as ethical boundaries of the reality it describes so that descriptive accuracy of the discipline can be restored.

I am very grateful to Geoffrey Brennan and Hayden Wilkinson for not only assembling the principal defences of modern mainstream economics but for refining, elaborating and, in some respects, qualifying the claims in its support. At the same time, I am disappointed that I have hitherto failed to express my thoughts with sufficient clarity so as to avoid the misunderstandings contained in their paper. At the risk of being unduly outspoken, I will try to rectify this deficiency.

Their critical approach to critiquing economics rests on two major components. First, they reconfirm their confidence in the fundamental tenets of mainstream economics with some concessions and qualifications. Second, they deny that economic theory can be held responsible for the admittedly troubling state of the world. I shall deal with these two matters separately.

P. Róna (✉)
Director of Las Casas Institute's Economics Programme, University of Oxford, Oxford, UK

P. Róna et al. (eds.), *Homo Curator: Towards the Ethics of Consumption*, Virtues and Economics 8, https://doi.org/10.1007/978-3-031-51700-6_8

8.1 The Tenets of Mainstream Economics

8.1.1 The Distinction Between Economic Phenomena and Economic Science

While I agree that, for some purposes it may be at least provisionally useful to make this distinction, in making it, two claims I make and defend are avoided instead of refuted. The first revolves around the notion of 'science', and the second around the question whether economic phenomena, as the authors appear to imply, are natural kinds in the usual philosophical sense of term, or, instead cultural contrivances that, albeit cultural and therefore not natural, can be innocent of any economic theory let alone modern economics.

8.1.2 Is Economics a Science?

In footnote 3 the authors concede that "the term 'science' here may be contentious", and proceed to dispose of the problem by stating that by science they mean "just systematic intellectual enquiry' – without any particular presumptions as to methodology" and thereby fail to deal with the cornerstone of my case. Simply put, it is that it will not do to apply the method of any "systematic intellectual inquiry" to any subject placed under intellectual scrutiny. Even if we stayed within the domain of natural laws, the methodologies of, for example, biology and physics diverge. The laws of heredity have nothing to do with the laws of physics and even within the laws of physics the theories of quantum phenomena and the theory of relativity operate with very different mathematical concepts namely the four dimensional Riemann space in the case of the former and the infinite dimensional Hilbert space in the case of the latter.

When we come to the social sciences, the divergence from the ontology of any branch or aspect of the natural sciences is even greater than the differences among the natural sciences. Economics cannot therefore be lifted into a domain populated by the natural sciences with the sleigh of hand labelling of them all as instances of systematic intellectual inquiry. It would take an unacceptably generalised formulation of the unicity of reality (an idea to which I, in any case, do not subscribe) to found a claim for analogies between the cannons for the comparison of the short stories of de Maupassant and Chekhov in the systematic intellectual inquiry known as comparative literature on the one hand with the computational rules for calculating position and momentum variables in elementary quantum mechanics on the other simply on the basis that they are both being subjected to systematic intellectual inquiry.

The economics Brennan and Wilkinson defend rely, confusingly and inconsistently, on two incompatible methodologies. The first one, an early version of which is set out in Menger's Methodenstreit and relied upon by, for example, Mankiw, is the inductive method with which models are created on the basis of generalised observations. The second is the Walrasian or deductive method where only those phenomena are classified as economic that are instantiations of some abstract, universal principle, distilled independently of the reality to which, after distillation, they can be applied. The Arrow-Debreu model of general equilibrium, built on fourteen assumptions none of which can be verified and nine of which cannot be true in the world as we know it is perhaps the quintessential example. This sort of model making assumes that there are universal conditions of human behaviour from which conclusions can be drawn with the guidance of mathematically expressible logic. The validity of the model rests not on its empirical confirmation but on the rigour of the logic with which its conclusions are reached. This methodology, despite its heavy reliance on mathematics, is the very negation of science.

A science then consists of a properly defined subject matter that exists independently of the theory with which it is studied, and a set of theories/tools shown to be appropriate to its study. How that appropriateness is determined is, of course, a subject onto itself. Modern economics does not satisfy either of these two criteria, and, therefore it is not a science. Daniel Hausman's fudge, "The separate and Inexact Science of Economics" (Hausman 1992) does not work, because the question is not its separateness – as noted above the science of heredity is quite separate from physics but there is no question as to its scientific status – nor is it one of exactitude – as Jacque Monod has shown genetics has as much to do with chance as it has with necessity – but, rather, the lack of a domain independent of the theory with which that domain is studied. Both methods – Menger's and Walras' – described above create their own domain.

8.1.3 Economic Phenomena vs. Economic Theory

This brings me to the authors' distinction between economic phenomena and economic theory, the crucial plank of their critique. In their view there are economic facts that exist independently of theory just as, for example, the lowest energy level of helium exists independently of the method developed by Kinoshita and Bazley for its calculation. According to Brennan and Wilkinson, ancient Greeks hunted lions and self-interest led them to over-hunt recasting the tragedy of the commons to an earlier age, providing a purported factual foundation for the claim that self-interest is a timeless universal principle upon which the edifice of economics as a science may be erected. There are at least three problems with this claim. If self-interest is, in fact, such a universal, Brennan and Wilkinson's own example (a conjectured version of ancient Greek history) means that humanity is heading towards its inevitable extinction on the wings of the determinist economic theory favoured by Brennan and Wilkinson, an outcome that presumably Brennan and Wilkinson do not welcome. If untrue, we need a different economic "science" from the one defended by Brennan and Wilkinson, since, by their own logic, the one they defend leads to catastrophe. Second, humans are not dinosaurs. They do not go mindlessly to their own extinction, but respond to the danger their collective and individual behaviour may have created. It is not science to ignore this propensity simply because mathematical model building cannot do otherwise. Accordingly, there has never been a showing that self-interest is the sole motive for human action or even that it overrides all others to a degree where it can provide an adequate foundation for the sort of theorising independently of the phenomenon about which the theory is formulated that characterises the sciences. Third, there is no foundation for the claim that there are eternal, immutable universal human propensities relevant to economic life. There is undoubtedly an instinct to live and reproduce, but they hardly provide an adequate foundation for, say, equilibrium theory. What sort of universal economic principle can we articulate that would encompass the motivations of, for example, eight out of the fourteen Afghan tribes that have no conception of private property nor any rules of exchange outside and independent of the kinship rules that bind the tribe together on the one hand, and the operations of a hedge fund manager on Wall Street aided and abetted by the pronouncements of economics professors at eminent universities)?

8.1.4 N. Gregory Mankiw vs. Adam Smith

Another way to illustrate the contrast between the idea that the economy is a separate reality from the theories about it is to contrast N. Gregory Mankiw's view of the subject with that of Adam Smith. Mankiw writes in his *Principles of Economics* (2011, 21).

> Economists try to address their subject with scientific objectivity. They approach the subject of the economy in much the same way as a physicist approaches the study of matter and a biologist approaches the study of life. They devise theories, collect data, and analyse these data in an attempt to verify their theories.

Adam Smith sees the heart of economic life as the necessary consequence of the human faculty of reason and speech:

> The offering of a shilling, which to us appears to have so plain a meaning, is in reality offering an argument to persuade one to do so and so as it is for his interest... And in this manner everyone is practicing oratory on others through the whole of his life (Smith 1910, 12).

Mankiw sees the subject as theories about existing, mind independent objects and their properties, while Smith's notion places it firmly in the domain of human intentionality. According to Mankiw, the subject matter is just like matter, harbouring data, which is there to be "collected" for the verification of some causal generalisation. For Adam Smith the essence of the subject consists of the "argument to persuade". Matter exists regardless of what scientists make of it, how they define or classify it; the valence of oxygen molecule does not depend on where it is placed or misplaced in Mendeleev's Table. Economic objects, on the other hand, come into being, they acquire their economic as opposed to their physical properties through the ministrations of the Smithian 'argument to persuade'. The economically significant properties of physical objects and services are the terms and conditions for their acquisition, ownership, exchange and consumption – all of which are always subject to the 'argument to persuade' particularly in an open, democratic society -rather than the sorts of properties that the physicist or the biologist might investigate. Objects become economic objects as the fruit of human thought that conceives of them in economic terms and human action that turns them into the subject of contingent events. As objects of thought and action, they are intentional, ontologically subjective objects, and are unlike ontologically objective objects such as matter, lakes, mountains or element. Thus, 'money', a piece of paper with specific size, colour design and printing is endowed with the specific but contingent properties and functions by the collective intentionality with which it is created and circulated. The piece of paper is an objective, corporeal object, but its significance is not a function of its physical properties. Its characteristics, such as its purchasing power or exchange value depends not on the quality of the paper on which it is printed but on what people make of it, what rules govern its use, etc. In short, its economic properties are subjective and contingent.

If economic objects are mind dependent, the Brennan-Wilkinson case collapses, and the misinterpretation of my position, set out under 1.3 in their paper does not save it. My claim is not that economic phenomena "do not exist independently of any conscious awareness of them", but that they come into being as the result of human intention and action. The components of economic life are not natural kinds. They are entirely culturally formed. The satisfaction of fundamental physical needs is an inadequate foundation for economic theory; animals also have fundamental physical needs but they not operate economies, do not know anything about inflation or the money supply.

The further claim that "Just because a phenomenon exists only subjectively, it does not follow that any and all predictions involving that phenomenon are only subjectively true" and the yet further one, that "not all phenomena studied in economic science are purely subjective", are iterations of the same misunderstanding. My claim is not that the perception of economic phenomena is subjective, but that it is formed by human intentionality. They are subjective not in the sense that a variety of notions can be formed about an otherwise objectively real something, but that they are mind dependent, that they exist because human mental activity and consequent action gives rise to them. The rise in the price of potatoes over a specified period of time at a specified location is an objective fact, but what brings it about is a series of contingent human judgments about a whole host of issues. Indeed, I explicitly recognise and claim that while economic phenomena are ontologically subjective, their perception may be and often is epistemologically objective. So, the issue is not how the objects of the economy are perceived, but, rather, how they are constructed and constituted, what rules authorise, legitimate, protect and foster their existence, and, as a second order problem, what is the truth value of an admittedly objective perception of an ontologically unstable, variable and constantly changing reality. The claim I make is that the model making techniques of modern economics – fixing the flux and flow of that reality and isolating it from what are deemed to be 'exogen' factors into stationary objects such the equilibrium price – involves the falsification of the ontological nature of that reality. Economics, in short, makes things out of contingent processes.

If the subject matter of economics were about "an ancient Greek hunter killing a lion or a farmer chopping down a tree" Brennan and Wilkinson would be entirely right in claiming that it is "about objectively real" phenomena. But economic theory is not about the number of trees chopped down or the number of lions killed, if it could do no more than predict the extinction of lions on the basis of the prevailing rate of kills it would hardly contribute anything more than what common sense produces. Economics is about the formulation of law-like generalisations with both predictive and explanatory power, about the supply and demand for chopped down trees and the consequent price formed through their interaction. But, the road from the "objectively real phenomenon", from the brute fact of the chopped down tree to the price received is strewn with Mill's "disturbing causes", including Smith's rhetoric about the value and desirable properties of the chopped down tree versus observations about its defects, not to mention the terms and conditions of licensing tree chopping, inflationary expectations, the actions of Extinction Rebellion, etc. etc. It is these Millian disturbing causes and their contingent interaction that make economic phenomena ontologically subjective, and it is their elimination in the formulation of economic theory that renders economics a false science.

It is simply not true that I have claimed that "economic science has no predictive power whatsoever".

What I have claimed is that its predictive power rests not on the properties of the brute facts constituting economic life, but on the mind dependent objects, the regulation through custom, laws, habits, advertising, etc. of human behaviour. These rules together with the economic objects to which they give rise, are all mind dependent and the limited predictive power of economics is the direct consequence of the ontological subjectivity of economic life. The claimed fact that the operation of human free will in making choices can be predicted with 60% statistical accuracy – not exactly the sort of result with which a physicist or chemist would be content – is an indication not of some sort of immutable human nature, but the conditioning with which free will is guided.

But this is not the end of the economist's problems. The chemist will predict with very close to 100% accuracy how each and every pair of hydrogen molecule will combine with an oxygen molecule under specified conditions to form water anywhere in the world as compared to the behavioural economist who will make a prediction about how the percentage of his selected group of paid volunteers will choose from among the alternatives preselected by the administrator of the experiment but cannot make a 60% accurate prediction about how any single one of them will choose. What then is the subject of the "objective reality" that is predicted with 60% accuracy? How generalisable is the result of an experiment conducted only at a specific time and place in the context of a specific culture and, typically with a specific age group (students)?

In summary, the Brennan-Wilkinson claim is that economics provides knowledge about a reality that exists independently of it, whereas I claim that the reality about which knowledge is provided is created and sustained by the very knowledge that purportedly informs us about it. Economic reality and theories about it are a mottle where the components have endless reflexive relationship and can be isolated from each other only at significant ontological cost. Economic reality and theory, in the immortal words Thomas Hobbes are both "made with words". The claim I make, therefore, is not that economics "produces false beliefs" but that it contrives and justifies the reality that is harmful to humanity and its habitat. That reality is not false; it is real enough, but it is not a necessary one.

8.1.5 Homo Economicus

Brennan and Wilkinson next defend homo economicus as the valid paradigm for the analysis of economic action after conceding that it:

> is an extreme simplification of a realistic human agent. Human agents routinely fail to act in ways that are representable by utility functions: they exhibit inconsistent beliefs; their preferences are often incomplete and/or intransitive; they show computational shortcomings when comparing available actions.

Two questions arise. First, what happened to the "objective reality" of the economy, so eloquently defended by the authors hitherto if it is agreed that the agent of that "reality" is an "extreme simplification", someone who concededly does not exist? "Extreme simplification" implies that all other characteristics of the agent could be isolated and removed so as to be left with the one in question. But what is the truth value of this assumption? Are Brennan and Wilkinson offering a novel causal theory under which a non-existent agent with the singular property of utility maximisation gives birth to "objective reality" or is that objective reality there independently of the agent? If the former, how are we to explain the complexities of that reality? If the latter, why do we need the agent model? Is economic reality not brought about by "human agents who routinely fail to act in ways that are representable by utility functions..."? If it is, why do we study reality, pace Milton Friedman with the aid of an admittedly unreal contrivance acting on the basis of admittedly false assumptions?

Second, science does not study inexistent objects and in its pursuit of knowledge it does not rely on contrivances and assumptions that cannot be true. In the process of studying the properties of an element or compound, it will isolate the object of its inquiry from other elements if and only if the isolation can be accomplished without causing changes in the properties of the object under study. Whatever the merits of homo economicus, this contrivance is alien to science, where, again pace Milton Friedman and his followers at the Chicago School, a law-like generalisation is accepted if and only if each and every of its assumptions is independently verified. Science simply does not provide a home for hypotheses built on patently false assumptions.

But what are the claimed merits of the non-existent homo economicus? There are two. First, in the words of Brennan and Wilkinson, recapitulating the standard textbook description of the rational agent:

> Agent Rationality: for each agent there is a consistent relation between the agent's actions, beliefs and desires, such that the agent's actions are those that maximise-satisfaction, subject to that agent's beliefs. As well, it is commonly postulated that this relation (and so too the agent's desires, or preferences) is representable by a utility function (or preference function) such that the actions an agent chooses are those among the available actions that maximise (expected) utility (or preference satisfaction).

The authors go on to explain that "An agent can satisfy Agent Rationality with any set of preferences over outcomes whatsoever,"

Does this mean anything? In fact, both components of this notion collapse under the "impregnable circularity" noted by Joan Robinson (1962, 26): "Utility is a metaphysical concept of impregnable circularity; utility is the quality in commodities that makes individuals want to buy them, and the fact that individuals want to buy them shows that they have utility." Similarly, an agent is rational if he acts so as to maximise his utility and the fact that he is maximising his utility is the proof that he is rational. His preference is "revealed" according to Samuelson's gloss on this notion by the agent's actions and the agent's rationality rests on his revealed preference. Suffice it to say, that it is sad to see the rationalism of Leibniz, Spinoza and Kant reduced to such banality.

After having stated that homo economicus is "an extreme simplification of a realistic human agent", the authors proceed to note that its standard uses "are purely descriptive rather than prescriptive". In short, we have, as the foundational paradigm of economics an 'extreme simplification' that is nevertheless descriptively valid. But what sort of descriptive validity can be reasonably claimed for a paradigm that admittedly fails to capture the actual properties and propensities of real economic agents? Walras at least acknowledged that his model was an abstraction, an idealisation that did not rest on descriptive truth value. The distinction between the descriptive and the prescriptive is part of the strategy to mimic the natural sciences, but does it does not conceal the ontological vacuity of homo economicus.

8.2 The Corrupting Effects of Economic Science

The authors reject my claim that economic theory has a corrupting effect on humanity with the help of the descriptive/prescriptive distinction, claiming that economics is a science concerned with what is rather than with what should be. Theory has no responsibility for what is since it is only concerned with extracting the law-like regularities of a reality that exists independently of it. The claim that economics is a science has been dealt with and refuted above. But to argue that the stimulation of economic growth and within it of consumption (aka utility maximisation) is an 'is' rather than an 'ought', that it is what the extremely simplified homo economicus wants after we have deprived him of all other human qualities, to argue, in other words that this non-existent paradigm is nevertheless an 'is' and its postulation is not the basis for the formulation of behaviour modifying (aka incentives) policies, laws and institutions, but simply a matter of how things in fact are, is to pretend that

Western consumer society did not arise on the back of demand led economic policies, and to pretend that these policies had nothing to do with the economic theories that grew up from Mill to Samuelson et al., and to further pretend that the stimulation of consumption is unrelated to environmental degradation, that the distribution of wealth and income is not the product of policies carried out with the support of economic theory but of just how things and human nature are in fact.

The descriptive/prescriptive dichotomy upon which this claim rests – now abandoned by all branches of the social sciences with the exception of economics – collapsed with the demise of logical positivism. It is the companion piece of the fact/value dichotomy derived from Hume's maxim to the effect that an 'ought' cannot be derived from an 'is'. Perhaps the first undertaker of the Humean dictum was John Dewey, followed by A.N. Prior, Alasdair MacIntyre, John Searle and Philippa Foot each of whom had shown in a variety of ways that the 'ought' can indeed be so derived, and culminated in Vivian Walsh's "Sen after Putnam" (2003); in Hilary Putnam's *The Collapse of the Fact/Value Dichotomy* (2002), and *The End of Value-Free Economics*, a volume of essays edited by Putnam and Walsh (2012) concentrating specifically on the futility of this notion in economics. The foundations upon which Brennan and Wilkinson defend homo economicus and mainstream economics were conclusively destroyed at the latest by the early years of this century even if the economics profession has chosen not to take notice of this development, continuing to insist – alone among the social sciences – on the applicability of logical positivist methodology.

Finally, after having argued that economics is a descriptive rather than a prescriptive science, they proceed to claim that mainstream economics provides the means with which the problems society faces can be solved. But if economics is about the 'is' and we follow Hume, what is there to 'solve', how can economic theory show us the solutions, how things ought to be? If economic theory is capable of providing good solutions to our problems, it is, ex hypothesi also capable of providing bad ones.

8.3 The Homo Curator Project

The homo curator project is about the construction of a discipline unburdened by the need to be on par with the natural sciences. Instead of the sort of description that serves to underpin mathematically representable theorising, the formulation of some law-like generalisation, its first task is the elaboration of a methodology, similar to the one developed anthropology, that leads to descriptive fullness and accuracy. Its next task is the formulation of criteria and the mapping of processes for deciding what should be done. It sees economics as a decisional discipline where what happens is not determined, not defined on the basis of what laws can be elicited from what is through mathematical logic from premises that may or may not enjoy evidential confirmation, but, rather what we want to happen in light of the fullest possible description of what is. This is not to deny that there are recurring regularities and propensities in economic life that can be the subject of statistical measurement and representation, but it does mean the abandonment of exceptionless hypotheses of universal applicability, and it does mean that only evidence based modelling has credibility even where the actual prediction of the model finds some degree of empirical confirmation. Instead of the clearly unsustainable pretence of being a science concerned with what is (whereas, in fact, it is the contingent ideology of capitalism) economics is seen as a discipline concerned with what should be. Needless to say, descriptive fullness includes objective limitations on what can be done, but the paradigm of homo economicus is not among them.

These are my specific responses to the Brennan – Wilkinson objections. There is, however, a deeper problem with economics that this exchange of views does not address: economics deals only with that fraction of the earth's resources that are subjected to economic transactions, and ignores the impact of those transactions on resources that are not part of it. The polluted air and water is not a part of the exchange of the goods whose production brought about the pollution. The utility maximising *homo economicus* excludes from his calculation of maximum utility any and all factors that do not have a market price. Modern economic theory is about exchange value and, as it will be shown below, exchange value is only a part of economic reality. It has no relationship with Creation, but only with those components of Creation that have direct bearing on its search for utility maximisation. The result is that the output of economic analysis cannot be made compatible with physical reality; it radically misprices the costs involved in the production, distribution and consumption of the factors of economic life, and deviates in significant ways from actual economic decision-making.

There is near scientific unanimity to the effect that an average atmospheric temperature increase of more than 2 °C will render global warming irreversible. Global net human-caused emissions of carbon dioxide would need to fall by about 45% from 2010 level, reaching net zero levels by 2050. In order to obtain a just distribution of this burden between the industrially developed and the developing nations, developed economies would have to reduce emissions to below 20% of their current level between now and 2030. World economic growth for the past three decades has averaged about 3%, accompanied by annual average increase in CO_2, methane and other environmentally damaging emissions of about 2%. Given this correlation and the absence of any paradigm for growth that does not entail a growth in dangerous emissions, the predicament facing us is obvious: economic growth as a policy target must not only be abandoned, but outright reversed because the constraints set out above cannot be met under any known economic growth model. Even the radical reformation of farming and food production, transport, particularly air travel cannot meet these constraints.

In parallel with global warming, biodiversity is collapsing and the oceans are dying. There are now 60% fewer vertebrates than there were in 1970. In 1960 about 6% of seabirds had plastics in their stomachs; that proportion today is 90%. Humanity is consuming each year 1.8 times the renewable natural resources that the earth produces. There is therefore an urgent need not only to limit the emission of noxious gases with the help of appropriate regulation, but, more generally, to redefine what, how and how much we consume. The issue we are facing is not simply how to produce less air pollution, how to prevent global warming or how to prevent the destruction of the oceans, but, rather, what to do with an economy that consumes a great deal more natural resources, including energy, than can be replaced by artificial or natural processes. This imbalance between the available natural resources and their consumption under the economic model that governs the world economy cannot be overcome through technology, nor can it be curtailed with the concepts and tools of modern economics. This claim is defended first through an examination of what is the Galilean proposition about mathematics as the key to an understanding of nature, subsequently extended to all of reality, and, second, with the help of Aristotelian economics. The severity of the crisis, the very real possibility, indeed the likelihood of a collapse of our ecosystem brings back to the forefront that oldest of all philosophical questions: "How should we live?"

Economic reality forms economic theory and economic theory affects the economy. There is a reflexive relationship between theory and reality that is altogether absent or present only to a very limited extent in the natural sciences notwithstanding Schrödinger's cat. Our perceptions of the physical world affect the theories we form about it, but do not alter it. In contrast, the economy changes in response to our actions and our actions change as our sense of economic processes changes. The search for law-like regularities resembling the hypotheses of the natural sciences has been the great project of modern economics. This search and the belief that such principles, independent of time and place, may be found has been and remains its fundamental objective. It is buttressed by the assumption, that whatever ontological differences there may be between incorporeal social reality and the corporeal world of the natural sciences, there is an underlying unicity. Accordingly, the methods developed by the natural sciences, in particular the use of mathematics, may be fruitfully applied in the social sciences in general and in economics in particular. It follows from these premises that ethical considerations in the formulation of economic decisions need not be taken into account. Where do these assumptions and beliefs come from?

Descartes is customarily seen as the father of modern philosophy and Galileo as the founder of modern science. In fact, Galileo's revolutionary contribution – the idea that the language of nature is written in mathematics – is also a philosophical, specifically an ontological proposition. It separates those aspects of natural objects that are measurable from those that are not, and prescribes that the former is the proper subject of scientific inquiry while the latter should be left out of scientific consideration. The modern, perhaps more practical variant of this notion was formulated by Lord Kelvin in 1883 in the following terms, just as modern economics was acquiring its present mathematicised form:

> I often say that when you can measure what you are speaking about, and express it in numbers, you know something about it; but when you cannot measure it, when you cannot express it in numbers, your knowledge is of a meagre and unsatisfactory kind; it may be the beginning of knowledge, but you have scarcely, in your thoughts, advanced to the stage of science, whatever the matter may be (Lord Kelvin 1910, 73).

There is, of course, despite the similarities. a deep difference between the two. Whereas Galileo postulates that mathematics is embedded in the objects of nature, that it is a constituent part of the object, Lord Kelvin simply claims that measuring is the indispensable tool to an understanding of natural objects. A third view, with particular relevance to economics, was formulated by Leon Walras to the effect that numbers represent reality more precisely than language (Walras 1954 [1926], 71). This view ascribes representational capability to mathematics.

Although both Galileo and Lord Kelvin express this claim in terms that can be read to encompass all of reality, they were both interested in discovering the properties of corporeal objects and did not explore the applicability of this notion to social processes. What can be measured was for them a given. It is the physical properties of size, shape, location, weight and motion of corporeal objects, expanded subsequently to temperature, molecular composition, malleability, conductivity, etc. If Galileo's great insight – restricting the study of objects to their measurable properties – was the foundation of the spectacular success of the natural sciences, his approach, as he admits, does not encompass the reality of the object in its entirety. The insight, however, provided the foundation for the notion that only the measurable is real, that what is not measurable is a chimera, a subjective illusion, and, as such, not part of objective reality (Goff 2019). Because ethics cannot be quantified, it is not a part of *homo economicus* and it could not form part of any science that deals with objective reality after Galileo's revolution and the extended application of his insight to all of reality. In its most extreme form this separation of the quantifiable from the unquantifiable has led to the denial of human consciousness, a denial reaching a high point with the behaviourism of John B. Watson and B. F. Skinner and an even more extreme form in the neurophilosophy of Patricia and Paul Churchland's "eliminative materialism" (Churchland 1988, 2013). The framing of the issues relating to the economic life along Galilean terms does not put the sort of constraints on consumption that could ensure the survival of the earth, first because the pricing mechanism of economic theory prices only "economic" goods, that is to say only goods that can be made the subject of exchange, and second, because it does not contain any restraints on what may be turned into an exchangeable good.

It was not always so. Aristotelian Epicurean and Stoic economic theory were all anchored to versions of the notion of virtue, and out of the seven deadly sins of subsequent Christian theology no less than three were explicitly economic sins. The chaos that has developed around the interpretation of Aristotle's Nicomachean Ethics 5.5 and Politics 1. 8–10, generally accepted as containing Aristotle's thought on economics is reflective not of any serious difficulty with the text, but, rather, it springs from the sudden discontinuity in economic thought that developed during the last third of the XIXth century (Meikle 1995). If the subject of our inquiry is how to live, the attention must be directed to the sorts of character traits that are conducive to a happy life, in short, to the virtues that one should cultivate in order to have the right character traits. For Aristotle the context in which this can be accomplished is the *polis*, the broad community in which the individual lives. Virtues, therefore, are traits with a constructive or positive impact on the community as opposed to the modern economic ideal, the maximisation of individual utility and they are developed through interaction with the community as opposed to conformity to the idealised model utility maximisation. Economic actions in the Aristotelean view are a part of the overall spectrum of human behaviour, guided as they are by virtue or the lack thereof. These actions are not a separate and isolated domain with its own law-like regularities, but, rather, part of how to live the good life. The conception of economic activity as part of the human condition was shared by the leading thinkers of the Scottish Enlightenment, most notably by Adam Smith, where the dividing line was between the Stoics and the Epicureans. At the same time, the conditions for the break with virtue ethics was laid by Humean metaphysics which sublimated the Aristotelian distinction between substance and attribute:

> 'Tis confest by the most judicious philosophers, that our ideas of bodies are nothing but collections form'd by the mind of the ideas of the several distinct sensible qualities, of which objects are compos'd, and which we find to have a constant union with each other. But however these qualities may in themselves be entirely distinct, 'tis certain we commonly regard the compound, which they form, as ONE thing, and as continuing the SAME under very considerable alterations (Hume 2009 [1739–40], 145).

Aristotle accepted that exchange value cannot be explained in terms of use value and provided a clear metaphysical explanation for it. Use value is seen as a category of substances, as the nature of things, determined by their substance. Use value is a matter of quality resting on the particular properties of an object. Exchange value is a matter of quantity, it is an attribute. It is homogeneous and it lacks species. Adam Smith, Ricardo and Marx all accepted the metaphysical gap between use and exchange value; Jevons, Walras and Menger thought that they found a way to bridge that gap based on the Humean rejection of Aristotelean metaphysics. In particular, they thought that the notion of utility justifies Humean metaphysics and provides the concept with which the difference between use and exchange value can be overcome. But the gap nevertheless exists because there is no metaphysically acceptable commensurability between use and exchange value.

This abandonment of the distinction between quantity and quality opened the way to an inflationist notion of measurement, permitting the eventual birth of an economics based entirely on the measurable properties of economic reality or, after World War II, the construction of measurable surrogate realities that were built on the Humean abolition of the distinction between substance and attribute. These structures *ab ovo* eliminated ethics, particularly virtue ethics from economic theory. Use value is linked to the virtues of prudence and sobriety exchange value results in the pointless and virtueless chase of profits as exchange value pays no heed to the nature of the substance being exchanged. The subordination of the former to the role played by the latter in modern economic theory has necessarily meant that ethical theories of any and all kind could no longer be a part of economics.

Recently some interesting attempts have been made to repackage virtue ethics as a form of rational behaviour.[1] For example, Christian U. Becker proposes:

---

[1] It is a measure of the seriousness of the break with Aristitelian metaphysics that as distinguished a thinker as Joseph Schumpeter (1954) could assert that „Even Aristotle... presented an exceedingly poor and above all 'pre-scientidfic' picture of economicswhich does not differ substantially

> The economic model of the human actor, *homo economicus*, is a theoretical model that cannot refer to virtues and, one might say, cannot develop virtues in a broader sense. However, the *homo economicus* model can influence the self-understanding and actions of individuals and, by this, may become a kind of virtue – a character trait and identity – by itself. Self-interested utility maximisation may become a normative concept, and people may train themselves to approximate "perfect" rational utility maximisers. This way, the theoretical model of the *homo economicus*, constructed for the purpose of explaining economic interaction results by mathematical analysis, transforms into a practical guidance or a model for character-formation and self-identity (Becker 2016).

The attempt, however, fails as it misconstrues both virtue and rationality. Virtue is not conformity to the idealised model of utility maximisation, but, rather, the development of character traits with social value and recognition, and it is not a matter of reason, understood as the rationalist innate knowledge or innate concept thesis. Virtue is not a given but a character trait hammered out through social interaction.

The same mechanism that expelled virtue ethics from its domain also expelled Christian ethical thought from economics. Of the seven cardinal sins of Roman Catholic theology and confessional practice, codified by Pope Gregory the Great (540–604) three are economic. They are *avaritia* (greed), *gula* (gluttony) and *luxuria* (lust, excessive pleasure seeking). They resemble, indeed derive from virtue ethics in that they all connect to the welfare of the community, but they go beyond virtue ethics in that they are sins against God. They all involve excessive consumption and this excess is not only a *malum* against fellow human beings but also a violation of the order of God's Creation. The three anti-consumption sins echo the Aristotelian distinction between natural and unnatural ends, reflected in the distinction between use and exchange value and are there to secure a harmonious relationship between human beings and Creation or, in Aristotle, nature by curtailing unnatural propensities.

These limitations on consumption were altogether removed from economic theory with the utilitarian commitment to there being no incommensurable values and to the concomitant doctrine that commensurability is secured by exchange value. Aristotelean theory with its juxtaposition of use value and exchange value as two fundamentally separate categories sets the stage for the struggle between ethics and economics, a struggle that cannot find a harmonious solution, but provides an entirely legitimate foundation for both. The utilitarian invention of utility as the link between the two destroys the autonomy of use value, renders everything commensurable and invests exchange value with the exclusive property of providing the means for measuring. Use value and ethics are edited out of the picture and consumption has no limits. Without the limits posited by virtue ethics or indeed Catholic theology, money, the quantitative expansion of exchange value, becomes the end of economic life. John Meynard Keynes thought this turn was mainly due to the moral perversion of humanity; Marx thought that the causal chain went the other way, that something in the nature of money brought about the moral perversion of humanity.

---

from that of laymen of all ages" before proceeding to nevertheless acknowledge Aristotle's important contributions and achievements.

The claim defended in the passages above is that it is neither. Ethics was removed from the domain of economic science because the utilitarians and subsequent modern economic theory defined its boundaries so as to remove it from the scene of the Aristotelian eternal battle between use value and exchange value.

References

Becker, Christian U. 2016. Aristotelian Virtue Ethics and Economic Rationality. In *Economics and the Virtues*, ed. Jennifer A. Baker and Mark D. White. Oxford: Oxford University Press.

Churchland, Paul M. 1988. *Matter and Consciousness*. MIT Press.

———. 2013. Consciousness and the Introspectiion of 'Qualitative Samples'. In *Consciousness Inside and Out: Phenomenology, Neuroscience, and the Nature of Experience*, ed. R. Brown. Dordrecht: Springer.

Goff, Phhilip. 2019. *Galileo's Error: Foundations for a New Science of Consciousness*. London: Penguin Random House.

Hausman, Daniel M. 1992. *The Inexact and Separate Science of Economics*. Cambridge: Cambridge University Press.

Hume, D. 2009, [1739–40]. *A Treatise of Human Nature,* ed. David Fate Norton and Mary J. Norton. Oxford: Oxford University Press.

Kelvin, Lord. 1910. "Lecture on Electrical Units of Measurement", delivered on 3 May 1883. In *Popular Lectures and Addressses*, vol. I. London: Macmillan & Co.

Mankiw, N. 2011. Gregory. In *Principles of Economics*, 6th ed. South-Western College Pub.

Meikle, Scott. 1995. *Aristotle's Economic Thought*. Oxford: Clarendon Press.

Putnam, Hilary. 2002. *The Collapse of the Fact/Value Dichotomy*. Cambridge, MA: Harvard University Press.

Putnam, Hilary, and Vivian Walsh. 2012. *The End of Value-Free Economics*. London: Routledge.

Robinson, Joan. 1962. *Economic Philosophy*. New York: Routledge.

Schumpeter, J. 1954. *Economic Doctrine and Method*. London: Routleddge.

Smith, Adam. 1910. *The Wealth of Nations Alfred*. New York: A. Knopf.

Walras, L. 1954 [1926]. *Elements of Pure Economics*. London: George Allen & Unwin.

Walsh, Vivian. 2003. Sen after Putnam. *Review of Political Economy* 13 (3): 315–394.

Chapter 9
Economics and Three Faces of Prudence

Edward Skidelsky

Abstract Modern economics does not have much use for the classical scheme of virtues and vices. Yet, it appears to recognise prudence, or something lying in the same general region as prudence. In classical philosophy, prudence is the virtue of practical rationality, or rationality in action. Economics too has a theory of rationality in action. This paper asks if this is a good theory – if the actions prescribed by economics are indeed the actions that an ideally prudent counsellor would prescribe. As I argue in what follows, there is reason to think that they are not, and the reason is to be traced back to the crucial dimension of time that is neglected in the economic theory of rational action.

Visitors to the National Gallery in London may be tempted to linger for a moment over a cryptic canvas by Titian. Three human heads are shown emerging from a single trunk. One, an old man, looks back; another, a man in his prime, looks straight at us; a third, a beardless youth, looks forwards. Below them are the heads of three animals, a wolf, a lion and a dog. Clearly, this is an allegory of some kind. But of what, exactly? The answer lies in the barely legible motto running along the top of the canvas: "From the experience of Past … the Present acts prudently … lest by its action it spoil the Future." This, then, is an allegory of prudence, which encompasses in one act an awareness of past, present and future. The three-headed monster at the bottom presents more of a puzzle. Is it the companion of the Egyptian god Serapis, later identified with Apollo, as Erwin Panofsky (1955) argued in a classic essay? We need not dwell on the problem here.

E. Skidelsky (✉)
University of Exeter, Exeter, UK
e-mail: E.B.H.Skidelsky@exeter.ac.uk

P. Róna et al. (eds.), *Homo Curator: Towards the Ethics of Consumption*, Virtues and Economics 8, https://doi.org/10.1007/978-3-031-51700-6_9

Titian was not the first or last artist to represent prudence as a figure with three heads. The conceit was common in the Renaissance, having (like many such conceits) its origins in antiquity. Cicero's *De Inventione* speaks of three "parts" of prudence: memory, intelligence, and foresight:

> Memory is the faculty by which the mind recalls what has happened. Intelligence is the faculty by which it ascertains what is. Foresight is the faculty by which it is seen that something is going to occur before it occurs.[1]

A rhyming triplet commonly attributed to Seneca but in fact written by the sixth-century Spanish bishop Martin of Braga neatly summarised the same thought: prudence consists in "the memory of the past, the ordering of the present, the contemplation of the future" (*in praeteritorum recordatione, in praesentium ordinatione, in futurorum meditatione*). To medieval imaginations, such texts irresistibly suggested an image of a head with three faces, or a face with three eyes. "Prudence, allas, oon of thyne eyen thre/ Me lakked alwey", says Chaucer's Cressida, lamenting her decision not to steal away from Troy with Troilus.[2] Titian needn't have strained too hard to fuse this idea of a three-faced or three-eyed prudence with the common motif of the three ages of man to create the image in the National Gallery.

But what exactly is the meaning of the "three faces of prudence", considered abstractly? "Prudence", recall, is the standard translation of *phronesis*, or practical wisdom, the virtue by which we know how best to feel and to act in the situation that confronts us. This is distinguished by Aristotle from *sophia*, or theoretical wisdom,

[1] *De Inventione*, II,53. Quoted in Burrow (2000, 39).

[2] Chaucer, *Troilus and Criseyde*, V.744–9. Quoted in Burrow (2000, 37).

the virtue by which we come to know abstract truths about the world, and in particular about what is highest and most sublime in the world, the gods and the fixed stars. *Sophia* and *phronesis* have a distinct relationship to time. *Sophia* concerns what is necessary and unchanging. It lifts its possessor out of the temporal stream, assimilating him, if only momently, to the eternity of God or the gods. *Phronesis*, by contrast, has to do with human conduct, whose field is the here and now. It reveals to us the *kairos*, the "hour of action", unique and unrepeatable. Prudence, one might say, is the virtue whose sphere is time; and so it is fitting that it should be represented by Titian in the form of a three-headed figure, turned simultaneously towards past, present and future.

The part of prudence concerned with the past is *memoria*, memory – a faculty which, in a world short of books, occupied a position vastly more important than it does today. Memory was not just a deposit of factual information, such as might be gleaned from an encyclopaedia or downloaded off the internet. It was a storehouse of maxims and exemplars, to be called to mind in moments of crisis and perplexity. The memory of humanity as a whole made up its history – the "school of prudence", as it was often called. History taught its students the permanent possibilities of human action. It showed what might be done, feared, or hoped for. Of course, this view of history rested on the assumption that human nature is as unchanging as "the sky, the sun, the elements", as Machiavelli put it, an assumption which few of us now share (1997, 18). It is clear to us that human needs and aspirations evolve, that not everything which is possible or advisable *in abstracto* is possible or advisable for us now. But even if human nature evolves, it is history which shows us where we are in that process of evolution, and hence what options are open or closed to us. No one wants to be that paradigmatic figure of modernity, the "man out of time", tilting at windmills as if they were giants, or fighting the current war as if it were the last.

The part of prudence concerned with the future was *providentia*, literally "foreseeing" – a meaning preserved, in attenuated form, in the modern English "provident", "provision" and "provide". *Providentia* was the ability to see one's actions as having effects stretching far into the future, and ultimately, for Christians, into eternity. It cautioned its possessor against impetuosity and haste. Clearly, foresight of this sort was a key virtue in peasant communities, where the autumn harvest had to be made to last through winter. Medieval preachers urged their rural congregants to follow the example of those great savers among the species, the ant, the squirrel and the bee. But rulers, too, were expected to display *providentia* in all things. A fifteenth-century English mirror for princes, the *Active Policy of a Prince*, counsels the young Edward, son of Henry VI, to make provision for his household, the commons, the law, and the army, concluding with a general statement of the doctrine of the "three parts" of prudence:

> Thinges past, remembre & wele devide;
> Thinges present, considre & wele governe;
> For thinges commyng, prudently provide;
> Al thinges in his tyme peise & discerne.[3]

[3] Quoted in Burrow (2000, 44–5).

The division of prudence into three parts was a rhetorical device, for ease of exposition. In reality, as Titian's painting nicely shows, the three parts were thought of as operating in tandem: prudence acts in the present, drawing on the past, in anticipation of the future. Extrapolating somewhat, we might say that prudence integrates all three regions of time into a unity. It fashions life into an ongoing narrative, in which each moment is subordinate to the pattern of the whole. Different vices upset this subordination in different ways. Self-indulgence exalts the present at the expense of the past and future. Nostalgia wallows in the past at the expense of the present and future. And avarice attaches supreme value to the future at the expense of the past and present. All these vices are opposed in a special way to prudence, which bids us to look on life as an integrated whole, not as a succession of temporal parts.

9.1 Prudence Among the Economists

Economics does not have much use for the classical scheme of virtues and vices. However, it does recognise prudence, or at least something lying in the same general region as prudence. Prudence, recall, is the virtue of practical rationality, or rationality in action. And economics also possesses a theory of rationality in action. To act rationally, according to this theory, is to act so as to maximise one's expected utility, utility being defined as a ratio of satisfied to unsatisfied preferences. If economics possesses a theory of prudence, it makes sense to ask if this theory is a good theory – if the actions prescribed by economics are indeed the actions that an ideally prudent counsellor would prescribe. As I shall argue shortly, there is reason to think that they are not.

First, however, I must address a doubt concerning the very idea that economics has a theory of prudence. Economics is often said to be a positive, not a normative science, meaning that its goal is to describe how people *do* in fact act, not to prescribe how they *ought* to act. Utility maximisation must be understood in this light, as a theoretical postulate, not an ethical ideal. Economics does not *enjoin* agents to act so as to maximise their own utility. It assumes that they do so already, deriving from this assumption testable hypotheses about their behaviour. It therefore has nothing corresponding to prudence, if prudence is understood as the virtue of rationality in action.

Thus runs the official line. *Un*officially, however, economists are as swift as anyone to recommend certain courses of action as rational and to denounce others as irrational; indeed, they see themselves as especially qualified to do this. Here for example is Greg Mankiw, author of a bestselling undergraduate textbook, on the subject of opportunity costs:

> Because people face trade-offs, making decisions requires comparing the costs and benefits of alternative courses of actions. In many cases, however, the cost of an action is not as obvious as it might first appear.

> Consider the decision to go to college. The main benefits are intellectual enrichment and a lifetime of better job opportunities. But what are the costs? To answer this question, you might be tempted to add up the money you spend on tuition, books, room, and board. Yet this total does not truly represent what you give up to spend a year in college.
>
> There are two problems with this calculation. First, it includes some things that are not really costs of going to college. Even if you quit school, you need a place to sleep and food to eat. Room and board are costs of going to college only to the extent that they are more expensive at college than elsewhere. Second, this calculation ignores the largest cost of going to college—your time. When you spend a year listening to lectures, reading textbooks, and writing papers, you cannot spend that time working at a job. For most students, the earnings given up to attend school are the largest single cost of their education (Mankiw 2007, 5–6).

The assumption underlying this passage is that most students are naturally pretty bad at calculating opportunity costs, that this is something they need to be taught to do. Similarly, they need to be taught to focus on marginal costs, to disregard sunk costs, and much else besides. Economics is "freakanomics" – a thoroughly unnatural, counterintuitive way of thinking. But of course, these frequent injunctions to think rationally about decision making make sense only on the assumption that agents are *not* maximally rational, which contradicts what the very same economists say elsewhere. The truth is, economics is schizophrenic. It *does* embody a substantive ideal of rationality – a doctrine of prudence, if you like – only its commitment to the positivist ideal of *wertfrei* social science renders it incapable of admitting the fact.

Let me proceed. If economics has a theory of prudence, the question arises: is it a good one? Do its verdicts agree with those of an enlightened common sense, unencumbered by special theoretical commitments? Those who have answered "no" to this question have usually focussed on the supposed egoism of *homo economicus*. My focus in what follows is somewhat different. I want to argue that economic prudence is defective because it neglects the dimension of time. It has only one eye, not three.

This neglect of time follows directly from a central principle of economic thought. The preferences whose satisfaction constitutes utility are necessarily *present* preferences, since only these have actual existence. We have no reason to seek to satisfy past preferences, unless we have some higher-order present preference for so doing. Similarly, we have no reason to seek to satisfy future preferences, unless (again) we have some higher-order present preference for so doing. Of course, most people *do* care at least a bit about honouring past commitments and ensuring their own future well-being, and this gives them reason to act accordingly. But the economist, qua economist, cannot recommend such care as "rational" or regret its absence as "irrational". Rationality, for him, is a property of what we do by way of satisfying our preferences, not of those preferences themselves. These latter are, as the saying goes, "given".

The counter-intuitiveness of this approach to time comes out especially clearly in the standard economic treatment of two topics – sunk costs and addiction. Let me take them in turn.

9.2 Sunk Costs

Judith is a PhD student in economics, in her fourth and final year. She has lost all interest in her subject and all desire to pursue a career based on it. Her urgent wish is to become a dancer. Should she quit immediately? Or should she slog on for another year and obtain her unwanted degree?

If Judith has taken to heart the lessons of her own discipline, she will have no difficulty answering this question. Three years of studying is a "sunk cost" – a cost which has already been incurred and should therefore have no influence on her decision making one way or the other. Those three years are irrecoverably lost, whether or not Judith choses to complete her degree. Of course, Judith might – on account of a puritanical upbringing, let us say – have an aversion to leaving projects unfinished; and this aversion may provide her with a reason for finishing the PhD. But if she has no such aversion, then she has no such reason. *The point is that there is no reason, from the economic point of view, for feeling such an aversion in the first place.* It is just a brute "preference", beyond the reach of scrutiny or debate.

Those of us unschooled in the mental habits of economists might look at Judith's dilemma in a different light. Even if we could say with certainty (which of course we cannot) that a degree in economics will be of no future use to her, there is still, we might feel, a certain value in finishing what one has begun. It expresses the virtues of perseverance and thoroughness, and a kind of loyalty to one's past self. It habituates one to pursue similarly hard courses of action in the future. To invest time or money in a project is a mark of resolution, and we think well of people who keep their resolutions, even if they have no current interest in doing so.

Another example of the same sort of dilemma comes from the Catholic economist Mary L. Hirschfeld. Suppose, she writes

> I have purchased a season pass to the opera. On the day of the fourth opera, I am just exhausted from work and really do not feel like going to the opera. I have paid for the ticket whether I go to the opera or stay home, and the cost of the ticket therefore is not relevant. To an economist, all that matters is whether the marginal cost of going to the opera (getting dressed up, driving downtown, and so on) is greater than or less than the marginal benefit (hearing the opera). If I am exhausted, the marginal cost of going is high and the marginal benefit is low, so I should rationally decide to stay home.

Many people in such a situation would feel obliged to go to the opera anyway, because they have paid for it. Economists dismiss such feelings as irrational. However, adds Hirschfeld,

> from the perspective of the cultivation of virtue they may not be irrational at all. For starters, ignoring sunk costs is a way of disassociating oneself from past decisions. If part of cultivating virtue is developing a coherent self over time, the habit of disavowing past choices would be counterproductive (Hirschfeld 2018, 208).

That puts it just right. It is our interest in developing a "coherent self over time" which gives us a reason to honour past choices, even if we have no current desire to do so. "If the past is not to bind us, where can duty lie?" says George Eliot's Maggie Tulliver, as she wrestles with a dilemma rather more serious than whether or go to the opera not to. “We should have no law but the inclination of the moment” (Eliot 1985, 601–2).

Of course, in some cases it is right to disregard sunk costs, and such cases give the economists’ point its force. How many wars have been pointlessly prolonged in order that so much death “should not have been in vain”? This is the kind of vicious nostalgia mentioned earlier, which sacrifices present and future to the vampires of the past. Prudence consists in distinguishing those sunk costs which should be disregarded from those which shouldn’t, not in ignoring all sunk costs indifferently.

9.3 Addiction

The economic theory of addiction originates with the influential 1988 article by Gary Becker and Kevin Murphy (1988), “A Theory of Rational Addiction”. “Rational” is, of course, a deliberate provocation: Becker and Murphy know that addiction is widely regarded as a paradigm case of irrationality. They are using the word in the economists’ special sense, in which all behaviour is rational so long as it aims at maximising some consistent set of preferences. Their claim is that addictive behaviour is no less rational, in this special sense, than behaviour in general. The addict is like other people in that has certain preferences whose satisfaction he seeks to maximise. He is unlike other people only in that his preferences include a certain “time preference” – a strong preference for immediate over future benefits. Future benefits weigh only very weakly with him. In technical terms, he discounts them exponentially. In ordinary language, he is chronically impatient.

This means that the addict is never in a position in which the benefits of quitting outweigh (subjectively) the benefits of another hit. Of course, he knows that, looked at in the abstract, from outside of time, his life would be better off without drugs. But from his particular position in time, the attraction of another hit always looms larger. He has no reason not to go for it.

To simplify hugely, let’s consider a drug addict faced with the choice of whether to consume or quit. Let’s represent utility levels with numbers. If he consumes now, he will enjoy a utility level of 100, followed thereafter by 70 (as he continues to consume). If he quits, he will enjoy a constant utility level of 80.

Time	1	2	3	4	
Quit	80	80	80	80	…
Consume	100	70	70	70	…

If the addict could abstract from his position in time, he would clearly chose to quit, since that will give him the great utility overall. The trouble is, he can’t abstract from his position in time. He discounts the benefits of each temporal interval by a constant rate of, let us say, 60%. Thus the weighted utility to him at time 1 of future utilities at time 2, 3, 4 … can be represented as.

$$80 + 80 \times 0.6(48) + 80 \times 0.36(28.8) + 80 \times 0.216(17.3) \ldots = 200$$

$$100 + 70 \times 0.6(42) + 70 \times 0.36(25.2) + 70 \times 0.216(15.1) \ldots 205$$

Time	1	2	3	4	
Quit	80	48	28.8	17.3	… 200
Consume	100	42	25.2	15.1	… 205

The upshot is, he has another shot. He has no reason not to. He is behaving perfectly rationally, given his preference structure.

The Becker/Murphy model of rational addiction can be faulted on two counts, one empirical, the other conceptual. Empirically, it fails to represent the behaviour of most actual addicts. For it implies that addicts can never be inconsistent or in conflict with themselves: they are always, consistently, short-sighted. But as we know, most addicts are not like this. For periods of time, they desperately want to give up; they may even invest money in hypnosis, rehab courses and such like. But then when faced with the offer of drugs or alcohol, all their good resolutions go to the wind. Their behaviour is inconsistent.

This inconsistency cannot be accounted for on the Becker/Murphy model. According to that model, addicts discount future benefits consistently, at a fixed rate (60% in my model above), or exponentially, to use the mathematical term. Exponential discounting is "time-consistent". If a person values an earlier, smaller reward over a later, larger reward, he will always so value it, no matter how far in the future the two rewards lie. His utility function can be plotted thus.

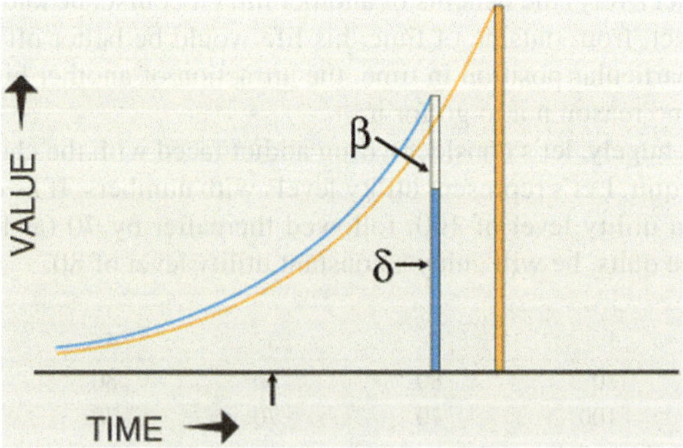

The crucial point about exponential curves is that they do not cross paths. At every point in time, the smaller earlier reward is preferred, at a proportionately constant rate, over the larger, later reward. This may be irrational in a deep sense (to be explored in a moment) but it is at least not inconsistent.

Most economists assume exponential discounting. This assumption makes their life easier, but it is not very realistic. Many experiments show this. If you ask a small child on Monday whether he would prefer a chocolate biscuit on Saturday or two chocolate biscuits on Sunday he will probably go for the latter. (Saturday/Sunday, what's the difference? It's light-years away, from his point of view.) But come Saturday morning, he may well think otherwise. He wants the one chocolate biscuit today, and the devil take tomorrow.[4]

In mathematical terms, the small child is discounting future benefits hyperbolically, not exponentially. In hyperbolic discounting, valuations rise slowly at first as one approaches the longed-for event, and then much more steeply. Crucially, this means that two hyperbolically shaped curves can cross paths, unlike two exponential curves, as this chart shows:

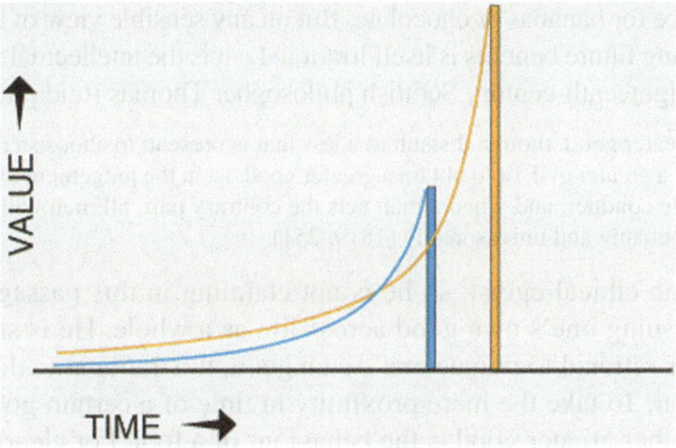

Think of this later event as "two chocolate biscuits on Sunday" and the earlier one as "one chocolate biscuit on Saturday". As you can see, the child's relative weighting of the two events switches as they come nearer in time. The curves cross paths. His preference for the smaller, earlier benefit is not just irrational (in the deep sense) it is also inconsistent with his erstwhile preference for the larger, later benefit.

Most of us are like this small child, to varying degrees. Benefits tend to loom large as they come closer in time, obscuring bigger but later benefits. Imagine walking towards a skyscraper located immediately behind a small house. For most of the distance, the skyscraper looms over the house in your field of vision. But as you get very close, the house completely obscures the skyscraper. This captures very nicely the state of mind of the addict. The week before the party, the benefits of abstaining weigh much more heavily with him than the pleasures of consuming. But as the hour of the party approaches, as he imagines the wine flowing, he changes his mind. He is, so to speak, too close to the house – he can no longer see the skyscraper in the background, though he knows in sense that it is still there.

[4] The classic study of this phenomenon is Ainslie (2006).

But the problem with the Becker/Murphy model goes deeper than this. Even if addicts did discount future benefits exponentially, not hyperbolically, it would still seem very strange to anyone unversed in economics to describe them as "rational". For addiction frustrates, often quite obviously, the addict's own long-term interests. Such behaviour is paradigmatically irrational, meaning that if a particular theory claims to exhibit it as rational, there must be something wrong with the theory. In fact, we might think of the Becker/Murphy paper as a *reductio ad absurdum* of the economic model of rationality. Its argument is valid; its conclusion is ludicrous; ergo, there must be something wrong with the premises.

The problem lies in the assumption that rationality (or irrationality) can be displayed only in behaviour that maximises (or fails to maximise) satisfaction of preferences, and not in the preferences themselves. On the Becker view, the addict's tendency to exponentially discount future benefits is simply another preference, no more or less rational than a preference for bananas or chocolate. But on any sensible view of the matter, massively discounting future benefits is itself irrational – it is the intellectual vice of *improvidence*. As the eighteenth-century Scottish philosopher Thomas Reid put it,

> To prefer a greater good, though distant, to a less that is present; to choose a present evil, in order to avoid a greater evil, or to obtain a greater good, is, in the judgement of all men, wise and reasonable conduct; and when a man acts the contrary part, all men will acknowledge that he acts foolishly and unreasonably (1819, 251).

Reid was not an ethical egoist, so he is not claiming in this passage that wisdom consists in pursuing one's own good across life as a whole. He is simply claiming that, where it is rational to pursue one's own good, it is rational to do so in a "time-neutral" fashion. To take the mere proximity in time of a certain good as reason to prefer it to another greater good is the behaviour of a fool. For clearly, what is now future will in the future be present, and what is now present will in the future be past. The "now" has no special value to it. Wisdom consists in standing outside the flow of time, in considering one's life *sub specie aeternitatis*, "from the perspective of eternity", as Spinoza put it – or at least, in approaching this ideal as nearly as is humanly possible. Someone who cannot do this is not just exhibiting a particular preference set; he is, ipso facto, irrational.

Defenders of Becker and Murphy might at this point say that I am making heavy weather of their talk of "rationality". The fact is that "rationality" functions within economics as a quasi-technical concept, with only loose connections to "rationality" as we commonly understand it. Once this is pointed out, the appearance of conflict vanishes. We might, if we like, agree to speak of "economic-rationality" and "common-rationality", adding that addicts possess the former but not the latter. Or we could treat "rationality" in the economist's sense as specifying the minimal conditions upon rational action, which we can bulk out if we like with further, stronger conditions.[5] In any event, we should not elevate what is clearly just a semantic confusion into a substantive disagreement.

[5]These two strategies of conciliation were suggested during the conference discussion by, respectively, Geoffrey Brennan and David Rose.

I am not convinced. Of course, scientists do sometimes give a technical sense to everyday words, and legitimately so: think of how evolutionary biologists use "altruism" in connection with insects or even plants. But we are not outraged by this eccentric use of the term because there is no possible danger of confusing it with the common one: no one could be so foolish as to imagine that biologists are claiming that bees or slime moulds are *altruistic* in the usual sense. But when economists describe addicts as "rational" it is natural to take them as advancing a special interpretation of our common concept of rationality, rather than a special concept of "economic-rationality". For it is not *just* economists who understand rationality in this way. The conception is broadly diffused in our culture, and has been ever since the seventeenth century.

Those creatures are the wisest who attain,By surest means, the ends at which they aim

wrote Lord Rochester (2012), summarising the doctrine of his intellectual master, Thomas Hobbes. In short, the economists' use of "rational" should be treated as embodying a substantive – and substantively false – claim about what rationality really *is*, and not just as a linguistic oddity.

9.4 Conclusion

I have argued that economics does have – contrary to the protestation of many economists – a normative doctrine of practical rationality, and that it is a flawed one. In identifying utility with the satisfaction of *current* preferences, economics cannot account for the peculiar irrationality of failing to honour past choices, or of discounting future risks. It gives us a mutilated prudence – a prudence with only one eye.

The argument can be extended. If someone who is massively improvident cannot defend himself against the charge of irrationality by saying "I don't care about my future welfare", then why should someone who is cruel or unjust be able to defend himself against the charge of irrationality by saying "I don't care about other people's welfare"? If prudence embraces a concern for one's future self, irrespective of current desires, why shouldn't it embrace a concern for other selves, again irrespective of desires. As Philippa Foot has said, "Either you have to accept that it isn't contrary to rationality to imprudently ignore one's future well-being, or you have to accept some conception of practical rationality that makes reference to things other than what one cares about."[6] But that is a topic for another occasion.

[6] Alex Voorhoeve, *Conversations on Ethics* (Oxford: Oxford University Press, 2009), p. 104.

References

Ainslie, George. 2006. *Picoeconomics*. Cambridge: Cambridge University Press.

Becker, Gary S., and Kevin M. Murphy. 1988. A Theory of Rational Addiction. *Journal of Political Economy* 96 (4): 675–700.

Burrow, John. 2000. The Third Eye of Prudence. In *Medieval Futures: Attitudes to the Future in the Middle Ages*, ed. J.A. Burrow and Ian P. Wei. Wood bridge, Boydell & Brewer.

Eliot, George. 1985. *Mill on the Floss*. London: Penguin.

Hirschfeld, Mary L. 2018. *Aquinas and the Market: Toward a Humane Economy*. Cambridge, MA: Harvard University Press.

Machiavelli, Niccolo. 1997. *Discourses on Livy*, trans. Julia Conaway Bondanella and Peter Bondanella. Oxford: Oxford University Press.

Mankiw, Greg. 2007. *Principles of Economics*. Mason: South-Western.

Panofsky, Erwin. 1955. *Titian's Allegory of Prudence: A Postscript, in Panofsky, Meaning in the Visual Arts*, 146–168. Garden City: Doubleday.

Reid, Thomas. 1819. *Essays on the Powers of the Human Mind*. Vol. III. Edinburgh: Bell and Bradfute.

Wilmot, John Earl of Rochester. 2012. Satire Against Reason And Mankind, *The Norton Anthology of English Literature*. The Restoration and the Eighteenth Century. Volume C. 9th Ed. New York: New York City, 2012. pp. 2301–2307, Lines 1–225.

Part III
Way Forward

Chapter 10
Trust as the Basis to Social Inquiry

Dominic Burbidge

> *In the case of all things which have several parts and in which the totality is not, as it were, a mere heap, but the whole is something beside the parts, there is a cause...*
>
> —*Aristotle, Metaphysics, 1045a*

> *The chemical combination of two substances produces, as is well known, a third substance with properties entirely different from those of either of the two substances separately, or of both of them taken together.*
>
> —*John Stuart Mill, A System of Logic (1859)*

Abstract Through recent developments in the study of trust and social capital, social science methods are frequently breaking with previous homo economicus persuasions and assumptions. The chapter theoretically considers this by exploring how social science methodology can be reoriented in its fundamentals in order to appreciate the change. In terms of the philosophical currents underlying the social sciences, there is ongoing divide between, on the one hand, individualistic and analytical approaches to interpreting social phenomena and, on the other, approaches that take more holistic and organic views of society. It is suggested that the study of trust as interpersonal, habitual and exhibited in human networks steps between these views, offering what I hope is a refreshing basis to social inquiry.

The social sciences have summed society's parts and found them less than equal to the whole. The measurement of individual units has poor predictive power as to their collective direction, unlike studies in the pure sciences. The problem lies in the analytical lens that social scientists have used to approach and understand the parts. The dominating argument is that society is a network of interests. This argument is shamelessly deployed in utilitarian accounts of the rational individual, though it is

D. Burbidge (✉)
University of Oxford, Oxford, UK

Canterbury Institute, Oxford, UK
e-mail: dominic.burbidge@politics.ox.ac.uk

P. Róna et al. (eds.), *Homo Curator: Towards the Ethics of Consumption*, Virtues and Economics 8, https://doi.org/10.1007/978-3-031-51700-6_10

also present at the other end of the spectrum in the intensely society-centred approach of Marxism. There is need to offer an understanding of the parts of society that matches the whole. Society is not a network of interests but a network of trust.

Something has been missed in the steady application of analytical research to society. By analytical research I refer to the application of analytic philosophy and scientific sentiments to the study of politics, society and economics. The general trend unleashed imitations of pure science methodologies onto social questions. Understandings of the parts of society (persons, families, social networks) were squeezed into interpretations of physical determinism and the image of homo economicus, as a lady squeezed into a corset that does not fit. This has resulted, first of all, in a methodological cycle of theory formulation, theory application and empirical observation, through which the concept of the "model" attempts to bridge the embarrassing gap between theory and reality. The model is, essentially, a description of society that fits with theoretical assumptions of parts of society, precisely an exercise in making sure the whole is a summation of the parts. In the words of one economics textbook, economists' models 'provide simplified portraits of the way individuals make decisions, the way firms behave, and the way in which these two groups interact to establish markets' (Snyder and Nicholson 2008, 3). Such research based on model formulation can be labelled "castaway" social science. There is a well-known joke: two economists are castaways on a desert island with only a can of baked beans which they cannot open. One cries, "How are we going to eat?" and the other answers, "Let us assume we have a tin opener." When the castaway methodology is applied to social science research, a particular model and a particular theory of the person are adjusted towards symmetry until the model and the unit of analysis, usually the individual, are synonymous. This **increases the distance of the study from empirical realities**, though the method is maintained under the excuse that analytical rigour is gained, an exercise in 'blackboard economics' (Coase 1988, 28). The irony is that analytical rigour is not attained. Aristotle's comment is worth meditating on: 'In the case of all things which have several parts and in which the totality is not, as it were, a mere heap, but the whole is something beside the parts, there is a cause'. Put in the negative, when things are just a big heap, and the parts are the same as the whole, without any particular unity, we cannot infer causality. As such, castaway social science nullifies the search for causality. In the same way, if assumptions of the individual have reached symmetry with assumptions of the model such that they are equivalent, no theory of causation can be added. It is only when the final display achieves a beauty, pattern, synthesis or self-sufficiency not in the original parts can we say the outcome was caused. Within the social sciences, the dominance of the castaway has come through popularity for neoclassical economic interpretations of the individual and institutions. Studies start with these assumptions and they are then identified as causal accounts.

The gap that has since formed between, on the one hand, self-fulfilling prophecies of models and, on the other, the freshness of reality through empirical observation has provided space for this generation's more enriching social science research. The approach consists of in-depth and empirically detailed critiques of models.

Despite its merits, however, methodological disappointment usually follows when the conclusions of such studies are, ultimately, that reality is more complicated. In a second gross generalisation, therefore, I term this approach the "critical caveman". The critical caveman enters the cave of his friend and sees the paintings of deer and hunters on the wall. He reprimands his friend: "You are inventing an arbitrary dichotomy between us and them." A critical caveman achieves much but is, ultimately, battling against the castaway's constant attempt to simplify the parts of society such that they may quickly and easily predict the direction of the whole. So long as the mainstay of social science is the reduction of complex wholes to the summation of individual parts through the medium of the model, the critical caveman will find employment but grudgingly, for the vocation of a researcher thirsts for conclusions that make sense of things. Instead, critical cavemen coalesce on the fallibility of "knowledge production".

The critical caveman is in a tug-of-war with the castaway and neither is willing to let go. In some ways it is appropriate they do not let go, for they are thoroughly interdependent.

What can be done? The analytical research agenda has missed something very small and yet of particular importance to the social science endeavour, and this small thing might just be enough to persuade the castaway and caveman to drop the rope. That, at least, is the argument here. What has been overlooked? Put simply, human communities function through trust. The model of the individual used in the social sciences—the hungry atom—has no capacity to trust. A new understanding of the parts of society is needed.

10.1 What Is Society?

That model of the hungry atom—that cacophony of Hobbes' science and neoclassical economics' equalising individualism—rose as part of the search for necessary forces at play in human beings' social dynamics. The context of its rise, through other thinkers such as Locke, Smith, Bentham, Mill, Hayek and Rawls, came in distinction to those who viewed social interactions as a single, organic whole, theorists such as Rousseau, Ferguson and Durkheim. That alternative approach takes society as one with its own volition, self-reproduction and sheltered longue durée. The position returns focus to the very social nature of humans which makes the social sciences a distinct area of study. Here, society is certainly more than the sum of its parts but there is again only one category through which humanity is seen—at base the same problem as that of the castaway. Society is a social block; from the social scientist's perspective, presumed an indivisible whole.

Is there any way of avoiding this collapse into reductionism? Some light can be shed here by Aquinas, a thirteenth century theologian and philosopher. Answering the strange question of if it is safe to distinguish between someone's command and the commanded act that results, Aquinas makes a general comment on whether or not we are safe in distinguishing the same thing in different ways. He writes:

> Nothing prevents certain things being distinct in one respect, and one in another respect. Indeed, every multitude is one in some respect, as Dionysius says. But a difference is to be observed in this, that some are simply many, and one in particular aspect: while with others it is the reverse. Now "one" is predicated in the same way as "being." And substance is being simply, whereas accident or being "of reason" is a being only in a certain respect. Wherefore those things that are one in substance are one simply, though many in a certain respect. Thus, in the genus substance, the whole composed of its integral or essential parts, is one simply: because the whole is being and substance simply, and the parts are being and substances in the whole. But those things which are distinct in substance, and one according to an accident, are distinct simply, and one in a certain respect: thus many men are one people, and many stones are one heap; which is unity of composition or order. (Aquinas 1265–1274, I-II, q. 17, a. 4)

Deploying a distinction between the substance of something and its accidents, Aquinas is suggesting it is possible to consider distinct things as one, insofar as they are considered under one aspect. This logic he explicitly applies to a collection of human beings and notes that, whilst they cannot be considered one in substance, they are one according to an accidental feature. Many men are one people; that is to say, a society.

This logical form navigates the Scylla and Charybdis of individualism versus organic social wholes. How so? The position of viewing society as an organic whole commits the fallacy, described by Aquinas, of assigning substantial unity to something made up of many "beings", each substantially self-sufficient in their own way. Taking an individualistic perspective therefore seems to fit more neatly with Aquinas' distinction because each person is considered as one only under a particular aspect, that of their self-interest (which leads them to forms of social interaction in contexts of scarce resources and likely greater collective productivity). However, what is difficult here is that the particular aspect under which the species of humanity is being considered one is not that which makes it one. Indeed, as Hobbes' state of nature theory opines, fear and self-interest is precisely that which sets persons apart as adversaries. Nevertheless, as a first suggestion it helps us by reverse, for just as intentional disunity is a radically mistaken aspect under which to consider society one, its opposite, intentional unity, is the aspect which successfully captures society's essence. Now, intentional unity is the definition of trust; society is, therefore, a network of trust.

10.2 A Criticism

In the early 1970s, the philosopher Alasdair MacIntyre (1973a; see also 1971, 260–79) controversially asked whether a science of comparative politics was possible. Stated briefly, MacIntyre asks how we can consider those the social scientist studies as incapable of self-reflection on a par with the social scientist. His argument is of relevance here, for any suggestion about how the social sciences can be better orientated needs to more successfully answer this concern. It is argued that considering society as a network of trust instead of a network of interests meets the objection.

MacIntyre begins by questioning 'the assumption that it is possible to identify political attitudes independently of political institutions and practices' (1973a, 172). If it is not possible to identify political attitudes independently, it may be they are endogenous or a product of free will or randomness, and therefore cannot be tracked through law-like human sciences. For MacIntyre, his suggestion assaults the refusal within the social sciences to acknowledge human potentiality for self-reformulation of intention. The point is directed particularly at 1960s structural functionalism and efforts to analyse culture (Almond and Verba 1963; 1989) as able to explain social developments. MacIntyre's critique of the assumed ability to isolate persons' attitudes is wider, however, incorporating also a rejection of the same assumptions as appear in behavioural economics and other schools of thought within the social sciences. He posits that attitudes depend on intention, and that institutions cannot be interpreted without reference to intention. Trying to maintain a separation between attitudes and institutions is, therefore, null and void. He notes Wittgenstein as supporting this position by having held that 'we identify and define attitudes in terms of the objects toward which they are directed, and not vice versa' (MacIntyre 1973a, 172).

MacIntyre dethrones the claim to law-like generalisations which, in a positivistic manner, has often been used to legitimise the study of politics and economics as sciences. He identifies three areas where this claim is compromised. Law-like generalisations tend to be:

(i) hindered by the frequency of counter-examples;
(ii) encumbered by flawed attempts at cross-cultural categorisation; and
(iii) when apparent, observations of human rationality rather than anything expressly political (MacIntyre 1973a, 173–8).

These problems mean that, for findings in comparative politics, '*either* such generalizations about institutions will necessarily lack the kind of confirmation they require or they will be consequences of true generalizations about human rationality and not part of a specifically political science' (MacIntyre 1973a, 178, emphasis in original). Attempting to solve this disjuncture through analysing politics and political systems in terms of functional analysis is, according to MacIntyre, as flawed as positivists' accumulation of repeated observations. Often termed "structural functionalism", the approach seeks to interpret society's complexity from a macro-perspective, often viewing society as a set of evolved organisms in similar vein to the organic/holistic approach described above. MacIntyre (1973a, 179) notes functional analysis as inescapably vague, requiring 'no reliance on any factual generalizations'; 'merely a matter of drawing out the consequences of definition.' He dismisses how 'most political scientists who have tried to specify the functions in question have produced nothing but statements about institutions and their effects in which the word "function" may appear, but could be replaced not only without loss, but with gain' (1973a, 178–9). This is the same danger of tautology in the organic/holistic approach of Rousseau and Durkheim: researchers are drawn towards the attractiveness of affirming sociality and interdependence but end with the cry, "Society is functional interdependence which cannot be simplified through individualism!"—very much a critical caveman conclusion.

Although MacIntyre demonstrates the distance between political science's expressed aims and its actual achievements, he indicates also a different aim and method that could better serve the vocation of the social sciences. To pave the way towards this, he notes a key difference between Hobbes and Machiavelli, stating that it is Machiavelli who 'ought to be regarded as the patron saint of political studies and not Hobbes' (MacIntyre 1973a, 180). This chimes with comments in the book *After Virtue* (1985, *196*), where MacIntyre notes Hobbes' analysis as correct only if a society recognises external goods minus notions of virtue or internal goods (a society dominated, therefore, by human competition). In contrast to Hobbes' desire for predictability in the study of human behaviour,

> Machiavelli realized that in political life fortuna, the bitch goddess of unpredictability, has never been dethroned. To any stock of maxims derived from empirically founded generalizations the student of politics must always add one more: "And do not be surprised if in the event things turn out otherwise." (MacIntyre 1973a, 180)

This position appears, at first, difficult. It seems pessimistic on whether any stable understanding of the social, political and economic can be held to. If everything may, in the end, turn out otherwise, the threat of counter-examples is crippling of the search for reliable or predictable knowledge. However, MacIntyre proceeds to demonstrate how the Machiavellian position is less an appeal to randomness and more an appeal to knowledge through praxis. MacIntyre quickly notes the value of historical experience, and explores history as human intentions impacting culture over time. This returns the reader to his initial rejection of the assumed independence between attitudes and institutions, and affirms how a connection between the two can be effectively studied through accumulated historical knowledge (Blakely 2013, 50–2). Interestingly, the argument reopens a door for the social sciences by way of comparative histories, holding constant similar examples of human intention and exploring their heterogeneous impact on diverse cultures over time (MacIntyre 1973a, 181–3). The approach seeks to furnish the study of politics and economics with understandings of necessary conditions for institutional change without claiming positivistic certainty:

> What I want to suggest is that it is characteristic of the causal knowledge which history does provide us with that the antecedent conditions in terms of which we explain historical outcomes are sometimes necessary conditions for the occurrence of some specific outcome, but are never sufficient. If this is so, then the patterns which we discern in comparative history will always be de facto guides yielding Machiavellian maxims, rather than Hobbesian laws. (MacIntyre 1973a, 183, emphasis in original)

The position is thus one of studying politics and economics in terms of both the moral and empirical lessons that can be drawn from examples of when human intention is applied to societies and the forming of institutions. Using the simple distinction between necessary and sufficient conditions, the social sciences are seen as unable to approach sufficient causal knowledge but able to nurture wisdom in human affairs through reference to necessary conditions that helped bring about past scenarios.

As part of demonstrating the value of this alternative approach, MacIntyre contrasts the "political scientist" with the "political agent". Crucially, he notes how the beliefs and attitudes of political agents can be reflected upon by themselves, which means they become subject to human intention and reinterpretation. Given this reflective capacity in political agents, their position is suggested by MacIntyre to be indistinguishable from that claimed as the realm and remit of political scientists (1973a, 184). MacIntyre's parting shot is that the claim amongst political scientists of being "value-free" is, therefore, simply a position of promoting the abandonment of values in politics (1973a, 188). This turns the reader to again question the worth of political science, and reveals a dogmatic side to positivistic claims (explored more extensively in MacIntyre 1973b). For the purposes of this chapter, however, the point is less how normative the underlying commitment to neutrality is so much as the problem of how social science makes sense of things given the contingency of human scenarios, the complexity of human interactions, and the inability to distinguish between the cognitive capacities of researchers and the researched. If we really are equal, how can one view others as predictable in their interpretations of society without removing one's own powers of interpreting society?

10.3 Answering the Criticism

MacIntyre's argument was not welcomed. Much as Machiavelli's belief in '*fortuna*, the bitch goddess of unpredictability' (1973a, 180, emphasis in original), the piece was digested by social science readers as 'an obscurantist salvo' and of the view that 'some answers are unknowable [...] because it is impossible to sort out the impact of institutions from the impact of the conditions under which we observe them' (Przeworski 2004, 527–8; see also Ware 2011, 412–3). MacIntyre became viewed as one of those who 'resist numerical analysis' (Gerring and Thomas 2011, 21), and his piece deployed as a straw man against which one can counter that empirically grounded research does, in fact, achieve something (Landman 2002, 890–1; Kaviraj 2013, 24–5).

But MacIntyre's discourse cut deeper than simply doubting the progress of social science. The argument that our model of the self-interested individual does no justice to humanity is given velocity as he reorients discussion back to the assumed capacity of researchers for self-reflection. Within the social sciences we are trying to model others, doing it in a way that, if successful, would need in the same breath to fully explain humanity's capacity to model and remodel things. This problem permeates the writings of Hobbes who, counterproductively, seeks to inform the reader about how *everyone else* is motivated by self-preservation. In the introduction to *Leviathan*, Hobbes (1651, 8, emphasis in original) writes:

> … there is another saying not of late understood, by which they might learn truly to read one another, if they would take the pains; and that is, *nosce teipsum, read thyself:* which was not meant, as it is now used, to countenance, either the barbarous state of men in power,

> towards their inferiors; or to encourage men of low degree, to a saucy behaviour towards their betters; but to teach us, that for the similitude of the thoughts, and passions of one man, to the thoughts, and passions of another, whosoever looketh into himself, and considereth what he doth, when he does *think, opine, reason, hope, fear*, &c: for these the constitution individual, and particular education do so vary, and they are so easy to be kept from our knowledge, that the characters of man's heart, blotted and confounded as they are, with dissembling, lying, counterfeiting, and erroneous doctrines, are legible only to him that searcheth hearts. And though by men's actions we do discover their design sometimes; yet to do it without comparing them with our own, and distinguishing all circumstances, by which the case may come to be altered, is to decipher without a key, and be for the most part deceived, by too much trust, or by too much diffidence; as he that reads, is himself a good or evil man.

Hobbes makes the same distinction here that MacIntyre made between attitudes and institutions or practices. However, whereas MacIntyre questions the assumption that they can be held distinct, here Hobbes (1651, 8) speaks of the necessity of their distinction, for the hearts of man cannot be trusted ('blotted and confounded as they are, with dissembling, lying, counterfeiting, and erroneous doctrines'; see also Jenco 2012, 177). Hobbes rejects comparing human experiences against our own, for we may be good or evil people, and so the way we reason about others' motivations will bear this bias. Instead, he searches for the key that will unlock knowledge of human behaviour universally, and calls in his next paragraph for neutrality:

> He that is to govern a whole nation, must read in himself, not this, or that particular man; but mankind: which though it be hard to do, harder than to learn any language, or science; yet, when I shall have set down my own reading orderly, and perspicuously, the pains left another, will be only to consider, if he also find not the same in himself. For this kind of doctrine admitteth no other demonstration. (Hobbes 1651, 8)

And here lies a grave mistake. For Hobbes is asking the reader to think impartially in order to understand the volition of human beings, but taking as his criterion of verification whether one sees the same image of the person in oneself. If, as is the case with Hobbes, the image of the person holds no self-reflective capacity, how can we reflect on the truth of its constitution in ourselves?

Hobbes' intention is noble, though the extent of his failure in connecting an interpretation of the human person with a capacity for self-reflection spawns the beastly division between castaway and caveman that we see today. However, to argue with MacIntyre that the scientific endeavour should be replaced with the more humble search for historical awareness and Machiavellian maxims is a needless scaling down. The mistake of Hobbes was not his attempt at general, impartial knowledge but his reduction of human intentions and motivations to self-interest. This mistake does not hold for viewing society as a network of trust because trust as intentional unity—the definition given in this chapter—leaves open the question of what particular intentions are at play at any given time, tracing merely the impact of their unity. Whether motivated by fear, hatred, love or happiness, persons form relationships, modes of cooperation and institutions that help generate social change. MacIntyre's questioning of the assumption that attitudes can be held distinct from institutions and practices is an accurate critique of Hobbesian individualism but not of social scientists who view society as a network of trust, for their attitudes may be endogenous to practices and the forming of institutions and yet observable externally—not individual, subjective and unknowable motivations but manifested unities of intention, inwardly endowed and yet outwardly exposed. The academic community is also a network of trust, and so its interpretation of others through the social sciences is conducted in terms of one group exploring others' social manifestations of intentional unity, with the academic community united around virtues of truth and humility. Intentional disunity will always be there; it is possible for us each, as Hobbes affirms, to lie to our friends. But the creation of a den of thieves requires a den, something that mimics our collective understanding of what we are doing and reinforces the intentional unity that lies at the heart of the common enterprise. For any social practice, some degree of intentional unity is required, just as any economic transaction depends to some degree on trust (Arrow 1972, 345–7). And, in the same way as the contract—whether verbal, written or in the form of a relationship—invariably accompanies a transaction, so too do institutions and practices invariably accompany common intention. We are not so unknowable at the social level as we sometimes maintain we are at the individual level. The social sciences capture trends of social unities of intention, and the simplifications towards self-interested human motivation for the sake of scientific reductionism were an unnecessary and unhelpful detour. We are moral animals with strong capacities for self-reflection, freedom of choice and personal deliberation (Smith 2003). When we are social we are known not through reduction to self-interest but through manifested networks of intentional unity.

10.4 Trust: The Fabric of Social Relations

This call for a reorientation of the social sciences comes alongside increased popularity in studying trust. But what is trust, and why define it as intentional unity? The recent emphasis was popularly ignited in the 1990s through the writings of Robert D Putnam (1993) who considered the value of "social capital" for explaining democratic success amongst devolved political units in Italy. Social capital, loosely defined, is the norms and networks that enable collective action. Rooting the approach in Tocqueville's *Democracy in America*, Putnam then penetrated a wider audience with a book called *Bowling Alone* (2000) which described the decline of associational behaviour in the United States since the 1950s. That group association, norms of cooperation and interpersonal trust form an essential part of successful societies has since been shouted from the academic rooftops, with supporters spread throughout sociology, political science and economics (Bjørnskov 2003, 2010; Collier and Gunning 1999; Heinemann and Tanz 2008; Helliwell and Huang 2008; Knack 2002; Knack and Keefer 1997; Svendsen and Svendsen 2009).

Does the idea of social capital appropriately reorient social inquiry through the notion of trust? As with any popular academic concept, it is important to note how social capital has suffered misuse, misappropriation and misdiagnosis. There is also strong criticism directed against its very existence. The economist Kenneth

J. Arrow (2000, 4) refused to accept social relations as a form of capital on the basis that they do not constitute deliberate sacrifice in the present for future gain. This is indeed an accurate criticism, for "capital" usually refers to stored value, not active value. In nevertheless maintaining empirically worthwhile contributions, the social capital literature has identified its effects for the outputs of economic growth, political efficiency and social harmony. Alternative attempts to get to grips with the causes of social capital have run into complicated evaluations of its definition and internal structure (Adler and Kwon 2002), which is a shame because it is the nature of social capital's input that interests us here. At present, the concept bears very little of the value alluded to previously of considering social relations as forms of intentional unity. Social capital remains a welcome popular approach to compensating for the gross inadequacies of having considered social relations in terms of motivations of self-interest but is still something of an economisation of human cooperation to fit positivistic social science trends (for insights on the connections between economic and social thought and the concept of social capital, see Farr 2004).

In a 2007 article, Putnam evaluates the distinction between "bonding" and "bridging" social capital. The bonding type refers to the norms of cooperation developed between those similar to one's own identity or natural social group. Bridging is alternatively understood as the norms of cooperation developed with those of other social groups. Putnam (2007, 143) identifies complications in making this distinction and notes how, 'without really thinking about it, we assume that bridging social capital and bonding social capital are inversely correlated in a kind of zero-sum relationship.' Not only is this indeed a misconstruction, the practice of distinguishing the two types also confirms the inadequacy of social capital as able to identify intentional unity more deeply. The idea that one type of cooperative unity is achieved through those of one's own social group and another type achieved through those outside puts identity-based variables in the position of determining factors for structuring human relations. However, at the heart of any valuing of interpersonal solidarity for interpreting social dynamics is the acknowledgement that interpersonal solidarity is a practice between individuals otherwise distinct. In our understanding of trust as intentional unity there can be no bonding without bridging and no bridging without bonding.

At the core of the innovation behind social capital studies is acknowledging the possibility of norms and networks of trust. This is interesting for noting social capital's outcomes for economic, political and social goals, though is revolutionary only if it can debunk both the castaway's insistence on economic individualism and the critical caveman's relativism. This social capital does, but only through the concept of trust as intentional unity that lies hidden as an unacknowledged ghost, working the social machine. Trust as intentional unity is a view of the parts of society that demarcates the analytical territory that must be covered in understanding how persons form a greater social whole. It is latent in the idea of social capital although almost entirely underexplored by that literature.

When Fukuyama (1995) wrote on trust he focused discussion on the cultural habits useful for economic activity. His piece encouraged a shift back to more cultural appreciations of social structures in order to explain differences between economies. The danger with this is if reference to trust and social coordination leads researchers to substitute analysis of the laws of unintended consequences with less detailed cultural allusions. Although trust as the key principle for interpreting society and social change is embedded in cultural habits, these are particular manifestations that neither vindicate nor falsify articulations on the methodological relevance of trust for the social sciences. Culture is of relevance for the study of trust because constitutive of common practices, social norms and habits, not because it acts as a deeper explanation of why certain peoples trust more than others. The key difference between a culturalist orientation towards trust and the present argument of deploying trust as the basis to social inquiry is that the definition of trust as intentional unity gives ultimate primacy to the freedom and creativity of human agency. Social norms and habits are expressions of that human coordination that arises from intentional unity in a society's members; the human choices, self-reflection and agency that form the process of trust must therefore be prior in analysis to cultural descriptions.

From the point of view of the researcher, these appeals to freedom and human agency should not, however, be confused with arguments for randomness in the forming of social behaviour, and nor can they be assumed unknowable. It is an appeal to engage with capacities for agent-based self-reflection in line with MacIntyre's criticism. Societies are knowable in an analogous way to friends being knowable: we get to know what they tend to like and not like, what they aspire to and what they judge right and wrong. We see how they change over time and reconstitute themselves when faced with changing circumstances. And yet, just as a friend's capacities for renewed self-direction linger and remain able to surprise, so too is society known by the researcher through habits of intentional unity, realising these intentions may be reconstituted as human self-reflection achieves new consensuses over collective goals. Rather than an appeal to randomness in human motivations, therefore, this is an endogenisation into the social sciences of human capacities for re-interpretation on a par with game theory's admission of persons' actions forming through reflective expectations of others' likely actions. The only difference with game theory is that here inclusion is also made of the ability of humans to re-define original preferences as well, as Amartya Sen (1977) imagines possible. Taking trust as the basis to social inquiry, the social sciences observe the way persons horizontally coordinate their interests with others to pursue social ends, and vertically coordinate their interests with how they view and constitute themselves. Intentional unity is a social fabric simultaneously fathomable as interpersonal and self-reflective.

10.5 Conclusion

This chapter has identified key trends in the social sciences and asked whether they can be improved. The contemporary difficulties and disagreements have been summarised as a tug-of-war between "castaways", those who form models that add nothing besides the assumptions they make about the parts of society, and "critical cavemen", those who frustrate the popularity of castaways through the questioning of assumed distinctions. The castaway and critical caveman depend on each other because the deficiencies of each provide justification for their respective filters. Behind this dilemma lies the question of how we view society in a way that the social scientist may productively explore. As things stand, there is ongoing division between those who take individuals as the unit of analysis and those who instead see society as an intrinsic whole.

The writings of Aquinas help provide room for flexibility, however, in seeing distinct beings as one under particular accidental features. That is how we can think of a collection of human beings as a society, he suggests. It is not that they must be one or exactly the same to be considered one; they are one in a certain respect. What aspect captures the social manifestations of humans such that the researcher can approach more general or universal interpretations? Here MacIntyre's criticisms were useful, for he identified the need for a view of the person that meets with a view of the researcher, just as a political agent cannot, due to his capacities for social reflection and pre-emptive action, ultimately be distinguished from the political scientist. In response to the general need for a view of society that contains both individuality of membership and reference to collectivity, in addition to the need for not reducing away the cognitive powers of the researched, I suggest considering society as a network of trust. Trust, defined as intentional unity, is that aspect under which humans can be seen as one. It allows for diversity in types of intention whilst still establishing when things are socially manifested. The argument rejects, of course, power-based theories and Marxist class-analysis as outside the discipline of the social sciences in exactly the same way as it rejects Hobbesian individualism as having made extreme and untenable assumptions about human motivation. It looks at institutions and practices as inextricably tied to common intention and understands the human person as capable of communicating desires, needs and aims as part of the process of cooperative behaviour. It is encouraged by the apparent renewed popularity in studying trust—sometimes under the difficult term "social capital"—and agrees with Elinor Ostrom (2000, 173) on how unfortunate it is if those movements are dismissed as 'just another fad', for their frustration with homo economicus contains the seeds for a wider re-growth of the social sciences. Viewing society as a network of trust meets directly MacIntyre's concern over the role of the researcher because academia is equal in its capacity for intentional unity, just as MacIntyre (2009) himself writes on the journey of a particular academic community as if it were the journey of a single society.

At its core the argument is very simple: social inquiry must have as its basis that which is most intensely social about human persons—unity of intention.

Bibliography

Adler, P.S., and S. Kwon. 2002. Social Capital: Prospects for a New Concept. *Academy of Management Review* 27 (1): 17–40.

Almond, G.A., and S. Verba. 1963. *The Civic Culture: Political Attitudes and Democracy in Five Nations*. Princeton University Press: Princeton.

———. 1989. *The Civic Culture Revisited*. London: Sage.

Aquinas, T., Summa Theologiae (1964–1981 [1265–1274]), (I-II) q. 17, a. 4., London, Blackfriars, http://www.newadvent.org/summa/1016.htm. Accessed 22/03/13.

Aristotle, Metaphysics, Book H 1045a. http://classics.mit.edu/Aristotle/metaphysics.8.viii.html. Accessed 24/05/11.

Arrow, K.J. 1972. Gifts and Exchanges. *Philosophy & Public Affairs* 1 (4): 343–362.

———. 2000. Observations on social capital, Ch 1. In *Social Capital: A Multifaceted Perspective*, ed. P. Dasgupta and I. Serageldin. Washington, D.C.: The World Bank.

Bjørnskov, C. 2003. The Happy Few: Cross-Country Evidence on Social Capital and Life Satisfaction. *Kyklos* 56 (1): 3–16.

———. 2010. How Does Social Trust Lead to Better Governance? An Attempt to Separate Electoral and Bureaucratic Mechanisms. *Public Choice* 144 (1/2): 323–346.

Blakely, J.W. 2013. *Three Political Philosophers Debate Social Science: Leo Strauss, Alasdair MacIntyre, and Charles Taylor*. PhD thesis, University of California, Berkeley.

Coase, R.H. 1988. *The Firm, the Market, and the Law*. London: University of Chicago Press.

Collier, P., and J.W. Gunning. 1999. Explaining African Economic Performance. *Journal of Economic Literature* 37 (1): 64–111.

Farr, J. 2004. Social Capital: A Conceptual History. *Political Theory* 32 (1): 6–33.

Fukuyama, F. 1995. *Trust: The Social Virtues and the Creation of Prosperity*. New York: The Free Press.

Gerring, J., and C.W. Thomas. 2011. 'Quantitative and Qualitative: A Question of Comparability'. Extended version of chapter published. In *International Encyclopedia of Political Science*, ed. B. Badie, D. Berg-Schlosser, and L. Morlino. London: Sage.

Heinemann, F., and B. Tanz. 2008. The Impact of Trust on Reforms. *Journal of Economic Policy Reform* 11 (3): 173–185.

Helliwell, J.F., and H. Huang. 2008. How's Your Government? International Evidence Linking Good Government and Well-Being. *British Journal of Political Science* 38 (4): 595–619.

Hobbes, T. 1998 [1651]. *Leviathan*. Oxford: Oxford University Press.

Jenco, L. 2012. From Constitutional Listening to Constitutional Learning. *Chicago-Kent Law Review* 88 (1): 171–184.

Kaviraj, S. 2013. On the Historicity of "The Political": Rajaniti and Politics in Modern Indian Thought, Ch 1. In *Comparative Political Thought: Theorizing Practices*, ed. M. Freeden and A. Vincent. Oxford: Routledge.

Knack, S. 2002. Social Capital and the Quality of Government: Evidence From the States. *American Journal of Political Science* 46 (4): 772–785.

Knack, S., and P. Keefer. 1997. Does Social Capital have an Economic Payoff? A Cross-Country Investigation. *Quarterly Journal of Economics* 112: 1251.

Landman, T. 2002. Comparative Politics and Human Rights. *Human Rights Quarterly* 24 (4): 890–923.

MacIntyre, A. 1971. *Against the Self-Images of the Age*, 260–279. London: Duckworth.

———. 1973a. Is a Science of Comparative Politics Possible? Ch 10. In *The Philosophy of Social Explanation*, ed. A. Ryan. Oxford: Oxford University Press.

———. 1973b. Ideology, Social Science, and Revolution. *Comparative Politics* 5 (3): 321–342.

———. 1985. *After Virtue: A Study in Moral Theory*. 2nd ed. London: Duckworth.

———. 2009. *God, Philosophy, Universities: A Selective History of the Catholic Philosophical Tradition*. Lanham: Rowman & Littlefield.

Mill, J.S. 1859. *A System of Logic*. New York: Harper and Brothers. http://www.isnature.org/Files/Mill1859-Composition_of_Causes.htm. Accessed 24/05/11.

Ostrom, E. 2000. Social Capital: A Fad or a Fundamental Concept? Ch 9. In *Social Capital: A Multifaceted Perspective*, ed. P. Dasgupta and I. Serageldin. Washington, D.C.: The World Bank.

Przeworski, A. 2004. Institutions Matter? *Government and Opposition* 39 (4): 527–540.

Putnam, R.D. 1993. *Making Democracy Work: Civic Traditions in Modern Italy*. Princeton: Princeton University Press, with Robert Leonardi and Raffaella Y. Nonetti.

———. 2000. *Bowling Alone: The Collapse and Revival of American Community*. New York: Simon & Schuster.

———. 2007. E Pluribus Unum: Diversity and Community in the Twenty-First Century. *Scandinavian Political Studies* 30 (2): 137–174.

Sen, A. 1977. Rational Fools: A Critique of the Behavioral Foundations of Economic Theory. *Philosophy & Public Affairs* 6 (4): 317–344.

Smith, C. 2003. *Moral, Believing Animals: Human Personhood and Culture*. New York: Oxford University Press.

Snyder, C., and W. Nicholson. 2008. *Microeconomic Theory: Basic Principles and Extensions*. 10th ed. Mason: South-Western.

Svendsen, G.T., and G.L.H. Svendsen. 2009. *Handbook of Social Capital: The Troika of Sociology, Political Science and Economics*. Cheltenham: Edward Elgar.

Ware, A. 2011. Exceptionalism, Political Science and the Comparative Analysis of Political Parties. *Government and Opposition* 46 (4): 411–435.

Chapter 11
A Deeper Humanity: The Family as the School of an Inclusive Economy

Joseph Rice

Abstract This paper addresses one particular understanding, based in the Catholic intellectual tradition, of ethical and anthropological foundations of the formation of social and economic attitudes in the family, and how these might be related to the understanding of humanity at the foundation of participation in an inclusive economy. What is at stake is how the primordial subjectivity of the human person, formed in the family, may be related to the formation of social and economic attitudes in the wider society. Building on the position, expressed in the Vatican II document *Gaudium et Spes* (52), that "the family is a kind of school of a deeper humanity," I will investigate the development of the notion of "humanity" in the thought of Karol Wojtyła (the future Pope John Paul II) to situate the question of economic inclusion in a context of human ecology. I will treat the question of human consumption within this perspective, as related not only to the human vocation to participate in community, but also to the consequences for persons of consumerist attitudes.

11.1 The Question: Examining Anthropological Assumptions

Amid the vicissitudes of life under a pandemic, added to the pressures of an ecological crisis, it is natural to be concerned for the integrity of our socio-economic systems. Efficient economies are not necessarily effective economies. Even before the pandemic, some economists have warned that we risk becoming inured to the human costs not only of markets that crash, but also of markets that soar. When the increased wealth of a few heralds the worsening poverty of many, the widening gap between rich and poor appears as *prima facie* evidence that a system designed for human flourishing is somehow deviating from its intended purpose (Piketty 2014, 571).

J. Rice (✉)
Seton Hall University, South Orange, NJ, USA
e-mail: Joseph.Rice@shu.edu

P. Róna et al. (eds.), *Homo Curator: Towards the Ethics of Consumption*, Virtues and Economics 8, https://doi.org/10.1007/978-3-031-51700-6_11

Some contemporary theorists have proposed new ways to organize economic activity to address economic exclusion, not just as inequality of opportunity, but also as inequity of outcomes. They propose to reset an inhuman system that installs a widening disparity between haves and have-nots (and, according to a scientific consensus, even threatens the integrity of the biosphere) (Schwab 2021; John Paul II 1989, 6–7). The goal, an inclusive economy, is one in which all, not merely a few, benefit from a reasonably sustainable approach to living standards, economically but also culturally. Inclusive economies are theoretically sustainable, adding value through economic activity rather than taking it out; exclusive economies extract value to enrich the few, at the expense of the many. As market forces do not guarantee inclusive economies, these theorists propose rethinking our integrated social systems—economic, political, and cultural—so as to guarantee an equitable distribution of growth, productivity, and sustainability to all participants, worldwide. The goal is an integrated global social reality that prioritizes humanity over profit.

People are more important than things, and it is good to put humanity first. But which understanding of "humanity"? *Homo sapiens? Homo faber*? *Homo economicus*? *Homo viator*? Every economic or social model incorporates certain assumptions; if we change the assumptions, we can change the direction in which a model will tell us to go (Rodrik 2015, 25–29). Here, the assumption is anthropological, which means that, downstream, it will also be ethical. So we naturally ask, "What does it mean to be human, and what should we humans do to live up to that?"

In the context of this symposium on the notion of *homo curator*, I therefore address one particular understanding, based in the Catholic intellectual tradition, of ethical and anthropological foundations of the formation of social and economic attitudes in the family, and how these might be related to the understanding of humanity at the foundation of participation in an inclusive economy. What is at stake is how the primordial subjectivity of the human person, formed in the family, may be related to the formation of social and economic attitudes in the wider society. Building on the position, expressed in the Vatican II document *Gaudium et Spes*, that "the family is a kind of school of a deeper humanity" (52), I will investigate the development of the notion of "humanity" in the thought of Karol Wojtyła (the future Pope John Paul II)[1] to situate the question of economic inclusion in a context of human ecology. I will treat the question of human consumption within this perspective, as related not only to the human vocation to participate in community, but also to the consequences for persons of consumerist attitudes.

[1] I will refer to John Paul II as "Wojtyła," except when referring explicitly to his papal teachings.

11.2 Participation in the Humanity of Others

Wojtyła collaborated, as Archbishop of Krakow, on the 1965 Vatican II document *Gaudium et Spes*. By then, he had developed a philosophy of marriage and the family expressed in *Love and Responsibility* (1986). *Gaudium et Spes* used the term *communio* to describe human community as both a fact and a project. The project is human to the extent that it is divine; God has created human persons to live first in union with him, and then with each other. "Community," in light of its primary theological analogue, *communio personarum*, reflects a likeness to the Trinity in human relationships centered on the truth about the good of persons; this likeness founds these relationships to the extent that they form the personal "I" (*Gaudium et Spes* 24).

Wojtyła sees the Trinity as the Source and pattern of every *communio personarum*. In the Trinity, there is a triple relation of existence (for, from, and in union with Someone), expressed in divine love, fatherly, filial, and unitive, that is reflected in human love (Szczepaniec 1995, 83–94). Józef Tischner has suggested that Wojtyła's play *Radiation of Fatherhood*, which formulates this idea, depicts God, 'not [as] an Absolute Solitude but [as] an Absolute Interaction" (Quoted in Weigel 1999, 912, note 88; von Balthasar 1989, 141–43; Wojtyła 1999, 279ff.). The mutual gift of human spouses open to life and love imitates the reciprocal love of two absolutely perfect divine Persons, which necessarily seeks the inclusion of a third to share Their Love (Richard of St. Victor and Angelici 2012, XI, 126). Thus Wojtyła reports that, theologically, the likeness of humans to God consists not only in our spiritual nature, but also in our capacity to enter into a *communio personarum* (1974b, 350; Szczepaniec 1995 83–94), and that we speak most properly of a *communitas* when that *communio* includes more than two persons (1978, 14).

Etymologically, *communio* (*communis*, from *cum munus*) connotes the union of persons around a public common good, task, or end, involving a dimension of trust ("Communis" 1982). Theologically, *communio* denotes the bond that forms a community, and the fact of the community formed by the bond (Wojtyła 1984, 119), implying mutual confirmation and strengthening of exclusively human relationships (Wojtyła 1974b, 353; cf. 1986, 31). Ecclesiologically, *communio* is more than community or society (*communitas*), more than mere togetherness, in part on account of the human vocation to self-gift, and in part because the teleology of a human community of persons is toward what Wojtyła calls "union in truth and love." *Communio* denotes a relation proper only to persons, who mutually bestow (and accept) the good, to (and from) one another (Wojtyła 1973, 16; cf. John Paul II 1981, 21, 49, 51, 59, 60, 61, 65).[2]

In Wojtyła's view, therefore, *communio* refers to the inter-personal sharing of values, as well as the interior potential of participation that belongs to persons as such (Boniecki 2000, 374). *Communio* signifies two persons maturing through parallel *I-Other* relations into an *I-Thou*, and eventually a *We*; *communitas* refers

[2] Unless otherwise specified, all translations herein are my own.

to a *We* of more than two persons (Wojtyła 1978, 14). In *communio* the individual "not only preserves his own nature but realizes himself definitively" (Wojtyła 1980, 120).

The commandment to love one's neighbor as oneself follows directly from the commandment to love God above all things, revealing an unsuspected foundation: something godlike in man that makes human community possible. *Gaudium et Spes* affirms that Jesus "implied a certain likeness" between the union of the divine Trinity, and human community "in truth and charity," so that "man, who is the only creature on earth which God willed for itself, cannot fully find himself except through a sincere gift of himself" (*Gaudium et Spes* 24, §3; cf. 12, 18, 19, 21). Wojtyła (1974a, 166) will later describe this likeness, leading to a mutual gift of self between God and man, and between man and man, as evidence of a "law of the gift" inscribed by the Creator in human nature.

Communio is a union formed in truth and charity, and identified with an act of pure self-gift—a mutual bestowal of goodness between or among persons (Wojtyła 1980, 61). The gift of self implies not only loving, but also allowing oneself to be loved; through it, the good of one becomes the good of all, "precisely because that good has become a gift" (Wojtyła 1980, 136). Thus "*communio* signifies a stable immanent dynamism of the community, ... from multiplicity and complexity towards unity ..." while also upholding that same complexity and multiplicity in the unity of the community (Wojtyła 1980, 140; cf. 1978, 14; John Paul II 1981, 21, 49, 51, 59, 60, 61, 65; Boniecki 2000, 374). *Communio* is at the center of human dignity, and of what it means to be human.

The gift of self, culmination of every authentic human act (cf. Wojtyła 1994, 151–53, 431), is most clearly seen in marriage and the family (Wojtyła 1975b, 59–76). (Wojtyła's analogous application of *communio* to marriage and the family, reflecting the Trinity as primary analogue, recalls a similar analogy by Augustine).[3] Accordingly, *Gaudium et Spes* calls the family "a kind of school of a deeper humanity".[4] The Latin *uberior* ("Uber" 2020: "deeper") connotes that, in the family, one learns to live a richer, "more fruitful," and "more productive" humanity.

It is from this notion of humanity that Wojtyła develops his theory of social participation; in his 1981 apostolic exhortation *Familiaris Consortio*, John Paul specified how the gift principle from *Gaudium et Spes* is to be applied: by building the communion of persons in the family, through service, sharing, and caring for those who are less able to care for themselves (1981, 21). In his 1994 *Letter to Families*, he clarified that "the life of nations, of states, and of international organizations 'passes' through the family ..." John Paul argued that the idea, founded in Enlightenment premises, that "a man is 'more' human if he is 'only' human" has contributed to the potential alienation of each man from everything human, and so has a negative effect on the family that humans are naturally called to resist.

[3] Augustine, *De Trinitate* 8, 10, 14.

[4] "Familia schola quaedam uberioris humanitatis est." (*Gaudium et Spes* 52; cf. 47–52).

> The family is in many ways the first school of how to be human. Be human! This is the imperative passed on in the family—human as the son or daughter of one's country, a citizen of the State, and, we would say today, a citizen of the world. ...

John Paul therefore presents the family as the realistic foundation of a civilization of justice and love (1994, 1, 12, 16–19).

Shortly thereafter, John Paul addressed young people in Rome, to mark the opening of the United Nations International Youth Year (IYY) dedicated to the theme Participation–Development–Peace:

> The family, in fact, is not only a community: it is a *communio personarum*. That means that each one of the members of the family *participates in the 'humanity'* of the others ... Great, therefore, is the importance of the family as a *school of participation!* And thus it is a great loss when this school of participation is lacking, when the family is destroyed (1985).

In the same discourse, John Paul clarified that, more than the simple social fact of being together with others, participation means to be fully oneself through being, dwelling and acting[5] together with others in relation to a common good and common values, and that these come into clearer focus in the family. Participation is learned first in the family, but also in a community, in a nation, and in the Church in its natural and supernatural dimensions. One participates in true and authentic development through a just balance between "being" and "having," which leads to progress in establishing a civilization of justice and love. Authentic participation is the key to peace, more than a mere absence of war, founded in fraternal charity (1989, 16–17).

As a communion of persons, the family is the first, and irreplaceable school of participation, teaching the love of God and a *consequent* love of neighbor. The family is the place in which one learns to speak one's first words, to experience one's first love, and to experience that humans are not reducible to things, animals, or numbers, but are persons, with a vocation to love and be loved that begins in a relationship with God, who is infinitely faithful and infinitely selfless (John Paul II 1985).

11.3 The Primordial Subjectivity of the Family

In *Man and the Family*, Rocco Buttiglione[6] emphasized the example that children receive in the context of the family: when the atmosphere in a family centers on obligation and debt, rather than on love and gift, children embark on a mistaken

[5] Wojtyła uses the formula *istnieć, bytować, działać* (1976, 8), recalling the three perfections (esse, *vivere, intelligere*—(Aquinas, *In III Sent.*; cf. Aquinas, *In III Sent.*, procemium) cited by Epimenides (Fragment from Cretica, c. 600 BC) and St. Paul (Acts 17:28) as evidence of a divine context for human action.

[6] The Hon. Rocco Buttiglione (1948–), Italian politician, professor of political science, member of the Pontifical Academy of Social Sciences, and close friend and disciple of Wojtyła from about ten years before he became pope, is often reputed the leading living authority on Wojtyła's philosophy.

trajectory, one that closes off for them "the original way through which man arrives to the point of becoming conscious of himself and of the sense of his own existence." "Only the power of God," Buttiglione concluded, "can rescue" a child from such a mistaken path (1991, 14–15).

Buttiglione raises a question of primordial subjectivity. In psychology, this term refers to the kind of gradual self-actualization that one person (typically, an infant) experiences through a primary contact with another (typically, its parents), beginning even from the womb (cf. Norman 2001, 83–84; Trevarthen 1993, 121–73; Trevarthen 1979, 321–47; Verny and Kelly 1981). Phenomenologically, the term is used in distinction from "transcendental" subjectivity (Husserl 1997, 106–07). Wojtyła's usage, neither completely foreign nor simply reducible to either approach, occurs in his treatment of the family, especially in his papal texts where it refers to human parenthood as a participation in God's creative act, and to the natural family as a school that forms persons to be able to participate in the humanity of others (cf. John Paul II 1994, 6).

Primordial subjectivity is formed, for Wojtyła, in reference to God, the Creator, or "Source," of all that exists. Analogously, John Paul recognizes something equally unique and essential in the family, implying a proper subjectivity, with its own moral imperative (1981, 17). To speak of the family as having its own subjectivity is to treat the family as a community, a "We",[7] founded in the I-Thou of husband and wife, in relation to the Source (Wojtyła 1965, 10; cf. 1974b, 358–61; 1975a, 17–31). To understand the primordial subjectivity of the family as a human *communio personarum*, then, it is appropriate to examine the bond formed between husband and wife in relation to the Source. In order to do that, however, we will first need to address Wojtyła's intricate treatment of the notion of humanity.

11.4 Exegesis of Wojtyła's Notion of "Humanity"

For Wojtyła, "humanity" is both metaphysical (human nature), and axiological (human dignity), reflecting his peculiar philosophical method (which he once described (2002, 281) as placing his work "on the frontier of the perennial philosophy and modern phenomenology"), as well as his theological reflections (1979a, 214–17) on human dignity in *Gaudium et Spes*. He links human dignity (*dignitas*) with moral fulfillment (*bonum honestum*), citing the similarity of the terms in Polish (*godność–godziwość*), and he favors a *sui generis* approach to moral value that reconciles teleology and normativity in the metaphysical transcendence of *esse* (*verum ut bonum*) (1991, 48–49). He intends this approach to be accessible to philosophers to whom pre-Enlightenment strictures and structures may appear foreign and unjustified; it also responds to what Alasdair MacIntyre (1984, 54–55) has represented as a break with the tradition among post-Enlightenment moral philosophers who

[7] Husserl (1997, 107).

"eliminate any notion of man-as-he-could-be-if-he-realized-his-*telos*," leaving "behind a moral scheme composed of two remaining elements whose relationship becomes quite unclear": "on the one hand a certain content for morality: a set of injunctions deprived of their teleological context ... on the other hand a certain view of untutored-human-nature-as-it-is." If morality has its origins in a project "to correct, improve and educate that human nature," these philosophers set off on a path that would end in a discrepancy between their conception of human nature, and the proposal of moral rules at odds with that conception.

For Wojtyła, *moralitas* follows the human aspiration to strive toward the *bonum honestum*, and therefore toward *dignitas*, so that "the norm of morality serves, precisely, the closer determination and the actualization of the dignity of the person." When moral thinking is deprived of its teleological relationship to being (*esse*) and truth (*verum*), it loses its normative power, slips into arbitrariness, and eventually collapses into a descriptive pursuit of the acceptable (1991, 48–49).

Human dignity may be understood, then, in terms of the natural destiny, or self-teleology, of the human person, which is not reducible to *homo faber* (man's efficient causality in relation to nature), or even to *homo sapiens* (if understood merely functionally). The identity of *homo*, for Wojtyła, is a spiritual identity; the finality of a human being is "spiritual to the core." Human dignity is not a *fait accompli*, or "a fact well-elaborated by people, in both the collective, as well as the individual, sense," but "a calling and a postulate" (1979a, 216). It is most experienced in the context of an I-Thou relation to God, especially in the act of prayer,[8] which John Paul observes is properly learned in the family (1981, 39, 55, 59–60).

On these grounds, Wojtyła warns that any tendency "for quantity to take precedence over quality," regarding persons must be revalued "according to the principle: the person, and the dignity of the person" (1979a, 216). One should never be "defined by quantity." Although it is common today to think in terms of "nations, continents, humanity, expressing all this in figures—so many thousands, so many millions, so many billions," doing so actually "disguises the essence of things ..." One must turn from the "numerical aspect to the person, to that concrete, human self, one and irreplaceable, which is found in a unique relationship with God. There is no other relationship which can define the person—this human *I*—in its unique and irreplaceable position as this relationship, this 'meeting point' with God, does. Person-God, God-person." Wojtyła concludes, "... when we pray, the God-person, person-God relationship manifests itself as the most fundamental and complete reality" (1984, 88). Wojtyła therefore defines human dignity, discovered in all human acts, but most clearly in the human act of prayer, as "the transcendent value of the person" (1976, 29).

Human dignity is, indeed, something we also recognize in verifying our ability to control and manipulate the natural order. We experience that we are conscious, free, autonomous subjects vis-a-vis a natural world that is none of these. In Wojtyła's

[8] "Prayer can be said to be a constitutive element of human existence in the world. Human existence is 'being directed toward God'" (Wojtyła 1979b, 135).

notion of conscience, Tadeusz Styczeń reports, we also come to know ourselves as "an autonomous subject, i.e., a center of actions that are conscious and free, and, at the same time, bound through truth'" (1982; Hilla 1991, 141; cf. Wojtyła 1994, 198–99). Wojtyła's emphasis on self-possession and autonomy in human action is balanced by an awareness that human dignity comes primarily from man's relation to God (Buttiglione et al. 1984, 25–37; cf. 113–17). For Wojtyła, human autonomy is a relative autonomy, relative to truth: "the tension that exists between the objective order of norms and the inner freedom of the subject-person is discharged by truth, by the conviction of the truthfulness of the good" (1994, 208–9).

In all, Wojtyła affirms a Christian tradition that human dignity is rooted in man's creation as *imago Dei* (Genesis 1:27), on the grounds of which Augustine described humans as *capax Dei* (De Trinitate 14, 2, 4; 14, 8, 11; cf. Bonaventure, *In I Sent.* dist. 3, part 2, art. 1, q. 2). Thomas Aquinas refers in this context to the human potential not only to act, but to act freely, which elevates humans above creation, making it possible for humans to know and love God (*ST* I-II, prologue).

11.5 Participation in the Humanity of Others

Following the principle of human dignity all the way to its roots, for Wojtyła, implies an Augustinian journey into the "inner man," *homo interior*, which Buttiglione and Styczeń, Wojtyła's two closest followers, have each separately characterized as a kind of "hidden man," or *homo absconditus*.[9] This is the inner space into which one enters to find oneself in the presence of God. It is the realm of conscience.

In his poem "Thought: Strange Space," Wojtyła characterizes this realm as containing a specific kind of weight, the gravity of the human spirit as ordered to God, its last end.[10] This is the space in which one also thinks things "through to the end," seeking "the fundamental reasons why," and a "foothold in knowledge of … the Creator" (1979b, 9–10; 1998, 172–73; Boniecki 2000, 169). It is a space in which the *itinerarium mentis ad Deum* of reason meets the *itinerarium mentis in Deum* of faith. It is the space of the human vocation, and of each human's own journey. Echoing Marcel's *homo viator* (1945), Wojtyła calls it "*itinerarium hominis*," the way of discovering an absolute foundation for one's humanity in a world of contingent things (1979b, 13–14). It is the deepest experience of being a person, the root of the human potential to participate in a community (cf. Galarowicz 1994, 275–77).

[9] Presenting at the same conference, Buttiglione compared Wojtyła's "hidden man," to the "hidden God" of Pascal, while Styczeń compared Wojtyła's *homo absconditus* to the *Deus absconditus* of Isaiah 45:15 (Buttiglione et al. 1984, 19, 129–34).

[10] "Myśl jest przestrzenią dziwną" (Thought: Strange Space) (Wojtyła 1998, 78–88, esp. 86–87).

Wojtyła defines "participation" in two senses: first, as a property of human persons that enables us to act together with others in a way that respects them as persons, and second, as a capacity to recognize the same property in the humanity of others. Of the two Polish terms that we translate as "humanity," Wojtyła is using *człowieczeństwo* (the concrete sense, "human-ness" or "man-ness"), not *ludzkość* (the more common, universal sense of "people-ness"). In both senses, participation is founded in humanity not as an abstraction, in which the property of being human is first induced, then applied deductively to each person, but as a value, concretely grounded, and recognized in conscience (1976, 20–21).

Conscience, then, is the *locus*, for Wojtyła, of a fundamental experience of personhood. In conscience, one is an eyewitness to oneself and one's own acts (cf. 1984, 90), rediscovering how truth, freedom, spirituality, and transcendence are all related in human action, conditioning one's fulfillment as a person. Here, the experience of one's own humanity in relation to God (actualizing the first sense of participation) founds one's participation in the humanity of others (second sense of participation), making it possible to see each "other" as a "neighbor" (1976, 20–21).

We cannot see God—although we perceive his presence interiorly, through intellect and will—but we can see our neighbor (cf. 1 Peter 1:8; 1 John 4:20). The basis of participation is not an action or series of actions, but the potential that is humanity. We recognize the presence of a neighbor, experiencing the humanity of the other through a kind of conscious approximation, starting with the recognition that the one in front of me is irreducible to the status of a thing (Wojtyła 1978, 11). As the potential to participate inheres in us to the extent that we are human, so human dignity inheres in every human being, regardless of age, defect, infirmity, or ability to perform social or ethical acts.

11.6 Alienation: Denials of Participation

For Wojtyła, participation denied takes two fundamental forms: individualism, and anti-individualism (including "objective totalism"). Participation leads to a mutual recognition of the good of oneself and another (including by implication the common good) (1986, 30 ff.); its denial leads to the subordination of one of these goods to the other (1994, 312–13; cf. 1979a, 439–40).

Both positions fail to recognize how far the good of the person and that of the community, properly understood and authentically affirmed, may be mutually interdependent. Each denies participation: individualism denies its first meaning (on which the second depends), valuing the good of the individual over the common good; objective totalism proposes the reverse, relocating primordial subjectivity from the family to the state, so that an ersatz 'common good' might prevail at the expense of the pursuit of individual goods.

In his lectures on Catholic Social Ethics (1958, 2018) delivered in Kraków starting in 1953,[11] Wojtyła ascribed the roots of individualism to the Enlightenment, while opposing Nazism, Fascism and other contemporary forms of totalism.

Josef Pieper (1989, 65–66) has similarly argued that totalitarian regimes "claim the right to define in complete detail the specifics of the *bonum commune*." For Wojtyła, both errors, individualism, and objective totalism, are rooted in "an identical way of thinking about man" (1994, 314–15; cf. 312–15), for they follow on one's understanding of humanity.

One foil for Wojtyła's opposition to totalism was the Austrian Othmar Spann (1878–1950), whose dubious interpretation of Aristotle and Aquinas placed "primordial subjectivity" in a social whole to which humans would exist in a partial and potential relation. Wojtyła used Spann's arguments as an occasion to describe an ideal relationship between the individual and the state, while refuting Spann's misuse of Aristotle, and his misinterpretation of Aquinas (*ST* II-II, 64, 5; II-II, 65, 1) on the ordering of parts to wholes. Wojtyła cited Aquinas—"Man is not ordained to the political community according to all that he is and according to all that he has … . But all that which man is, and which he is able to do, and has, is ordained to God"—(Aquinas, *ST* I-II, 21, 4, ad 3. cf. Wojtyła 1958, 63–81, esp. 72–75)[12] in a way that calls to mind a similar position of Jacques Maritain from 1946: "The adage of the superiority of the common good is understood in its true sense only in the measure that the common good itself implies a reference to the human person, whose ultimate good is God himself. The common good is always a *human* good" (Maritain 1966, 29–30; cf. Pius XI 1937, 30).

The literature is divided on whether and to what extent Wojtyła's early lectures on social ethics may accurately reflect his thought, then or later. The controversy is fueled by speculation that positions taken in the lectures—regarding capitalism, Marxism, and the possibility that both might be forms of totalism (Beyer 2020, 1127–30, 1132; cf. John Paul II 1991, 42)—might shed light on John Paul's future positions. Complicating the question, it is difficult to say how much of the lecture material is originally Wojtyła's, or derivative of his mentor Jan Piwowarczyk from whom he took over the course on short notice. Although situating Wojtyła, and by implication, John Paul II, on a continuum between communism and capitalism would be interesting, it will be more useful to parse his approach to participation and alienation, which is more fundamental (cf. Beyer 2020). Here, it may suffice to note that John Paul II (1994, 312–13) indicts both individualism and objective totalism for the same essential error, in a way consistent with the earlier lectures (1958, 1998).

[11] Wojtyła's lectures (1958, 2018) were at least partially derived from the lectures of Wojtyła's mentor Jan Piwowarczyk (1960, 1963). The extent of Wojtyła's sole authorship of this early, derivative work is uncertain; one may safely cite it to confirm Wojtyła's positions elsewhere, but not to challenge them. Beyer, the editor, suggests (2020) that the 2018 text may be hermeneutic for the later thought of Wojtyła and John Paul II, but his sources don't support a definitive conclusion. No other scholar could publish such a text, Wojtyła himself declined to publish it, and its attribution must be carefully weighed throughout.

[12] Wojtyła (1958) incorrectly lists the citation as I-II, 24, 4.

Historically, Wojtyła's interest in participation, alienation, and the value of humanity grew out of his experiences under two totalitarian systems. Born in 1920, as Poland recovered its existence and its freedom after a century and a half of partition (attributable in part to an overused parliamentary veto), Wojtyła knew the price of freedom, and the ease with which it could be lost if abused.

Hannah Arendt (1973, 1975) reports that totalitarian systems exchange the common good for the good of the state, so that persons exist for the state instead of for God and each other. Adolf Hitler (1999, 298) described this exchange as the subordination of "the interests of the ego to the conservation of the community." Totalitarian systems falsify the conscience, where humans discover their origin and end in God, leaving them rootless and superfluous apart from the state. The freedom and dignity of the person then become functional in service of the whole. The result is a strange mix of conformity to the whole and neglect of the neighbor[13] held together by a utopian ideology, and immune to the data of experience. Supplying the form of the social whole, the ideology relieves its devotees of a responsibility to seek the truth about the common good. Thus dehumanized, the society loses its sense of solidarity, and falls completely under state control. Solitude, the essential condition for dialogue, is the antidote to the sense of rootlessness, superfluousness, and loneliness that make a society vulnerable to the appeal of a totalitarian ideology. An accurate understanding of human dignity is essential to participation in a common good.

11.7 A Non-Exchangeable Gift of Self

Human dignity, for Wojtyła, naturally seeks expression in a community, founded around a common good, in relation to which participants make a mutual "gift of self." He pictures Adam, the first man, spontaneously affirming creation as a gift to which the only adequate response is give himself away to God and others. Wojtyła, who counseled married couples as a young priest, saw the gift of self most clearly expressed in conjugal life, as well as in every authentic ethical act. Morally good human actions present a personal structure of self-determination, self-integration, self-possession, self-dominion, and self-gift, and potentiate one for further morally good actions and further self-gift (1994, 151–53). Giving oneself away, one opens a way to social communion. Here Wojtyła follows St. John of the Cross, from whom he assimilates (1981, 52) a paradigm of *communion – participation – transformation*. Participating in a common good, we transform ourselves and our communities.

Moral participation in a community resists quantification. The content of the gift of self is not something that can be measured, for it is the moral potential of a

---

[13] Similarly, Wojtyła (1994, 323–26) lists conformism (*konformizm*) and ducking responsibility (*unik*) as inauthentic attitudes that are opposed to participation, and inimical to dialogue.

person, disclosed in conscience, which St. Augustine called *pondus meum* (Confessions, 13, 9, 10), and Wojtyła describes as a "proper weight" of the person, a "nonexchangeable" core. In self-gift, one chooses being over having, dedicating one's own human potential to another's moral fulfillment, and confirming one's moral autonomy relative to God.

In his poetic and dramatic works, Wojtyła describes God as the Source of all things; in his treatment of conscience, the "given" discloses a transcendent Giver. One perceives the gift quality of both persons and things in moral action. Wojtyła identifies the conscience, where Giver and gift appear together, and truth and goodness appear as non-negotiable, as synonymous with the experience of personhood (1984, 90).

There are two kinds of actions in which the values of truth and goodness especially draw moral agents to affirm the presence of an Absolute Person or Source: religious acts, in the presence of an Absolute *Thou*, and conjugal acts, in the presence of a creative Source. In each, one perceives the duty of a just response, whether orienting one's life religiously to God, or welcoming God's creative action at the foundation of a family. These actions are able to give rise to families and communities that create person-centered cultures in a context of divine transcendence. In them, Wojtyła (1974a, 166) sees evidence of a "law of the gift, written in the being of the person." The awareness that the whole of reality is a gift from the Source makes persons aware of a call to respond in kind. In this response, religion and morality are "joined by a very profound bond" (1969, 247).

The gift of self takes place in the context of participation. In participation, one affirms the truth about the good that one seeks, while also affirming a potential for that good in the other persons with whom one acts together. Morally good actions culminate in a gift of self to God, in the affirmation of the truth about the good; actions together with others culminate in a gift of self to God and others when one places one's moral potential at the service of the moral fulfillment of others. Each form of the gift affirms human dignity as rooted in a moral and existential relation to the Source.

In this sense, the gift of self recalls Aquinas's *amor amicitiae*, which is compatible with a rightly-ordered *amor concupiscentiae*. Aristotle holds, "to love is to will the good for someone" (Rhetoric II, 4, 1380b 35); Aquinas adds, "one loves the good that is willed for the other with love of concupiscence, and that for which the good is willed with a love of friendship" (*ST* I-II, 26, 4, corpus). Both loves, the love of persons and the love of things, are resolved in the love of God, the last end of all, similar to the way that Wojtyła resolves the Kantian problem of autonomy, so that to give oneself away becomes a truly autonomous act, affirming a common *bonum honestum*, yet always open to the social or economic affirmation of the merely useful or pleasant.

Even when there is an exchange of goods, then, something non-exchangeable is expressed. What is affirmed in the gift of self is not reducible to quantity, or even to reciprocity; it is the irreducible value of persons, their dignity, the affirmation of which makes *communio* possible. John the Evangelist represents Jesus's self-consciousness at the Last Supper in a kind of dignity formula: aware that He "had come from God and was returning to God," He got up, dressed as a slave and proceeded to wash the feet of His disciples (John 13:3). The awareness of God as our origin and end is a recognition of the essential dignity that totalitarian regimes seek to erase by rendering humans as rootless and superfluous as things that acquire their purpose from the way that they are used. As long as persons are rooted and destined in God, then the worth of a person is not comparable to that of anything finite. If the value of a person can never be fixed, it can never be formulated in terms of exchange. The heart of Wojtyła's human ecology is the recognition that the value of a person is equal only to the love of God, which means that it is infinite, and non-exchangeable.

11.8 The Family and the Mutual Bestowal of Humanity

At the foundation of the life-giving and love-giving of a marriage and family, Wojtyła describes a "mutual bestowal of humanity"—a gift of self—that leads through fertile sexual relations to parenthood (1975a, 17). A marriage comes to be through the spouses' mutual recognition and acceptance of responsibility for each other in a gift of self, from which children may learn to love as a family (1986, 33, cf. 109–12). Humanity is a potential that is ordered to the moral fulfillment of knowing and loving God. Bestowing one's humanity in a gift of self means accepting responsibility for another in relation to God, committing one's own potential so that the other might know and love God. Conjugal intercourse rises to this level when spouses consent not just to a sexual act, but to the possibility of becoming parents through each other's fertility, recognizing the presence of the Creator and accepting responsibility for a new person created by Him. Conjugal intercourse builds the *communio* when spouses allow the humanity of a new person that may exist to be the root and fruit of their own participation in each other's humanity (1974b, 358–60).

Wojtyła affirms that spouses who mutually bestow their humanity gravitate together to God. Their unconditional acceptance of each other's fertility allows them to participate, through the creativity of God, in the creation of a new person. Becoming *participes Creatoris* (1986, 204, 219ff.) in the humanity of a new person, they irrevocably weigh together, so that without each other, they are weightless, morally adrift (1999, 216–17; 226–27). Their *communio* is a moral system—the man's fatherhood takes place through the woman's motherhood, and vice-versa— that depends on a fully conscious acceptance of responsibility. Through their shared flesh, the one flesh of the child unites them, but not only biologically. In fact, it is more correct to say that the spouses assist *at*, rather than *in*, the divine act of creation. Theirs is a fully personalistic, spiritual procreation, accepting responsibility for educating a new human being in truth and goodness. Such a marriage so unites the spouses that it is no longer proper to speak of authentic love directed outside of the marriage that is not rooted in the marriage itself (1975a, 18).

The integrity of that moral system depends, for Wojtyła, on the mutual acceptance of parenthood. "The meaning of the marital *communio personarum* and everything of which it consists, especially marital intercourse, is the child," and the family that grows as children enter the *communio* "to confirm, strengthen, and intensify [it]." (1975a, 21; cf. 48). Parents give themselves to each other through the child—not a potential person, but a real person with the full potential of its own humanity—who widens the circle of mutual bestowal of love that is the family, making it even more true and authentic (1975a, 21–22). More than a statistic, the birth of a child discloses the uniqueness of each person in the family (1974b, 348), and of the family itself as a *communio* "united around the reality of giving birth" (1975a, 28).

Spiritual procreation is the subject of *Radiation of Fatherhood*, in which Wojtyła follows Plato (Symposium 206e) in affirming *homo particeps Creatoris* above *homo faber*: "one must choose to give birth, even more than to create" (1999, 265). This radiation consists in freely accepting responsibility for another's moral fulfillment as a way to fulfill oneself in relation to God as Father and Source (1999, 271). To accept responsibility for another human being in a fatherly or motherly way is to radiate the creative presence of God for another human being; this is only possible when one is first willing to become a child in relation to that same creative presence (1999, 263). In Wojtyła's formulation, "one must step into the radiation of fatherhood; only therein does it all become the full reality" (1999, 265).

Wojtyła develops the notion of spiritual paternity and the radiation of fatherhood by reference to the experience of *Adam*, the first human, called to respond to the Giver of the gift of creation, rather than approaching creation as a set of givens.[14] In *Radiation of Fatherhood*, the protagonist "Adam" resolves his own frailty in a decision to depend on the power of God, step into the radiation of fatherhood, and accept responsibility for another (1999, 260–61, 274–77, 1986, 53).

Not all persons can reproduce biologically, Wojtyła avers, but all can procreate spiritually, educating others, and sharing with them the experience of humanity in relation to creation and Creator (1986, 232–33). Spiritual procreation thus appears as the primary human analogue for all parenthood. Parents, especially, are called to procreate spiritually within the family, and they are better prepared for it to the extent that they themselves have matured as persons, developing their own potential for self-determination, self-possession, self-dominion and self-gift. (cf. 1994, 151–53; 302 n. 73; 421–32).

For Wojtyła, humans participate biologically (1986, 53) and morally (1986, 53–56) in both divine creation and conservation. Morally, spiritual procreation extends beyond the conjugal act to a commitment to educate persons not only to function well in life, but to live the truth about the good. Education thus becomes a matter of forming good consciences, which Wojtyła identifies as integral to the establishment of any authentic community (1986, 32–3; John Paul II 2002). Pindar (476 BCE) advised, "learn and become who you are." Romano Guardini (1994,

[14] Urbankowski (1983) writes that, at the level of culture, "the proper seat of mankind," man appears not as "an artificial *homo economicus*, but as *Adam* who gives meaning even to things he has not created, whereby he creates them for the second time.

87–88) described education according to the *form*ation (Bildung) of a person according to an inward law of *form* (Bild), so that one becomes (actually) who one already is (in one's humanity). Wojtyła describes the experience of moral value as a kind of self-education leading to the self-expression of a person:

> In a moral value the very person expresses himself; that which he is will encounter that which *hic et nunc* he ought to be.... The moral value anticipated by the intellect and taken over by the wanting (the will) of the person, happens to be, in each act, excavated, as it were, from the dynamics of the being of this person, from the relation of who he is to whom he should be becoming (1986, 291).

Education is thus more a matter of habituating a person to the truth about the good, fulfilling the person's nature or form, than a transfer of information aimed at controlling one's environment.

Plato (Republic 508e) describes education as a habituation to perceive the Form of the Good. Aristotle adds that education means learning to delight in or to disdain what one ought to delight in or to disdain (Nicomachean Ethics II, 3, 1104b11; cf. Plato Laws 653aff.; Republic 401e–402a). For Wojtyła, both perspectives are present in the educing of a personalistic structure of human action that culminates in a gift of self. Educating each other in love, parents learn together that it is not reducible to affectivity, closed in on the self, or even confined to the I-Thou of marriage (1979a, 91); with their consciences formed to strive for the highest good (1986, 65–66), they are able to form their children, giving authentic witness to the meaning of the gift of self (1986, 65–66).

Wojtyła clarifies that the family is naturally a *communio*, and only then a society, as a complement and extension of the love of the spouses (1986, 65–66; cf. 55–56; 1974b, 352). It is "*irreplaceable* not only in its procreative function, but even more profoundly, in its *personalistic, communal function*... ." Any other social structure that seeks to protect humans from the danger of alienation "must be based on the family," especially when the other structure is "more powerful than the family." As part of the social order, every such structure must fulfill its personalistic function in order to be truly itself (1986, 65–66; 1975a, 22–23, citing *Gaudium et Spes* 24, 30–31).

John Paul (1981, 17) exhorts each family to live up to its unique dignity and responsibility: "family, become what you are." There is no other structure that can replace the family, for it is the primordial structure of the authentic *communio* without which a society cannot be itself. All *communio* begins with *communio* with the Source; as love of neighbor depends on love of God (1 John 4:20), one who refuses *communio* with the Source cannot enter into *communio* with others.

In *communio*, what is communicated is not merely some content, but one's very self. When one fails to transmit a given content, there is a breakdown in communication. When one merely transmits a content in a context that calls for a gift of self, there is a breakdown in *communio*, exposing participants to the danger of alienation. As a first step to considering alienation, it will be helpful to consider a model in which the family is considered less as a living structure of communion, and more as an abstract unit of analysis of production and distribution.

11.9 Familism: The Family as a Unit for Social Policy

Following Pius XII (1939, 61), who calls man and the family "the primary and essential cell of society," "anterior to the State," and "not to be considered from the narrow standpoint of national power," Wojtyła (1958, 140, 144) clarifies that the family, organized from within, "lives and acts" as the fundamental cell not only of the society but also of the nation (like the family, a natural society, in this case, one made up of families). A cell is not a unit, but a living member; the *communio* of society begins in the family. There can be no authentic society, certainly no nation, without the family, and the *communio* of each family is an expression of the dignity of each human person that participates in it.

Frank Knight describes the natural family as the minimal effective unit for socio-economic policy, more real than the individual for economic analysis. Knight prefers "familism" to "individualism" for describing the liberal social order, balancing the distribution of power and responsibility among families and other institutions, and between these and the political order, including the sovereign state. Families perdure across generations; individuals come and go; the family is more stable and permanent than the ephemeral individual, who participates economically thanks to family life. In the family, man learns the traditions and customs that found the social order. In it, we "become what we are," so that we can "live and move and have our being." making education a social policy issue. The family is a principle of the continuity of the wealth, culture, identity, and life of the society that depends on it (Knight 1939, 277, 283–4; 1941, 829; 1944a, 413; 1944b, 53–54; 1946, 87–88; 1948, 495–6; 1950a, 118, 120; 1950b, 520; 1951a, 8; 1951b, 223; 1953, 282, 285; 1957, 168; 1966, 166; 1967, 83; Knight and Merriam 1948, 89, 97).

As human mortality challenges this continuity, the family is the primary channel of inheritance, not only of property, but more importantly of economic, political, social, or psychological power. Accidental differences among the wealth, culture, politics, education, and social status of families lead to differential inheritance, inequality, insecurity, and injustice, leaving members of succeeding generations in unequal positions from which to engage in economic competition. Inequality then compounds itself, as inherited power is used to gain more power. Economic conflict may arise between present and future members of the same family, even through efforts to resolve inequality. What is just among parents may not be so among children (Knight 1929, 138; 1937, 108; 1939a, 277; 1942, 272; 1946, 87–88; 1950b, 520; 1951a, 20; 1966, 166, 174; Knight and Merriam 1948, 89, 91, 102).

A facile solution to inequality might be to abolish tangible inheritance; even if possible, solving differential property ownership would not solve inequality based on intangible, social inheritance, through which individuals not only come to be, but to possess economic attributes. It is through the family that the individual becomes what he is in all other respects, and that culture is perpetuated. Social continuity and progress, and cultural values, depend on preserving (and improving) the family and other institutions (Knight 1939b, 416–7; Knight and Merriam 1948, 102).

Abolishing property would not equalize power, consumption, or prestige. Abolishing capital accumulation would close a conduit for families in a free society to provide for succeeding generations. The urge to abolish in the name of equality may begin with property, but may extend to family inheritance, and even to the state substituting for the family, to the detriment of the family as an institution. Through the family, differential inheritance of property and culture perpetuates civilization. Socialism transfers functions from the family to an omnipotent state, and competition for power and goods from business to politics, at the expense of the family and the society (Knight 1936, 265; 1940b, 588; 1943, 137; 1948, 494, n. 20; 1950b, 520).

Efforts to eliminate inequality, insecurity and injustice can go too far, threatening continuity and progress in technology, knowledge, wisdom, and culture to the detriment of society. They can also err; some discussions confuse income distribution with wealth distribution, and all considerations of equality begin in reference to existing conditions that include prior inequality (Knight 1937, 105, 108; 1936, 265; 1938, 249; 1940a, 287–288; Knight and Merriam 1948, 104).

Inequality from differential inheritance can be mitigated through differential taxation and services like free education, but such measures eventually destroy incentive, and then freedom, civilization, or both. Radical redistribution requires absolute power, meaning complete loss of freedom. Prospective economic reform is therefore more of a moral and political question, because of its potential effect on the family (Knight 1939, 283–4; 1950b, 520; 1960, 32)

Seeking an ethical foundation for his analysis, Knight distinguishes freedom from power. Like Wojtyła, perennial philosophers including Aquinas (*In II Sent.* dist. 25, q. 1, prologus) have typically recognized three levels of freedom—freedom from constraint (including coercion or interference), freedom from necessity (culminating in freedom of choice), and freedom from error (ending in possession of the good). Knight restricts his notion to the first two, culminating in freedom of choice, often expressed as freedom of consumption. A person is therefore free if he does what he wants to do (whether or not he does what he ought to do), on the condition of free, mutual consent in all his transactions. Freedom means being able to make changes, and take chances, limited by concern for those not involved, or not consenting to a transaction, who might still be affected by it. Knight denies the third level: "Liberty need not lead to good results or to any results at all," resisting identifying freedom with "the good life" (a "'weasel' expression") or with conditions or institutions that might lead to it or make it possible (Knight 1939b, 422; 1940a, 265; 1940b, 586–9; Knight and Merriam 1948, 91).

Although he allows for strong political action that may uproot, overturn, or reconstruct "the very foundations of culture and personality," in its effort to foster effective freedom (i.e, freedom plus power, consistent with the general interest), Knight rejects authoritarianism (listing Catholicism alongside Nazism and Communism) as incompatible with freedom. Generally rejecting Christianity, in part for a perceived embrace of revolutionary Marxism, he counsels against seeing social questions through a moral lens, as if societal evil were the result of deliberate wrongdoing. Even the precept "do good and avoid evil" cedes, for him, to the question of how to define goodness and evil (Graham 1947, 940–2; Knight 1939b 403–422; 1940a, 289; 1940b, 586–9; 1950b, 522).

Knight further rejects the commandment to love on the grounds that it would have to extend beyond the family, as universal love, which seems to him unworkable. To love one's neighbor as oneself, which Knight conceives as an "emotional relation," is neither a "solvent for problems" nor a "reliable guide to conduct" (Knight 1939b, 403–4; 1940a, 287–288; Knight and Merriam 1948, 46, 103).

At first glance, Knight's position may seem parallel to Wojtyła's, in that both situate the family at the foundation of society. Knight's pro-family position is incompatible with Wojtyła's, however, even beyond the question of his polemic against Christianity. Wojtyła treats the family as a living cell; Knight, as an abstract unit for analysis. Wojtyła sees the family as participating essentially in a community; Knight, as accidentally contributing to shaping a social whole—it is not the reality of the family that is essential, so much as the functions that it fulfills. Knight rejects substitution of the family by the state, not as inherently false, so much as unworkable; his "subsidiarity" seems more pragmatic than principled. Knight's vision of the dignity, or worth, of the family is functional and actualistic; the family is to be valued, more than the individual, because of what it does for the system, and by that lens, for what it is. Wojtyła's vision is personalistic; the family derives its dignity from its members, not as individuals, but as *persons*, who are *capax Dei*, so that the dignity of the human person, and of the family, comes from God. The person and the family are "worth" the love of God that gives them origin. For Knight, the family is sometimes presented almost as the best "bad" solution to the problem of social continuity; if another institution could assume its role without fostering inequality, it might be preferable. For Wojtyła, marriage and family are the heart of a community founded on a gift of self learned therein, so that the community cannot be itself without affirming the good of the person and that of the family as one.

Knight's treatment of the family as a unit is consistent with an analytic vision that considers being through a lens of quantity, reflecting (while not entirely embracing) a tendency of liberal economic theory to take the individual (and the family as a unit) as merely "given" (Knight 1940, 286–87; 1941, 829). Wojtyła's preference for quality over quantity leads him to see the family, with Pius XII, as a living cell, participating in a wider community. Quantification is essential to abstract modeling of a problem, but it can mask the dignity of persons called to live it—not as a problem, but as a mystery. Not all humans respond effectively to this call. Some inequality stems from human and moral, rather than systemic, failure.

Wojtyła approaches the question of inequality in his analysis of what is exchangeable and non-exchangeable in the human person and the family (an exchangeable family reduces to the exchangeable attitudes behind it). The problem of inequality exists at the exchangeable level, but the failure to address it is a failure to live at the level of a deeper, non-exchangeable humanity. It is a failure of participation, and a problem of alienation.

11.10 The Exchangeable Man and the Problem of Consumption

One form that alienation can take is the reduction of a human to the value of a thing of exchange. Unlike Knight, Wojtyła (1979, 427) defines the human person as a "subject of morality," who happens to engage in economic activity, and not as an ephemeral subject of economy (the family unit), that happens to engage in actions of social or cultural significance. Defining the person economically may lead to its reduction to a commodity, an "exchangeable man." The primordial subjectivity of the family, in contrast, is naturally ordered to the formation of a "non-exchangeable man," a human whose value is discovered in relation first to God, then to the self, justifying the name "neighbor" (1976, 20–21). A human discovered only in relation to the self remains an object of alienation, a stranger (1994, 334, 1978; Tischner et al. 1994, 58–61; Buttiglione et al. 1984, 247–51). Economic systems founded on participation or alienation will tend to retain the orientation of their founding.

The distinction between an exchangeable man and a non-exchangeable man is central to Wojtyła's play *Our God's Brother* (1950a), retelling the life of St. Adam Chmielowski, who left an artistic lifestyle to serve the poor. Wojtyła (1999, 128) calls the play an attempt "to penetrate man," a reference to Adam, the human archetype, who, like every human since, has had to opt to live as exchangeable or non-exchangeable. The non-exchangeable man is one who has achieved enough moral integration, evidenced in the personal structure of self-determination, self-integration, self-possession, and self-dominion, to discern his dignity as a condition of self-gift.

In the play, Wojtyła argues that quantifying humans masks their transcendent value. When we don't see others as neighbors, we approach them as strangers. The exchangeable man, a form of *homo economicus*, appears as something finite and countable, like money. When we see ourselves in this way, we become fascinated with possessing and consuming things, as a way of increasing our perception of our own objective value.

In this way, consumption, and consumerism in general, can lead to an outcome comparable to that of totalitarianism: the separation of persons from an awareness of their transcendent dignity in light of their divine origin and end. The non-exchangeable man dwells in the inner life, what Augustine (De vera religione XXXIX, 72) called the "inner man," which Wojtyła (1986, 25) has described as centered on truth and goodness. The exchangeable man dwells in the outer life, his attention fixed on the changing and impermanent. Persons then become alienated from transcendence, incapable of participation, and reduced to interchangeable parts of a material or cultural whole.

Once we begin to define our worth by material standards, we may come to equate our dignity with what we desire or possess. We may mistakenly think of this equation as a condition of freedom, the exchange of labor or other human activity for finite rewards. We may begin to live according to a paradigm of obligation and debt, instead of one of love and gift.

11.11 Homo Curans—Homo Curator

John Hamilton (2013) has traced the etymology of "security" to a Roman anthropogonic fable describing man as *homo curans*: a curious mix of the earthly and heavenly principles humility (*homo*, from *humus*, earth) and solicitude (the goddess *Cura*). Cicero, who may have been first to coin *securitas* (from *se-cura*, without care), employed it to indicate a "care-free" path from anxiety to tranquility. Over the centuries, the notion of human care has also developed a positive meaning, related to the ability to make a gift of oneself in response to love.

Economic insecurity, manifested in a rising gap between rich and poor, ecological insecurity, manifested in projections of natural catastrophe, and political insecurity, manifested in reduced opportunities for social participation, all invite the attention of *homo curans*. Each of these questions is a matter of modeling, with a need for attention to the assumptions in play. Extrapolating from Hamilton's study, *homo curator*, the human guardian, will likely approach the *munus* of *communio* differently in each case, depending on the lived-experience of *homo curans*.

Homo curans becomes *homo curator* by deciding not only to care about, but to care for, a person or object. This distinction, between forms of positive and negative liberty (freedom "from" anxiety; freedom "for" persons), has a deeper foundation for John Paul II (1993, 64), for whom "freedom of conscience is never freedom 'from' the truth but always and only freedom 'in' the truth." That is, freedom is ordered to participation, or, in Wojtyła's formulation, "Freedom is for love."[15] The difference is a commitment to responsibility not unlike that experienced in the radiation of fatherhood. Hamilton (2013, ch. 5) offers Jesus as an example of *homo curator*, in that He sacrifices His life for His sheep. Wojtyła (1999, 265) describes the radiation of fatherhood as not something we do, so much as something we step into, giving ourselves away so that the love of God may be more palpable for persons in our care.

If we assume the responsibility of *cura* understanding it as anxiety and fear, our vocation as *homo curator* may be stunted by a solicitude about the future that is ultimately misguided. Caring for the earth is a natural law imperative, and a divine command; fearing for the earth is neither. If we assume the responsibility of *cura* understood as a form of love and self-donation, learned by participating in a community, then our vocation as *homo curator* may more closely resemble the living out of the radiation of fatherhood. This transformation is at the heart of what John Paul called the "ecological conversion":

> We must therefore encourage and support the "ecological conversion" which in recent decades has made humanity more sensitive to the catastrophe to which it has been heading. Man is no longer the Creator's "steward", but an autonomous despot, who is finally beginning to understand that he must stop at the edge of the abyss (2001, 4).

---

[15] Polish: "Wolność jest dla miłości" (Wojtyła 1986, 120). John Paul II used this phrase as the title of a chapter in a memoir (2005, 47–51).

If we seek to address problems like ecological collapse or economic exclusivity only out of a legitimate concern for the integrity of the given, we may restore a measure of control over the material world, but without recovering a necessary dimension of ourselves; we may unwittingly exchange one form of despotism for another. If we seek to address the same economic and ecological concerns out of a love of the Giver, we will carry out many of the same actions, but we will do so within a vision of hope, love, and gift, as stewards of creation, who seek to affirm it, rather than to control it.

Ecological conversion is only possible to the extent that one is aware of one's dignity as a person. Each human being's transcendence as *persona* appears most clearly within the family, and it risks being masked whenever there is a failure to acknowledge the priority of this primordial *communio*. Outside of the family, Wojtyła (1974b, 348) warns that the union of persons in *communio* may be misinterpreted as a quantitative unit of merely mathematical or statistical relevance.[16]

In the context of the radiation of fatherhood, ecological conversion follows the paradigm that Wojtyła (1981, 52) assimilated from St. John of the Cross: *communion – participation – transformation*. *Communio*, above all in the family, creates the conditions for a participation that transforms the way that we care, not only about, but for each other as neighbors—not strangers, and for creation as a gift—not a given. In this light, we may hope that a Ciceronian preoccupation with *securitas* may eventually yield to a creative *insecuritas*, in which we gradually learn to surrender all anxiety to the Giver so as to be free to care, and work together, as authentic stewards of the gift. "Perfect love casts out all fear." (1 John 4:18). On this foundation, John Paul (1978, 5) began his pontificate with the exhortation, "Be not afraid!"

11.12 The Great Renewal: An Invitation to Hope

In his 1990 World Day of Peace Message, John Paul II spoke of an impending ecological catastrophe coupled with "a new ecological awareness." To address the catastrophe and encourage the awareness, he endorsed coordinated action from biblical principles, appealing to the Genesis story of creation and the fall in the context of divine Redemption. (1989, 1–2).[17]

John Paul II (1989, 2–3) thus affirms: the assumptions for any model to address contemporary questions of social, political, cultural, or economic participation, as well as the ecological question and other difficulties, are ultimately anthropological;

[16] Wojtyła is not opposed to modeling, or statistical analysis, so much as to the reduction of the value of the person to some aspect of quantity.

[17] Years earlier, shortly before becoming Pope, Wojtyła (1979b, 23–24, cf. 20–21) had similarly exhorted Pope Paul VI to reflect on the stories of creation and the fall in the first three chapters of Genesis, so as to understand the situation of humans in a contemporary world influenced by Sartre and Marx.

the solutions will ultimately be ethical. The Genesis account relates the story of a primordial *communio* that chose alienation over participation, exchanging a human ecology of non-exchangeable harmony for one of exchangeable control. Only God can restore the primordial subjectivity of human civilization, destined for justice and love, by revealing "the deepest meaning of our humanity." The Great Renewal begins in participation, through which persons transform the culture, affirming it or challenging it according to the soundness of its anthropology (1995, 3, 6; cf. *Gaudium et Spes* 22).

For John Paul, the crisis is moral, a crisis of humanity; the dangers for ecology and economy are merely secondary effects. It stems from a "callous disregard for the hidden, yet perceivable requirements of the order and harmony which govern nature itself." It cannot be solved by better management of resources (1989, 5). It can be adequately addressed only by referring everything to the principles of humanity, and the transcendence of persons. Although the created world cannot damage itself, humans may gradually cease to live in harmony with their fellow creatures. To be willing to damage creation, however, one must first suffer damage oneself (1989, 7).

John Paul (1989, 7–10, cf. 16) lists a number of practical areas of concern; all depend on responsibility and fidelity to the human vocation in the face of what can even become contempt for humanity. He adds that "respect for life, and above all for the dignity of the human person, is the ultimate guiding norm for any sound economic, industrial or scientific progress." In this sense, the question becomes one of human ecology, the place of man in the order of creation. It is here that questions about consumption and the inclusive economy come into play. The universal destination of goods may counsel structural reforms to address the accumulation and squandering of resources by a few, while the many live in the misery of bare subsistence. Some international coordination of resource management may be necessary; the problem is not national, but human, and therefore global. John Paul therefore calls for "a new solidarity," within and among nations.

John Paul (1991, 36–38) evaluates consumerism within the ecological question as a moral problem requiring "simplicity, moderation, discipline, [and] a spirit of sacrifice," and calling for a non-political, non-ideological, forward-looking "education in ecological responsibility," founded in principles of authentic participation (1989, 13). "A true education in responsibility entails a genuine conversion in ways of thought and behaviour," and although all persons and organizations within society have a role to play, "the first educator, … is the family, where the child learns to respect his neighbour and to love nature." This respect and love are not utilitarian; they are founded in the value of persons and things not in relation to ourselves, but to God. Communion, participation, and transformation must begin in the natural family, as a matter of moral urgency, love and responsibility (1989, 14–15).

Ultimately, for John Paul, every ecological and social question is in some way connected to the question of human ecology, which conditions our potential to realize human dignity (1991, 38). Therefore, he observes:

> the first and fundamental structure for 'human ecology' is the family, in which man receives his first formative ideas about truth and goodness, and learns what it means to love and to be loved, and thus what it actually means to be a person. Here we mean the family founded on marriage, in which the mutual gift of self by husband and wife creates an environment in which children can be born and develop their potentialities, become aware of their dignity and prepare to face their unique and individual destiny (1991, 39).

Human ecology provides a context, for John Paul (1991), not only for ecological questions, but for social (economic, political, and cultural) questions as well. When a society becomes centered on the consumption of resources, the value of money and human commodification, it runs a greater risk of developing an unworkable economy, but the problems and solutions are anthropological and ethical. When humans are seen more as producers or consumers, than as moral subjects who produce and consume in order to realize a human vocation, "then economic freedom loses its necessary relationship to the human person and ends up by alienating and oppressing him" (1991, 39).

The logic of the economy cannot capture every human need. Some things simply cannot be bought or sold. Our models for understanding its logic and ecologic rest on assumptions, some of which are anthropological, with ethical consequences. Rectifying false assumptions requires attention to human dignity and to its realization in communion, participation, and transformation, which are learned in the family.

Homo curator therefore begins in the family understood not as an abstraction, but as a *communio personarum*. It begins as a maturing of *homo curans*, forming attitudes of participation, ecological conversion, and the dignity of the non-exchangeable. Once formed, these attitudes will tend to renew a society organically, resulting in just, workable policies that may affirm the primordial subjectivity of the family, creating a virtuous circle of renewal. If *homo curans* lives in a perspective of obligation and debt, rather than in one of love and gift, a perspective of fear rather than hope, the persons under his care will embark on a mistaken path, contributing to a vicious cycle of policies that subordinate humanity to the social whole, redefining the family as a statistical unit, commodifying persons, and installing the false inclusivity of totality and a defensive love of the farthest, based on an exchange of rights and power. Such a family is a cradle of consumption and consumerism for a society.

Truly inclusive economies and truly human ecologies affirm the truth about humanity and the primordial subjectivity of the family. They estimate human dignity not only in terms of equality, but in relation to the transcendent origin and destiny of the person. Their sustainability is that of human development, not human exchange. They affirm the good of the person, because they affirm the person as a good.

Depending on which vision one has, attempts to form an inclusive society may affirm humans as subjects in relation, or as parts of a merely objective whole. Following an adequate anthropology, the models we need will be models of renewal, not reset; their ethos, conversion, not control. The only workable solution is a just solution. John Paul calls us to seek that solution organically, in solidarity with the dignity of the human person, and a subsidiarity centered on the family.

Bibliography

Aquinas, Thomas. *In II Sententiarum.* (*In II Sent.*).
———. *In III Sententiarum.* (*In III Sent.*).
———. *Summa Theologiae.* (*ST*).
Arendt, Hannah. 1973. *The Origins of Totalitarianism.* New York: Harcourt Brace Jovanovich.
——— (1975) "On the Nature of Totalitarianism: An Essay in Understanding"; "The Great Tradition and the Nature of Totalitarianism" (lecture, New School for Social Research, New York, 1953); and "Totalitarianism" (lecture, Oberlin College, 1954); at *The Hannah Arendt Papers at the Library of Congress*, Library of Congress Series: Speeches and Writings File, 1923–1975.
Aristotle. *Nicomachean Ethics.*
———. *Rhetoric.*
Augustine. 400. *Confessions.*
———. 419 (?). *De Trinitate.*
———. 391. *De vera religione.*
Beyer, Gerald J. 2020. Karol Wojtyła's *Katolicka etyka społeczna* as Precursor and Hermeneutic Key to Pope John Paul II's Economic Teaching. *American Journal of Economics and Sociology* 79 (4): 1111–1145.
Bonaventure. *In I Sententiarum.*
Boniecki, Adam (2000) *The Making of the Pope of the Millennium: Kalendarium of the Life of Karol Wojtyła.* Translated by Irena Mirecki et al.; edited by Kazimierz Chwalek, Stockbridge, Massachusetts: Marian Press.
Buttiglione, Rocco. 1991. *L'uomo e la famiglia.* Rome: Dino.
Buttiglione, Rocco, Carlo Fedeli, and Angelo Scola. 1984. *Karol Wojtyła, filosofo, teologo, poeta...: Atti del I Colloquio internazionale del pensiero Cristiano organizzato a ISTRA – Istituto di Studi Per La Transizione: Roma, 23–25 settembre 1983.* Vatican City: Libreria Editrice Vaticana.
Epimenides. *Cretica.*
Galarowicz, Jan. 1994. *Człowiek jest osobą: Podstawy antropologii filozoficznej Karola Wojtyły.* Kraków: PAT.
Glare, P.G.W. 1982. Communis. In *Oxford Latin Dictionary*, 369–370. Oxford: Clarendon Press.
Graham, Frank D. 1947. Review of: *Freedom and Reform*, by Frank H. Knight (New York: Harper, 1947), *The American Economic Review* 37(5): 938–943.
Grondelski, John M. 1996. Social Ethics in The Young Karol Wojtyła: A Study-in-Progress. *Faith & Reason* 1–2: 31–43.
Guardini, Romano. 1994. *Letters from Lake Como: Explorations in Technology and the Human Race.*, Translated by Geoffrey W. Bromiley. Edinburgh: T & T Clark.
Hamilton, John T. 2013. *Security: Politics, Humanity, and the Philology of Care.* Princeton: Princeton University Press.
Hilla, Dieter Josef. 1991. Osoba jako zasada teologii moralnej wkład Karola Wojtyły – Jan Pawła II w wypracowanie podstaw teologii moralnej. Translated by Alfred Wierzbicki. *Ethos* 15–16, 140–155.
Hitler, Adolf. 1999. *Mein Kampf.* Boston: Translated by Ralph Manheim, Houghton Mifflin.
Husserl, Edmund. 1997. *Cartesian Meditations: An Introduction to Phenomenology.* Dordrecht: Translated by Dorion Cairns, Kluwer.
John Paul II. 1978. *Homily of His Holiness John Paul II for the Inauguration of His Pontificate*, St. Peter's Square (Oct 22).
——— (1981) Apostolic Exhortation *Familiaris Consortio* (November 22).
———. 1985. *Apertura dell'Anno Internazionale della Gioventù, Incontro di Giovanni Paolo II con i giovani in Piazza San Giovanni in Laterano*, Anno Internazionale della Gioventù (March 30).

———. 1989. *Message of His Holiness Pope John Paul II for the Celebration of the World Day of Peace, 1 January 1990*, Vatican City (Dec 8).
———. 1991. Encyclical Letter *Centesimus Annus* (May 1).
———. 1993. Encyclical Letter *Veritatis Splendor* (Aug 6).
———. 1994. *Letter to Families from Pope John Paul II, Gratissimam Sane*, 1994 — Year of the Family (Feb 2).
———. 1995. Apostolic Journey to the United States of America, Eucharistic Celebration, *Homily of His Holiness John Paul II*, Oriole Park at Camden Yards, Baltimore (8 October).
———. 2001. General Audience (Jan 17).
———. 2002. *Message for the 50th Anniversary of the Permanent Mission of the Holy See to the United Nations Organization for Education, Science and Culture (UNESCO)* (Dec 11).
John Paul, II. 2005. *Pamięć i tożsamość: Rozmowy na przełomie tysiącleci*. Kraków: Wydawnictwo Znak.
Knight, Frank H. 1929. Freedom as Fact and Criterion. *International Journal of Ethics* 39 (2): 129–147.
Knight, Frank H. 1936. The Place of Marginal Economics in a Collectivist System. *The American Economic Review* 26, no. 1, Supplement, Papers and Proceedings of the Forty-eighth Annual Meeting of the American Economic Association, 255–266.
Knight, Frank H. 1937. Economists on Economic Ethics. *International Journal of Ethics* 48 (1): 98–108.
———. 1938. Two Economists on Socialism. *Journal of Political Economy* 46 (2): 241–250.
———. 1939a. Bertrand Russell on Power. *Ethics* 49 (3): 253–285.
———. 1939b. Ethics and Economic Reform. III. Christianity. *Economica New Series* 6 (24): 398–422.
———. 1940a. Socialism: The Nature of the Problem. *Ethics* 50 (3): 253–289.
———. 1940b. Review of: *What Is Liberty?* by Dorothy Fosdick (New York: Harper & Bros., 1939). *Journal of Political Economy* 48(4): 586–589.
———. 1941. The Role of the Individual in the Economic World of the Future. *Journal of Political Economy* 49 (6): 817–832.
———. 1942. Science, Philosophy, and Social Procedure. *Ethics* 52 (3): 253–274.
Knight, Frank H. 1943. Review of: *Social Goals and Economic Institutions*, by Frank D. Graham (Princeton: Princeton University Press, 1942). *The Journal of Business of the University of Chicago* 16(2): 138–139.
Knight, Frank H. 1944a. Human Nature and World Democracy. *American Journal of Sociology* 49 (5): 408–420.
———. 1944b. Contribution to Westley C. Mitchell, Frank H. Knight, and Frank D. Graham, "Discussion." *The American Economic Review* 34, no. 1, Part 2, Supplement, Papers and Proceedings of the Fifty-sixth Annual Meeting of the American Economic Association: 48–57, 50–55.
———. 1946. The Sickness of Liberal Society. *Ethics* 56 (2): 79–95.
———. 1948. Professor Heimann on Religion and Economics. *Journal of Political Economy* 56 (6): 480–497.
———. 1950a. Comment on Professor Parsons' Article. *Journal of Farm Economics* 32 (1): 112–122.
———. 1950b. Economic and Social Policy in Democratic Society. *Journal of Political Economy* 58 (6): 513–522.
———. 1951a. The Rôle of Principles in Economics and Politics. *The American Economic Review* 41 (1): 1–29.
———. 1951b. Review of Theories of Welfare Economics, by Hla Mynt (Cambridge, Mass.: Harvard University Press, 1948). *Ethics* 61(3): 219–224.
———. 1953. Theory of Economic Policy and the History of Doctrine. *Ethics* 63 (4): 276–292.
———. 1957. Intelligence and Social Policy. *Ethics* 67 (3, Part 1): 155–168.

———. 1960. Social Economic Policy. *The Canadian Journal of Economics and Political Science/ Revue canadienne d'Economique et de Science politique* 26 (1): 19–34.
———. 1966. Abstract Economics as Absolute Ethics. *Ethics* 76 (3): 163–177.
———. 1967. A Word of Explanation. *Ethics* 78 (1): 83–85.
Knight, Frank H., and Thornton W. Merriam. 1948. *The Economic Order and Religion*. London: K. Paul, Trench, Trubner.
MacIntyre, Alasdair. 1984. *After Virtue: A Study in Moral Theory*. 2nd ed. Notre Dame: University of Notre Dame Press.
Marcel, Gabriel. 1945. *Homo viator; prolégomènes à une métaphysique de l'espérance*. Paris: Aubier, Éditions Montaigne.
Maritain, Jacques. 1966. *The Person and the Common Good*. Translated by John J. Fitzgerald. Notre Dame: University of Notre Dame Press.
Norman, Johan. 2001. The Psychoanalyst and the Baby: A New Look at Work with Infants. *International Journal of Psycho-analysis* 82 (1): 83–84.
Pieper, Josef. 1989. *Josef Pieper, An Anthology*. Translated by Richard and Clara Winston. San Francisco: Ignatius Press.
Piketty, Thomas. 2014. *Capitalism in the Twenty-First Century*. Translated by Arthur Goldhammer. Original title: *Le capital au XXI siècle* (Paris: Editions du Seuil, 2013). Cambridge: Harvard University Press (Belknap).
Pindar. 476 BCE (?). *Second Pythian Ode*.
Pius XI. 1937. Encyclical Letter *Mit brennender Sorge* (March 14).
Pius XII. 1939. Encyclical Letter *Summi Pontificatus* On the Unity of Human Society (October 20).
Piwowarczyk, Jan. 1960, 1963. *Katolicka etyka społeczna*. London: Veritas.
Plato. 360 BCE (?). *Laws*.
———. 375 BCE (?). *Republic*.
———. 385 BCE (?). *Symposium*.
Richard of St. Victor and Ruben Angelici. 2012. *On the Trinity: English Translation and Commentary*. Translated by Ruben Angelici. London: James Clarke & Co.
Rodrik, Dani. 2015. *Economics Rules: Why Economics Works, When it Fails, and How to Tell the Difference*. Oxford: Oxford University Press.
Schwab, Klaus (with Peter Vanham) 2021. *Stakeholder Capitalism: A Global Economy that Works for Progress, People and Planet*. Hoboken: Wiley.
Second Vatican Ecumenical Council. 1965. Pastoral Constitution on the Church in the Modern World *Gaudium et Spes* (December 7).
Styczeń, Tadeusz. 1982. "Miłość a sens życia: Nad encycykliką Jana Pawła II 'Redemptor hominis,'" in John Paul II, *Redemptor hominis: Tekst i komentarze*, edited by Zofia Józefa Zdybicka (Lublin).
Szczepaniec, Stanisław. 1995. Trójosobowy Bóg zasadą rozumienia *communio personarum* w nauczaniu Ojca Świętego Jana Pawła II. *Roczniki Teologiczne* 42 (5): 83–94.
Tischner, Józef, Józef M. Życiński, and George F. McLean, eds. 1994. *The Philosophy of Person: Solidarity and Cultural Creativity*. Washington: Paideia Press & The Council for Research in Values and Philosophy.
Trevarthen, Colwyn. 1979. Communication and Cooperation in Early Infancy: A Description of Primary Intersubjectivity. In *Before Speech: The Beginning of Interpersonal Communication*, ed. Margaret Bullowa, 321–347. Cambridge: Cambridge University Press.
———. 1993. The Self Born in Intersubjectivity: The Psychology of an Infant Communicating. In *The Perceived Self: Ecological and Interpersonal Sources of Self-Knowledge*, ed. Ulric Neisser, 121–173. Cambridge: Cambridge University Press.
Uber. 2020. In Charlton T. Lewis and Charles Short. *A Latin Dictionary*. Nigel Gourlay.
Urbankowski, Bohdan. 1983. The Romantic Theatre: Its Bounds and the Overstepping of Bounds. *Dialectics and Humanism* 1: 120–123.
Verny, Thomas R., and John Kelly. 1981. *The Secret Life of the Unborn Child: How You Can Prepare Your Baby for a Happy, Healthy Life*. New York: Summit Books.

von Balthasar, Hans Urs. 1989. *You Crown the Year with Your Goodness: Sermons Throughout the Liturgical Year*. San Francisco: Ignatius Press.

Weigel, George. 1999. *Witness to Hope: The Biography of Pope John Paul II*. New York.

Wojtyła, Karol. 1953–1958. *Katolicka etyka społeczna*, unpublished typescript. Kraków.

———. 1960. *Przed sklepem jubilera*.

———. 1965. Zagadnienie katolickiej etyki seksualnej: Refleksje i postulaty. *Roczniki Filozoficzne* 13 (2): 5–25.

———. 1969. Problem teorii moralności. In *W nurcie zagadnień posoborowych*, vol. 3, 217–249. Warsaw: Wydawnictwo Sióstr Loretanek-Benedyktynek.

———. 1973. Objawienie Trójcy Świętej a świadomość zbawienia w świetle nauki Vaticanum II. In *Z zagadnień kultury chrześcijańskiej / Kardynałowi Stefanowi Wyszyńskiemu, Prymasowi Polski*, ed. Wojtyła et al. Lublin: Towarzystwo Naukowe Katolickiego Uniwersytetu Lubelskiego.

———. 1974a. O znaczeniu miłości oblubieńczej (na marginesie dyskusji). *Roczniki Filozoficzne* 22 (2): 151–174.

———. 1974b. Rodzina jako 'communio personarum': Próba interpretacji teologicznej. *Ateneum Kapłańskie* 6683 (395): 347–361.

———. 1975a. Rodzicielstwo a 'communio personarum'. *Ateneum Kapłańskie* 67: 17–31.

———. 1975b. Rozważania pastoralne o rodzinie. *Roczniki Nauk Społecznych* 3: 59–76.

———. 1976. Osoba: Podmiot i wspólnota. *Roczniki Filozoficzne* 24 (2): 5–39.

———. 1978. Uczestnictwo czy alienacja. *Summarium* 7 (27): 7–16.

———. 1979a. *Aby Chrystus się nami posługiwał*. Kraków: Wydawnictwo Znak.

———. 1979b. *Sign of Contradiction*. New York: Crossroads (The Seabury Press).

———. 1980. *Sources of Renewal: The Implementation of the Second Vatican Council*. Translated (from revised Italian edition) by P. S. Falla. San Francisco: Harper & Row.

———. 1981. *Faith According to St. John of the Cross*. Translated by Jordan Aumann, OP. San Francisco: Ignatius Press.

———. 1984. *The Way to Christ: Spiritual Exercises*. Translated (from Italian) by Leslie Wearne. San Francisco: Harper Collins.

———. 1986. *Wykłady lubelskie* (Lublin Lectures). In *Człowiek i moralność, 3; Źródła i monografie*, ed. Tadeusz Styczeń et al., vol. 120. Wydawnictwo Towarzystwa Naukowego Katolickiego Uniwersytetu Lubelskiego: Lublin.

———. 1991. *Człowiek w polu odpowiedzialności*. Edited by Andrzej Szostek. Rome-Lublin: Instytut Jana Pawła II KUL.

———. 1994. *Osoba i czyn, oraz inne studia*, 3rd edition, edited by Tadeusz Styczeń, et al. Człowiek i moralność, 4. Lublin: Wydawnictwo Towarzystwa Naukowego Katolickiego Uniwersytetu Lubelskiego.

———. 1998. *Poezje • Poems*. Translated by Jerzy Peterkiewicz. Krakow: Wydawnictwo Literackie.

———. 1999. *Poezje i dramaty*. Kraków: Wydawnictwo Znak.

———. 2002. Letter # 57 (Wojtyła to Swieżawski, April 16, 1977), in "'Chociaż oczy słabną, nie słabnie miłość Kościoła,' Korespondencja między Stefanem Swieżawskim a ks. Karolem Wojtyłą (Janem Pawłem II) z lat 1953–2001" in Aleksander Fedorowicz, Tadeusz Fedorowicz, Stefan Swieżawski, and Karol Wojtyła, *Pełny wymiar: listy przyjaciół*, edited by A. Dobrowolski. Tarnów: Wydawnictwo Biblos.

———. 2018. In *Katolicka etyka społeczna (Kraków, 1953–58)*, ed. Gerald J. Beyer, Agnieszka Lekka-Kowalik, and Alfred M. Wierzbicki. Lublin: Wydawnictwo KUL.

———. *Miłość i odpowiedzialność*. Źródła i monografie, 111; Człowiek i moralność, 1. Lublin.

Chapter 12
Subexponantial Compound Interest: A Tool for Homo Curator?

Eörs Szathmáry

Abstract Our ability to successfully fight major challenges of climate change is diminished by rising social and economic inequality. One important source of inequality can be identified in the formula of compound interest which describes unlimited growth of monetary assets and debts based on the law of exponential growth. The paper suggests a novel way to calculate compound interest in times of crisis based on a mechanism that could mitigate the effects of economic competition and help achieve sustainable life on our planet.

12.1 Introduction

Rising inequality in societies is being acknowledged in several sources as a major problem (Bowles 2015, OECD 2015, Wilkinson and Pickett 2020). Inequality affects life of most people adversely, and it also harms our ability to successfully fight major challenges, including those stemming from local and global climate change (Wilkinson and Pickett 2020). Inequality has several sources, one of them being the phenomenon of compound interest (Bowles 2015). In this chapter I elaborate on a previous suggestion by von Kiedrowski and myself (von Kiedrowski and Szathmáry 2012) that advocated a novel way to calculate compound interest (Szathmáry 2023) as well as a new approach for central banks to regulate interests. The common method is to tune the interest rate, but—as we shall see—there is potentially another, complementary, mechanism that would mitigate the effects of economic competition that is ultimately linked to the exponential increase of assets

This work has been supported by the grant GINOP-2.3.2-15-2016-0 0 057 ("In the light of evolution: Principles and applications"). The author thanks von Kiedrowski for scientific stimulation and partnership for several decades and Professor Péter Róna for advice on the manuscript.

E. Szathmáry (✉)
Eötvös University, Budapest, Hungary

P. Róna et al. (eds.), *Homo Curator: Towards the Ethics of Consumption*, Virtues and Economics 8, https://doi.org/10.1007/978-3-031-51700-6_12

through compound interest. I see this suggestion as one that could help our efforts at achieving sustainable life on this planet.

12.2 Setting the Stage: The Appearance of Subexponential Growth

Compound interest implies exponential growth, expressed by the formula for the calculation of continuous compounding:

$$P(t) = P_0\, \mathrm{e}^{rt} \tag{12.1}$$

Where P_0 is the principal (the initial value) and $P(t)$ is the value of the asset at time t and r is the interest rate. This formula is exactly isomorphic to unlimited exponential growth in biology and chemistry:

$$N(t) = N_0\, \mathrm{e}^{rt} \tag{12.2}$$

where is the $N(t)$ number of individuals (in this case replicators) at time t and N_0 is the initial number of individuals. r in this case the Malthus parameter affecting the vigorousness of population growth, stemming from the differential equation:

$$\mathrm{d}N / \mathrm{d}t = rN. \tag{12.3}$$

Population numbers go to infinity in infinite time. Note that such growth can be expressed in terms of formal chemistry as an autocatalytic process in which A is catalysing its own formation from X, while producing waste substance Y:

$$\mathrm{A} + \mathrm{X} \rightarrow 2\mathrm{A} + \mathrm{Y}. \tag{12.4}$$

Unlimited exponential growth requires keeping the level (concentration) of X constant, in which case its value can be absorbed into the Malthus parameter.

Exponential growth has profound consequences for selection. Assume that there is another replicator type M that grows also exponentially but with a different Malthus parameter:

$$M(t) = M_0\, \mathrm{e}^{st}, \quad \mathrm{d}M / \mathrm{d}t = sM. \tag{12.5}$$

Now we can calculate growth of the two replicators relative to each other:

$$N(\mathrm{t}) / M(\mathrm{t}) = \left(N_0\, \mathrm{e}^{rt}\right) / \left(M_0\, \mathrm{e}^{st}\right) = K\mathrm{e}^{(r-s)t} \tag{12.6}$$

where K is a constant. Note that this is also an exponential equation, and if $r > s$ then

$$\lim_{t\to\infty}\frac{N(t)}{M(t)}=\infty \tag{12.7}$$

despite that fact that the number of both replicators tends to infinity also. The inferior competitor M is diluted out. This is the simplest hint at "survival of the fittest" (Szathmáry 1991). But growth is of course not unbounded in a finite world. For the considered two competitors this can be expressed as a pair of differential equations:

$$\frac{dN}{dt}=rN-N(rN+sM)/C \tag{12.8.1}$$

$$\frac{dM}{dt}=mM-M(rN+sM)/C \tag{12.8.2}$$

where $C = N + M$ is the total population number. The equation ensures that if $N_0 + M_0 = C$ holds then C does not change (it is a "constant of motion", or "first integral" of the system), so the replicators can grow only at the expense of each other. If, as above, N is the superior competitor then starting with both replicators being present the system converges to the following stable equilibrium:

$$\widehat{N}=C,\quad \widehat{M}=0 \tag{12.9}$$

which ensures that (7) holds again.

Now comes the lesser known, less trivial bit. Growth eq. (12.3) can be generalized to:

$$\frac{dN}{dt}=rN^{p} \tag{12.10}$$

where p is the growth order that for exponential growth equals exactly one. It is perhaps surprising that unless p is exactly one the selective consequences are qualitatively different. Integration of the above rate equation yields (von Kiedrowski 1993):

$$N(t)=\left(N_0^{\,1-p}+(1-p)rt\right)^{\frac{1}{1-p}} \tag{12.11}$$

With $p = 0$ we have linear growth and effectively no autocatalysis, so that is of no interest here. $0 < p < 1$ is in contrast of major interest. If we do the same exercise with the relative growths as for Eq. (12.6) we see that the stable ratio remains finite. For example, if $p = ½$ then

$$\lim_{t\to\infty}\frac{N(t)}{M(t)}=\left(\frac{r}{s}\right)^{2} \tag{12.12}$$

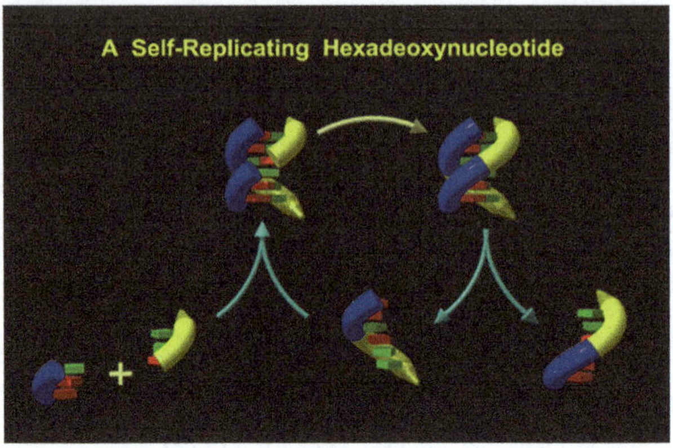

Fig. 12.1 The first artificial chemical self-replicator (von Kiedrowski 1986). The building blocks bind to the longer template. This catalysis the formation of a strong bind between the former (yellow arrow). The copy (indentical to the template) can spontaneously dissociate from the template. Re-association is also possible, which inhibits grows, entailing subexponential growth

implying dynamic coexistence with selectivity depending on the growth order p (von Kiedrowski 1993, Szathmáry and Gladkih 1989, Szathmáry 1991): the superior competitor has an advantage, but cannot oust the inferior one. This conclusion remains valid for a competitive system as an analogy to eq. (8). The table below shows how this stable equilibrium depends on the growth order:

p	1/2	4/5	9/10	0.99
$\widehat{N} / \widehat{M}$	$\left(\frac{r}{s}\right)^2$	$\left(\frac{r}{s}\right)^5$	$\left(\frac{r}{s}\right)^{10}$	$\left(\frac{r}{s}\right)^{100}$

Note that the last entry is very close to exponential growth, hence the very high selectivity. In a finite system this would already imply extinction of M.

Subexponential growth is real in chemistry. It was discovered by von Kiedrowski in 1986 in an experimental system of the first artificial self-replicating molecule (von Kiedrowski 1986). The principle of the process is shown in Fig. 12.1.

Since then, a rich zoo of replicators has been created in labs all over the world. For us here the question is what the implications for economics might be.

12.3 The Monetary Growth Order

The consequence for finance, economy and sustainability is that if a new method of calculating interests could be adopted, the central banks could set not only the classical interest rate (r) but also the monetary order (p). Emphatically, subexponential compound interest calculation would mitigate the rise of inequality.

It is instructive look at examples of how assets grow in the subexponential regime (Fig. 12.2).

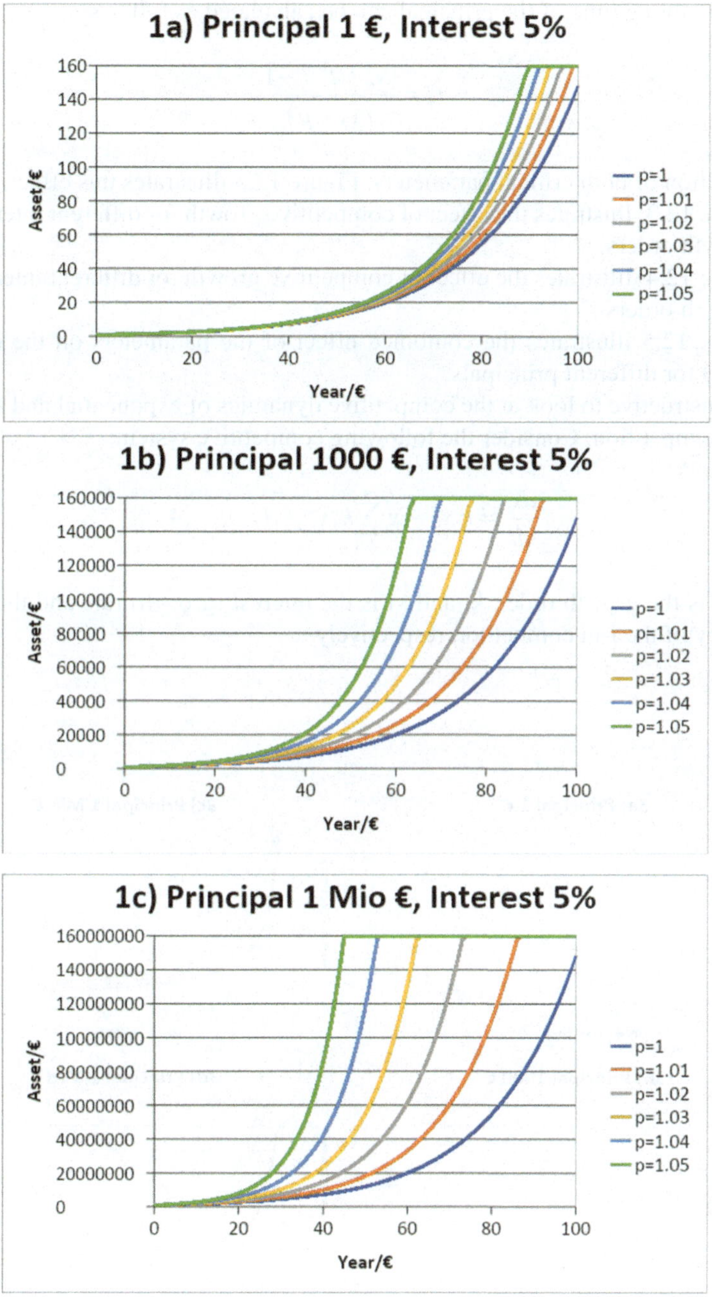

Fig. 12.2 Asset growth for the different principals in the exponential and subexponential domains (von Kiedrowski 1986)

The doubling time of the principal can be calculated as follows:

$$t_2 = \frac{N_0^{1-p} 2^{1-p} - 1}{r(1-p)} \tag{12.13}$$

as a function of both critical parameters. Figure 12.3 illustrates this effect.

Figure 12.3 illustrates the effect of competitive growth for different interest rates and growth orders.

Figure 12.4 illustrates the effect of competitive growth for different interest rates and growth orders.

Figure 12.5 illustrates the combined effect of the parameters on the doubling time (13) for different principals.

It is instructive to look at the competitive dynamics of exponential and subexponential competition. Consider the following competitive system:

$$\frac{dx_i}{dt} = k_i x_i^p - x_i \sum_{j=1}^{4} k_j x_j^p, \quad i = 1, \ldots, 4 \tag{12.14}$$

where p is the growth order, ki and xi is the interest (growth) rate and the relative frequency of the i-th competitor, respectively.

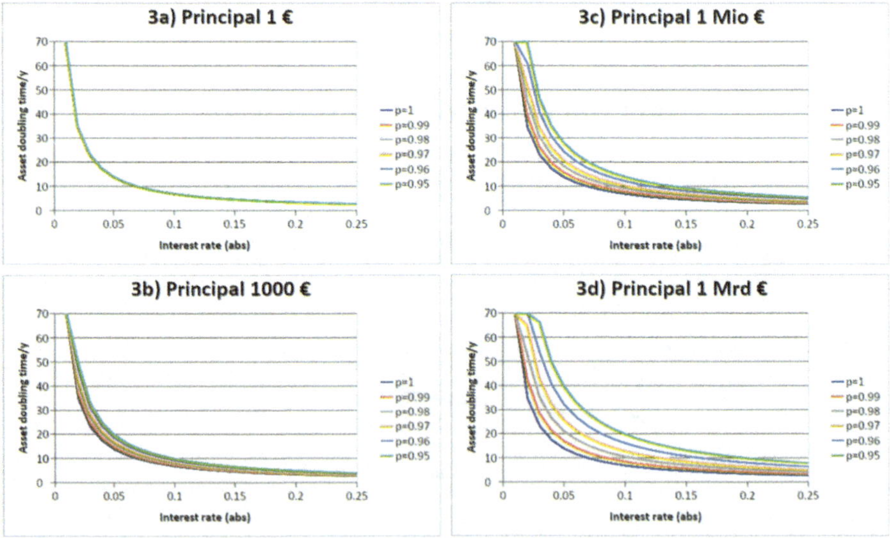

Fig. 12.3 Asset doubling times as a function of interest rate for different principals as a function of the monetary growth order and interest rate (von Kiedrowski 1986)

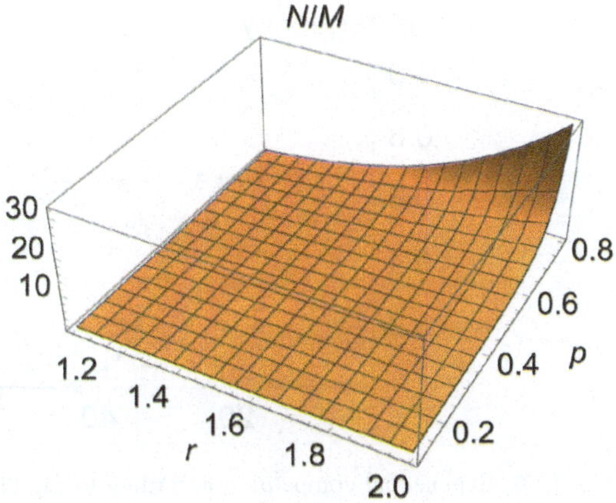

Fig. 12.4 The equilibrium ratio of fast (N) and slowly (M) growing assets while $s = 1$. Note the dramatic effect of the growth order on this ratio

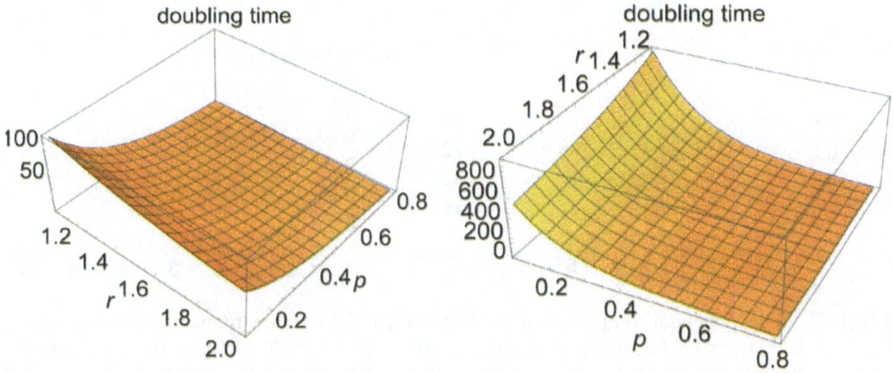

Fig. 12.5 Asset doubling times for $N_0 = 100$ and $N_0 = 1000$ as a function of the critical parameters

For exponential growth ($p = 1$, analogues to classical compound interest) the boring outcome is that the competitor enjoying the highest interest ousts all others (Fig. 12.6). The case for subexponential competition (here $p = 1/2$) is very different (Fig. 12.7). Whether you start with the most inferior or the most superior competitor, the outcome of subexponential competition is the same: stable dynamical coexistence of all types. Note especially how much faster competitive equilibrium is reached for the subexponential case. This is due to fact growth at low asset level growth is much faster (!) than exponential growth, favouring people or startups entering the system, providing a remarkable incubation effect.

Just as we wrote 11 years ago: "The subexponential compounding mechanism is thus an effective means to stop large assets and debts creating problems of the kind we see today" (von Kiedrowski and Szathmáry 2012, 11).

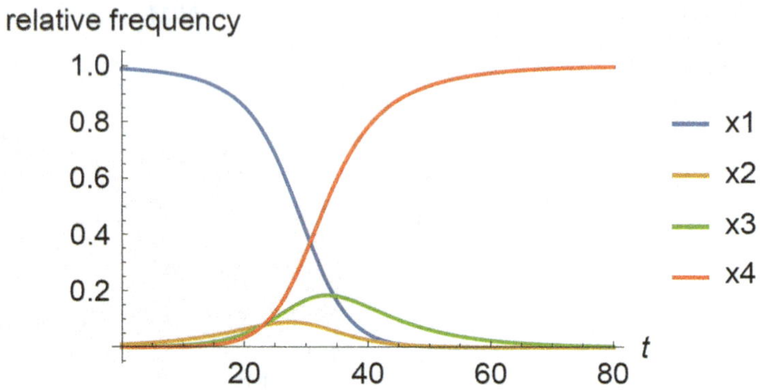

Fig. 12.6 Exponential competition according to Eq. (12.14). Growth/interest rates are: k1 = 1, k2 = 1.1, k3 = 1.2, k4 = 1.3. Initial asset values are: x1(0) = 0.9889, x2(0) = 0.01, x3(0) = 0.001, x4(0) = 0.0001

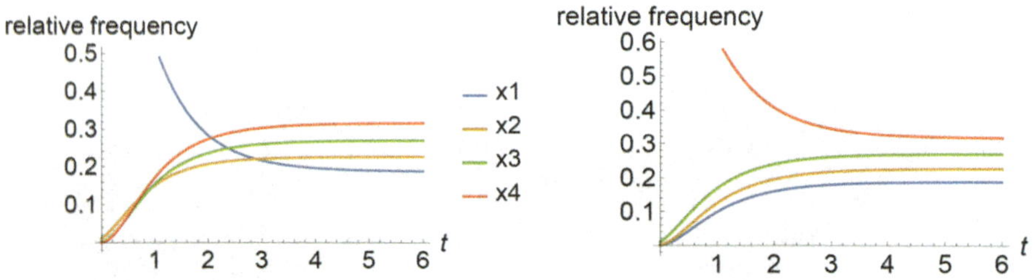

Fig. 12.7 Subexponential competition according to Eq. (12.14). Growth/interest rates are: k1 = 1, k2 = 1.1, k3 = 1.2, k4 = 1.3. Initial asset values Left: x1(0) = 0.9889, x2(0) = 0.01, x3(0) = 0.001, x4(0) = 0.0001. Initial asset values Right: x4(0) = 0.9889, x2(0) = 0.01, x2(0) = 0.001, x1(0) = 0.0001. Note the successfil invasion of the most inferior competitor, starting with the smallest asset value

12.4 Discussion and Outlook

In biological evolution fitness (the expected number of offspring) is maximized. This maxim is context-dependent. The environment evaluates how good replicators as "hypotheses" are for making a living in the particular environment. Naturally, the latter includes the other, competing and cooperating replicators. Humans have inherited aptitudes for both type of behaviour. Greed, broadly speaking, is also in our baggage. Subexponential compounding would run against it because asset growth would be self-inhibitory. The rich would get richer at diminishing rate. Do we face an invincible obstacle? Maybe not.

In the first supplement to Perpetual Peace Kant (1917) famously wrote:

> The problem of organizing a state, however hard it may seem, can be solved even for a race of devils, if only they are intelligent. The problem is: "Given a multitude of rational beings requiring universal laws for their preservation, but each of whom is secretly inclined to exempt himself from them, to establish a constitution in such a way that, although their

private intentions conflict, they check each other, with the result that their public conduct is the same as if they had no such intentions."

A problem like this must be capable of solution; it does not require that we know how to attain the moral improvement of men but only that we should know the mechanism of nature in order to use it on men, organizing the conflict of the hostile intentions present in a people in such a way that they must compel themselves to submit to coercive laws. Thus a state of peace is established in which laws have force.

There are indications that central banks are slowly but increasingly better aware of the issue of sustainability, including "green economy". 11 years ago, we thought that subexponential compounding could be a major step forward in the direction of stabilising economy and society as a whole. Less inequality favours societal well-being. Naturally, open questions are a legion, such as:

Which macroeconomic data are to be employed to set a growth order that improves the overall performance?
How does the monetary growth order affect the Pareto distribution, the Lorenz curve or the Gini index?
How do the latter statistical data change with time for an exponential versus non-exponential modes of monetary growth?
Should a change in the monetary growth order only affect new credits or should all assets and debts, including the existing ones, continuously feel the actual growth order as a feedback?
Is it necessary to introduce, for example, a European tax number in order to assign asset components spread over many bank accounts?
Should the correction by the monetary growth order become an issue of merchant banking (as proposed) or taxation (as an alternative)?" (von Kiedrowski and Szathmáry 2012, 12).
What would be the effect on other domains of the economy?
Could shadow banking undermine central subexponential compounding?

Clearly, the authors of the original suggestion (von Kiedrowski and Szathmáry 2012) are a chemist and a biologist, respectively, hence neither of us is a trained economist. These questions are for experts to analyse and resolve. But there is a precedent worthy of some attention. Sir Frederick Soddy earned the Nobel Prize in chemistry in 1921. In four books, including *The Role of Money* (2003 [1934]) he expressed concerns about the exponential growth by compound interest, and he saw – in a Malthusian fashion – war as a means to overcome the problems of caused by such growth. In Wikipedia we find the assessment "While most of his proposals – 'to abandon the gold standard, let international exchange rates float, use federal surpluses and deficits as macroeconomic policy tools that could counter cyclical trends, and establish bureaus of economic statistics (including a consumer price index) in order to facilitate this effort' – are now conventional practice, his critique of fractional-reserve banking still 'remains outside the bounds of conventional wisdom', although a recent paper by the IMF reinvigorated his proposals.

It may be time to reconsider. The future of technological civilisation may depend on this.

References

Bowles, J. 2015. The secular nature of inequality growth. https://riskandwellbeing.com/2015/05/21/the-secular-nature-of-inequality-growth/

Kant, I. 1917. *Perpetual Peace*. London: George Allen & Unwin.

OECD. 2015. *In It Together: Why Less Inequality Benefits All*. Paris: OECD Publishing.

Soddy, F. 2003 [1934]. *The Role of Money: What It Should Be, Contrasted With What It Has Become*, London, Routledge.

Szathmáry, E. 1991. Simple Growth Laws and Selection Consequences. *Trends in Ecology & Evolution* 6: 366–370.

———. 2023. A Radically New Way of to Tune Compound Interest and Some if Its Implications. In: *Integráció – Növekedés – Reform: Tanulmányok a 70 éves Halmai Péter tiszteletére.* Ludovika Egyetemi Kiadó, in press.

Szathmáry, E., and I. Gladkih. 1989. Subexponential Growth and Coexistence of Non-enzymatically Replicating Templates. *Journal of Theoretical Biology* 138: 55–58.

von Kiedrowski, G. 1986. A Self-Replicating Hexadeoxynucleotide. *Angewandte Chemie International Edition* Engl. 25: 932–935.

———. 1993. Minimal Replicator Theory I: Parabolic Versus Exponential Growth. *Bioorganic Chemistry Frontiers* 3: 115–146.

von Kiedrowski, G., Szathmáry, E. 2012. The monetary growth order. https://arxiv.org/ftp/arxiv/papers/1204/1204.6590.pdf

Wilkinson, R., and R. Pickett. 2020. *The Inner Level. How More Equal Societies Reduce Stress, Restore Sanity and Improve Everyone's Well-being*. London: Penguin Books; Reprint edition.

Index

P. Róna et al. (eds.), *Homo Curator: Towards the Ethics of Consumption*, Virtues and Economics 8, https://doi.org/10.1007/978-3-031-51700-6

The manufacturer's authorised representative in the EU is Springer Nature Customer Service Centre GmbH, Europaplatz 3, 69115 Heidelberg, Germany. If you have any concerns regarding our products, please contact ProductSafety@springernature.com

Printed and bound by CPI Group (UK) Ltd, Croydon, CR0 4YY
30/09/2026
02225573-0002